Gender, Church, and State in Early Modern Germany

WOMEN AND MEN IN HISTORY

This series, published for students, scholars and interested general readers, will tackle themes in gender history from the early medieval period through to the present day. Gender issues are now an integral part of all history courses and yet many traditional text books do not reflect this change. Much exciting work is now being done to redress the gender imbalances of the past, and we hope that these books will make their own substantial contribution to that process. This is an open-ended series, which means that many new titles can be included. We hope that these will both synthesise and shape future developments in gender studies.

The General Editors of the series are *Patricia Skinner* (University of Southampton) for the medieval period; *Pamela Sharpe* (University of Bristol) for the early modern period; and *Margaret Walsh* (University of Nottingham) for the modern period.

Published books:

Gender, Church, and State in Early Modern Germany:
   Essays by Merry E. Wiesner
Merry E. Wiesner

Gender, Church, and State in Early Modern Germany

ESSAYS BY

MERRY E. WIESNER

Longman
London and New York

Addison Wesley Longman Limited
Edinburgh Gate,
Harlow, Essex CM20 2JE,
United Kingdom
and Associated Companies throughout the world

*Published in the United States of America
by Addison Wesley Longman Inc., New York*

© Addison Wesley Longman Limited 1998

First published 1998

ISBN 0 582 292824 PPR
CW/ISBN 0 582 292832 CSD

British Library Cataloguing-in-Publication Data
A catalogue record for this book is
available from the British Library

Library of Congress Cataloging-in-Publication Data
Also available

Set by 35 in 10/12pt Baskerville
Produced by Longman Singapore Publishers (Pte) Ltd.
Printed in Singapore

Contents

Acknowledgements

The publishers would like to thank the following for permission to reproduce copyright material:

'Women's defence of their public role' was originally published in *Women in the Middle Ages and the Renaissance: Literary and Historical Perspectives,* ed. Mary Beth Rose (Syracuse, NY: Syracuse University Press, 1986). Used by permission.

'Ideology meets the Empire: reformed convents and the Reformation' was originally published in *Germania Illustrata: Essays Presented to Gerald Strauss,* ed. Andrew Fix and Susan C. Karant-Nunn (Kirksville, MO: Sixteenth Century Essays and Studies, 1992), pp. 181–96. Used by permission.

'The Reformation of the women' was originally published in *Archiv für Reformationsgeschichte. Sonderband Washington* (Gütersloh: Gerd Mohn, 1993), pp. 193–208. Used by permission.

'Frail, weak, and helpless: women's legal position in theory and reality' was originally published in *Regnum, Religio et Ratio: Essays Presented to Robert M. Kingdon,* ed. Jerome Friedman. Sixteenth Century Essays and Studies, Vol. 8 (Kirksville, MO: Sixteenth Century Journal Publishers, 1987), pp. 161–9. Used by permission.

'Paternalism in practice: the control of servants and prostitutes in early modern German cities' was originally published in *The Process of Change in Early Modern Europe: Essays in Honor of Miriam Chrisman,* ed. Phillip N. Bebb and Sherrin Marshall (Athens: Ohio University Press, 1988), pp. 179–200. Used by permission.

'Spinning out capital: women's work in the early modern economy' was originally published in *Becoming Visible: Women in European History,* 2nd edition, ed. Susan Stuard, Renate Bridenthal and Claudia Koonz (Boston: Houghton Mifflin, 1987), pp. 221–50. Used by permission.

'Guilds, male bonding and women's work in early modern Germany' was originally published in *Gender and History* 1 (1989): 125–37 and reprinted in *La Donna nell'Economia Secc. XIII–XVIII.* Serie II: Atti delle 'Settimane di Studi' e altri Convegni, 21 (Prato: Istituto Internazionale di Storia Economica 'F. Datini', 1990), pp. 655–69. Used by permission.

'*Wandervögel* and women: journeymen's concepts of masculinity in early modern Germany' was originally published in *Journal of Social History* 24/4 (Summer 1991): 767–82. Used by permission.

For Neil

Introduction

For several years, whenever I have written or given a talk about the history of women in early modern Europe, I have invariably used the word 'explosion' in the first sentence to describe what has happened to the amount of scholarship available. When I began graduate study in 1974 – only a little over twenty years ago – and decided I wanted to write first a master's thesis and then a dissertation on women, it was possible to read nearly everything that had been written about women in all countries of Europe for the period 1500–1800, and a good share of the material about medieval women as well. For many of the questions I wanted to look at, there were almost no descriptive studies available and certainly no theory, a fact which I had to impress upon some members of my dissertation committee who kept asking about comparable analyses and theoretical frameworks.

Those days now seem like a rosy, distant past, as book-length studies and collections about medieval and early modern women in Europe now number in the hundreds, and articles in the thousands. Added to these are hundreds of studies of gender, a word that was not even part of the academic vocabulary twenty years ago other than in linguistics, and scores in other related fields, such as the history of sexuality and the body. And instead of a lack of appropriate theory, the study of early modern women and gender is almost over-theorized, with every theoretical school seeming to have something to offer: post-colonialism offers ways to analyse the first European colonial ventures and their real and metaphorical impact on women; socialist feminism ways to examine women's changing work options and the values accorded men's and women's work; post-structuralism ways to analyse power relationships imbedded in the developing national languages; cultural materialism ways to

1

understand the meaning and significance of new consumer goods and changing economic structures; psychoanalysis ways to view both family relationships and witchcraft; new historicism ways to use literature by and for women in our analyses. Conversely, many of these theoretical perspectives use changes in ideas about gender and in the actual lives of women and men in the early modern period to support their case; proto-industrial capitalism, the growth of the state and its forces of social discipline, the witch hunts, encounters between European and non-European women and men, and the emphasis on the patriarchal family and lineage are all developments now viewed as central to understanding how the modern world became what it is. The picture is now a much more complicated one, and having spent the first decade of my academic career, along with many others, arguing that there was no development in early modern Europe that did not involve and have an impact on women, I sometimes wish our words had not been so widely heeded.

In some ways this sense of being enveloped by a flood of research comes from my perspective as a scholar whose first language is English, and would be even stronger if I specialized in English history, for studies of women and gender in early modern England vastly outweigh those of any other European country, and perhaps those of all other countries in Europe taken together. In part this results from the fact that much of the earliest work in women's history was done by English-language historians, who introduced their students to key texts and sources; those students in turn went on to explore gender and sexuality and to develop theory, but their geographic base remained England. The imbalance in terms of available materials has actually increased in the last fifteen years with the publication of key texts by and about early modern women in modern editions, a process that is continuing at a great rate today.[1] If we want our students to read original sources about early

---

1. The Brown University Women Writers Project is a primary sponsor of such editions, published by Oxford University Press in the series Women Writers in English, 1350–1850, edited by Suzanne Woods. Scolar Press also publishes a series of facsimile reprints, *The Early Modern Englishwoman: A Facsimile Library of Essential Works*, edited by Betty S. Travitsky and Patrick Cullen. Study of the works of English women writers will become increasingly easy in the near future when the Brown Women Writers Project will go on line. In 1996, Brown received $400,000 from the Mellon Foundation to make approximately 100 Renaissance texts written by women available through the Internet, and then to assess the impact of delivering these texts electronically instead of in the paper versions that the Brown project has provided up to now.

modern women, they will almost invariably be about women in England, for published sources from other parts of Europe are very limited and translations even more so.

In contrast to England, early modern Germany, or, politically speaking, the Holy Roman Empire, has been relatively under-studied, in both English and German. In part this is a language issue, for with the influence of bilingual instruction in schools in the US and the predominance of French theory in the academy, historians whose first language is English are much more likely to learn French or Spanish as their second. In part this is a reflection of the way academic fields have been defined, for to study Germany in the early modern period generally meant one was defined as a historian of the Reformation, a field that has been somewhat scep-tical of women's history. Those drawn to issues regarding women on the Continent in the early modern period were thus more likely to choose France or Italy as their focus.[2] In part this is a result of the initial hostility of the German academic system in both the west and the east to women's history and often to women historians, whatever their field.[3]

Despite the initial hostility, a small number of extremely dedicated German historians began to explore aspects of women's history in the early 1980s, and their work and that of their students has

2. This was also enhanced by the fact that several of the most prominent scholars and theorists in the field of early modern gender studies, particularly Joan Kelly, Natalie Zemon Davis, and Christiane Klapisch-Zuber, worked on France or Italy.

3. Two of the most important historians of women in early modern Germany, Heide Wunder and Christina Vanja, wrote in 1992 that 'female students and doc-toral candidates who inquired about "female people" received little attention from professors or thesis advisors. If not rejected outright, research on women's issues was under no circumstances encouraged or promoted . . . the historical brotherhood of Germany persistently resists (with only a few exceptions) women's history and up to now has hardly deigned to notice the results' (Ute Frevert, Heide Wunder, and Christina Vanja, 'Historical research on women in the Federal Republic of Germany', in Karen Offen, Ruth Roach Pierson and Jane Rendall (eds), *Writing Women's His-tory: International Perspectives* (Bloomington: Indiana University Press, 1990), p. 292. From the outside this appears to be changing somewhat. There are now three chairs of women's history in Germany – one at Bielefeld and two in Berlin – and seven more general women's studies centres. Only three of these are officially parts of universities, however – the others are either free-standing or affiliated with a university in an indirect way – and most of them were started with outside funding, so are not viewed as 'regular' parts of the university. There is clearly strong interest in women's and gender history, but younger women report that they are still dis-couraged from focusing specifically on women and are advised to leave anything they publish on women off their official curriculum vitae if they want to get a position. The chill also applies to foreign scholars known to work on women, par-ticularly if these scholars are themselves female, and has only been aggravated by the turmoil in German academia since reunification.

now created at least a small flood. Most of these scholars are very conversant with American and English theoretical and substantive works, and set their own work within a European-wide context. This cross-fertilization has not gone the other way, however, for, unlike the work of French and Italian scholars, very little of this German scholarship has been translated, so that generalizations made about women in early modern 'Europe' by scholars who do not read German usually do not include developments in this large part of the Continent.[4]

This collection is a small effort to address this problem, and provide English-language readers with a series of essays which focus largely on women and gender in early modern Germany. The volume begins, however, with a broader essay, 'Women's defence of their public role', which I wrote in 1983 as part of a workshop at the Newberry Library in Chicago. That title represents both the way I addressed the specific question posed by that workshop, 'How free were women in the Renaissance?', and how I conceptualized my research on women at that point, for the construction and nature of the public/private dichotomy was a very common topic in the early 1980s for women's historians. This essay includes material from many parts of Europe and lays out some general considerations of the three themes of the rest of the book – religion, law, and work.

The next nine essays, seven of them published before and two of them previously unpublished, look specifically at religion, law, and work in Germany. Each of these three sections is preceded by a brief introduction discussing research trends in scholarship pertaining to Germany and to Europe as a whole. In each section the articles are arranged in chronological order of publication, so that the reader can get some sense of how the historiography has developed. The final section, 'Reassessing, transforming, complicating: two decades of early modern women's history', explores several of the questions that have been central to the field, and assesses the ways the writing of early modern women's history has changed since 'Women's defence of their public role' was written.

4. Translations of works of French historians of women include: Christiane Klapisch-Zuber, *Women, Family, and Ritual in Renaissance Italy* (Chicago: University of Chicago Press, 1985); Christine Fauré, *Democracy Without Women: Feminism and the Rise of Liberal Individualism* (Bloomington: Indiana University Press, 1991); Genevieve Fraisse, *Reason's Muse: Sexual Difference and the Birth of Democracy* (Chicago: University of Chicago Press, 1994); Georges Duby and Michelle Perrot (eds), *A History of Women in the West*, 5 Vols (Cambridge, MA: Harvard University Press, 1992), Vol. 2 of which does include one essay by the German historian Claudia Opitz on medieval women.

The book ends with a descriptive bibliography of some of the materials available for further reading. Because of the 'explosion', or 'flood', or whatever metaphor you choose, I have not been able to include everything, so I have concentrated, when discussing English-language materials, on only those things that have appeared in the last three years or that specifically discuss Germany. Readers interested in earlier studies of other parts of Europe should consult the chapter bibliographies in my *Women and Gender in Early Modern Europe* (Cambridge University Press, 1993). When discussing German-language materials I have ranged more widely, though also with a preference for the most recent work.

Most of these essays were written while I was a member of the history department at the University of Wisconsin-Milwaukee and also for four years the director of the Center for Women's Studies there. I would like to thank my colleagues and friends in both history and women's studies for their advice and suggestions, and in particular the members of my Renaissance Women reading group: Margaret Borene, Martha Carlin, Janet Jesmok, Gwynne Kennedy, Gretchen Kling, Deirdre McChrystal, Jennifer Sansone, Sandra Stark. The volume was completed during the year I held the Association of Marquette University Women (AMUW) Chair in Humanistic Studies, and I would like to thank AMUW for its support which allowed me to complete this and many other writing projects. I would also like to thank Pam Sharpe, the editor of the Early Modern tier of the series, and Hilary Shaw of Addison Wesley Longman for their assistance and their willingness to take on a collection of essays as the first volume in a new series. The book is dedicated to my husband, without whom my life in these last ten years would have been very different and far too serious.

CHAPTER ONE

Women's defence of their public role[1]

The question which Joan Kelly posed a decade ago, 'Did women have a Renaissance?', is one which has led to a great deal of re-examination and rethinking of that particular period. Kelly examined courtly love literature, Castiglione's *The Courtier,* and the experience of Italian upper-class women to answer the question with a resounding 'no'. Instead of expanding opportunities and increasing liberation from ideological constraints, she argues, these women 'experienced a contraction of social and personal options that men of their classes . . . did not'.[2] Kelly further describes this contraction as a 'new division between personal and public life', a division which also relegated women to the personal, private realm.[3]

Kelly primarily uses prescriptive literature written by men to make her points, but the voices of actual women from the period indicate that they were aware of what was happening to them. They felt both the shrinking of opportunities in a variety of areas and the increasing split between public and private life. Their objections

1. As I explain in my Introduction to this volume, this article was written in response to one of the workshops in the conference 'Changing Perspectives on Women in the Renaissance' at The Newberry Library in May 1983, and it specifically addresses the question posed by that workshop: 'How free were women in the Renaissance?' It is very much a working paper, exploring a wide variety of disparate material with that particular question in mind, rather than culminating extensive research on one particular aspect of the issue. Much of the German material comes from city archives where I was carrying out research on working women. My thanks to the American Council of Learned Societies and the Deutsche Akademische Austauschdienst (DAAD) for their support for that research. All translations are my own, unless otherwise noted.

2. Joan Kelly-Gadol, 'Did women have a Renaissance?', in *Becoming Visible: Women in European History,* ed. Renate Bridenthal and Claudia Koonz (Boston: Houghton Mifflin, 1977), p. 139.

3. Ibid., p. 160.

to this growing constraint took on many different forms but generally centre on women's right to a public role. While male writers, officials, theologians, workers, and professionals were attempting to limit women's activities to the private realm, women consistently defended their public role.

These defences are closely linked to the question of the nature and degree of women's freedom in the Renaissance. Most scholarly discussions of female freedom focus on male definitions and limitations of that freedom – law codes, sermons, guild restrictions, prescriptive treatises, literary models. In all of these, the word 'free' would rarely have been used when referring to women. Classical authors, to whom the Renaissance writers looked for models of thought and language, would not have done so, as 'free' meant to them enjoying the rights and privileges of a citizen and possessing an educated capacity for reason, neither of which was possible for women. Italian humanists, while occasionally allowing women some rational capacity, sharply restricted the avenues by which a woman could develop that capacity; her course of study was to be neither as 'free' nor as 'freeing' as a man's. It is only in a religious sense that the word 'free' is applied to women in the Renaissance. According to Erasmus, a woman had the same 'free will', the same moral responsibility to do good, that a man did. According to Luther, of course, no one had free will, but a woman could receive God's grace and come to faith the same as a man, participating thereby in the 'freedom of a Christian' which resulted from this faith.

Philosophical discussions of 'freedom' as it was defined by male authorities may be leading us somewhat astray, however. While Renaissance women used a variety of philosophical, legal, rational, and religious justifications to argue their case, they in fact had a much more pragmatic definition of the word: 'freedom' to them meant the ability to participate in public life. Their voices tell us a great deal about female self-conception during the Renaissance, which never emerges when listening to male voices alone. It is true that women's sphere in most cultures has been defined by men, as have the limits of what is considered 'public' and what 'private'; but women have often objected to or ignored those limitations, and at no time more than during the Renaissance when they were aware that restrictions on them were increasing.

The contraction of women's public role, and their responses to it, occur in a variety of realms of life during the Renaissance and may best be explored realm by realm. It will also be instructive to look at examples from somewhat later periods, for this process continued over centuries, eventually restricting not only the upper-class women who are the focus of Kelly's study, but middle- and lower-class women as well. As Natalie Davis has noted, 'Women suffered for their powerlessness in both Catholic and Protestant lands in the late sixteenth to eighteenth centuries as changes in marriage laws restricted the freedoms of wives even further, as female guilds dwindled, as the female role in middle-level commerce and farm direction contracted, and as the differential between male and female wages increased.'[4]

The theoretical limits of female freedom in economic, political, and familial life were set by a variety of municipal, national, and regional law codes. These differed widely from area to area throughout Europe, but some general trends can be seen by examining changes in them from the thirteenth through to the seventeenth centuries.

In regard to the basic obligations and duties of citizenship, little distinction was made between men and women; all heads of households were required to pay taxes, provide soldiers for defence, and obey all laws. Beyond that, however, there were clear legal restrictions on what the female half of the population could do. Women differed from men in their ability to be witnesses, make wills, act as guardians for their own children, make contracts, and own, buy, and sell property. These limitations appear in the earliest extant law codes and were sharpened and broadened as the law codes themselves were expanded.

A good example of this process can be seen in the restrictions on women buying and selling goods, or loaning, borrowing, or donating money without their husbands' or guardians' approval. The earliest law codes (for example, Lübeck 1220–26) simply prohibited any woman from engaging in these transactions unless her occupation required it, an exception so broad as to make the law meaningless.[5] As the occupations that were to be excluded were described more specifically, this list shrank gradually over centuries. When one goes beyond law codes to actual court proceedings, however, it is apparent that women were making contracts, buying, selling, and trading goods all the time. Perhaps because

4. Natalie Zemon Davis, 'City women and religious change', in her *Society and Culture in Early Modern France* (Stanford, CA: Stanford University Press, 1965), p. 94.

5. Wilhelm Ebel, *Forschungen zur Geschichte des lübischen Rechts* (Lübeck: M. Schmidt-Römhild, 1950); Luise Hess, *Die deutschen Frauenberufe des Mittelalters* (Munich: Neuer Filser-Verlag, 1940), p. 52; A. Abram, 'Women traders in medieval London', *Economic Journal* 26 (June 1916): 280; Inger Dübeck, *Købekoner og Konkurrence* (Copenhagen: Juristforbundets Forlag, 1978), pp. 184ff.

theoretical restrictions were bypassed, evaded, or ignored in so many cases, we can find few objections by women when they were added or expanded.

Other types of legal restrictions began to appear in the sixteenth and seventeenth centuries and were opposed both by women and by individual men. Most areas began to tighten their system of guardianship, demanding that all widows and unmarried women choose a male guardian, who was to oversee their financial affairs and appear for them in court.[6] Women not only took these guardians to court when they felt their rights had been violated and demanded new guardians; they also objected to being required to have a guardian at all.[7] Women had appeared before city courts in the past in regard to financial matters and had been handling their own property and inheritance, they argued, so why did they now need male guardians to do the same things?

Some cities were very frank as to why they were requiring guardians; the Strasbourg city council demanded this expressly to prevent women from going into convents and deeding all their property to the convent, 'by which their relatives are disinherited and the city loses people who provide it with horses' (that is, taxpayers).[8] Because such personal decisions by women ultimately had repercussions in the public realm, the council felt they were really public affairs and thus should be placed under male control.

The prominent Catholic preacher and moralist Geiler of Kaysersberg opposed this move, seeing it as an infringement on individual women's opportunities to perform works of charity. In a sermon from 1501 he comments:

> Arranging a guardian for widows who are responsible and sensible persons is a novelty that has arisen in this city supposedly for the common good. In truth, as I will report, it is a self-seeking move by those who were in power... Everyone who is bothered by something always

6. Strasbourg, Archives municipales (hereafter AMS), Statuten, Vol. 24, fol. 62 (1464), Vol. 18, fol. 104 (1471); Augsburg, Stadtarchiv (hereafter AB), Verordnungen, Vol. 16, fol. 272–3 (1615), Anschlage und Dekrete, 'Erneuerte Witwen und Waisenordnung' (1668).

7. AMS, Akten der 15, 1633, fol. 26; Frankfurt, Stadtarchiv (hereafter FF), Bürgermeisterbücher 1608, fol. 184, 1609, fol. 136; Munich, Stadtarchiv (hereafter MU), Ratsitzungsprotokolle, 1522; Stuttgart, Hauptstaatsarchiv (hereafter ST), 1540 Witwen und Waisen Ordnung. My specific examples here are all German, but similar developments were occurring in other parts of Europe, as Natalie Davis has discovered in Lyons ('Women on top', in *Society and Culture*, pp. 124–51) and Pearl Hogrefe in England ('Legal rights of Tudor women and their circumvention by men and women', *The Sixteenth Century Journal* 3 (April 1972): 97–105.

8. AMS, Statuten, Vol. 18, fol. 104 (1477).

says it harms the common good, but it really involves his own affairs
... The Gospel tells us directly – if you want to be saved, go out and
sell everything you have and give it to the poor. It doesn't say to give
it to your heirs and relatives. This law is totally against the word of
Christ. It is a mockery of God, a haughty service of the devil to forbid
a pious person to give everything she owns for the will of God.[9]

The thrust of Geiler's argument here is that such decisions were
personal matters and should be left up to the individual woman
without city interference. He thus at least tacitly agrees with the
city council that women should not have a public role, but sets
the boundary between private and public differently. This line of
argument will emerge in male defences of women's activities in
other realms as well. Men, whether humanists, reformers, or political thinkers, often argued that the activity concerned – such as
writing, education, or inheriting an estate – was essentially private
and thus should be open to women.

Women's objections to guardians follow a very different line of
reasoning. This was a period when the division between public and
private was not as sharp and distinct as it would become later, and
when the household, as a legal and economic unit and as the location of most production, was clearly within the public sphere.[10]
City councils recognized this fact, for they taxed households, not
persons, as did Protestant reformers who spoke of the family as a
little commonwealth, from which basic unit the larger society was
made. Women also recognized this and were aware that they were
making 'political' decisions, or certainly decisions which had effects
beyond the immediate household, when they were planning something as simple as whether to cook fish or meat on fast days, whether
a political or religious refugee was to be fed, or what quality and
amount of food journeymen were to receive.[11] They, along with
their husbands, were held responsible by municipal and regional
authorities for maintaining order within the household and keeping children and servants under control.[12] Thus they saw their legal

9. *Die Aelteste Schriften Geiler von Kaysersberg* (Freiburg, 1877).
10. Heide Wunder, 'Frauen in den Leichenpredigten: Personen, Bilder, Rollen?',
unpublished paper.
11. I am grateful to Lyndal Roper for pointing this out to me, both in private
conversation and in her unpublished paper, 'Urban women and the household
workshop form of production: Augsburg 1500–1550'.
12. Heide Wunder sees this recognition of the wife's authority within the household and of her importance to the smooth operating of society as the reason why
numerous funeral speeches for women were not only written and given, but also
printed. (See note 10 above.)

and financial activities in the larger sphere as no different from, or
simply an extension of, those activities in which they were already
involved within the household.

Though Geiler and the women were arguing for the same thing
– women's ability to make financial decisions without the aid of a
guardian – and though the underlying issue was an economic one
which had little to do with women's rights *per se* – the tax base of
the city – and though none of the arguments was successful in this
case, the differences between their justifications are very important.
As the split between public and private hardened, and as the public
realm expanded to include education, administration of public welfare, and a growing number of occupations, Geiler's line of reasoning resulted in an ever-shrinking female sphere. The assertion by
the Strasbourg women that the household was part of the public
realm allowed for an augmented, or at least for a stable, female
sphere. Had the women's line of reasoning ultimately triumphed,
the gender divisions which evolved in early modern Europe might
have looked somewhat different. The advent of national governments
and the end of the household form of production may have made
the public/private, work/home, male/female divisions which did
develop inevitable, but the speculation is still an interesting one.

Along with increasing restriction of women's ability to make financial
decisions and to handle their own property, the Renaissance and
early modern periods saw a restriction of women's work. This issue
is very complex and may be partially attributed to nearly every major
economic change that was going on: the decline of the craft guilds
and the rise of journeymen's guilds, the shift in trade patterns, the
general inflation, the decline of old manufacturing centres and the
growth of new ones, formalization of training requirements, the rise
of capitalism. In addition to strictly economic factors, political and
ideological ones also affected women's work: the rise of territorial
states, dislocation caused by the religious wars, increasing suspicion
of unmarried women, secularization of public welfare, campaigns
against prostitution and begging, new ideas about women's 'proper'
role and ability to be trained. Whatever the reasons behind it, in
every occupation in which women's work was restricted, the women
themselves objected. In this arena we can hear most clearly the
voices of lower- and middle-class women defending their public role.

Some of the most vocal individuals were widows of master craftsmen. The earliest guild ordinances rarely mention widows, who
seem to have had unrestricted rights to carry on their husband's

shop after his death, or at least as long as they remained unmarried.[13] Beginning in the mid-fifteenth century, nearly every craft
began to impose limitations: widows could only continue operating
the shop for a few months or finish work that was already started
and could not take on apprentices, hire new journeymen, or buy
any new raw materials. Such restrictions were particularly strict in
crafts which were declining and whose craftsmen were thus feeling
threatened, or in those with strong journeymen's guilds, as the
journeymen saw widows as a block to their being able to open their
own shops.[14]

Individual widows frequently brought requests to guild authorities, city councils, ducal courts, and other governing bodies that
they be excused from the normal restrictions. Each used a variety
of tactics, stressing her age or infirmity, number of dependent children, good reputation, and quality products. These requests referred
primarily to the individual facts of the case, but an occasional supplication also mentioned widows' rights in general: 'I bring my
humble request . . . that the apprentice be allowed to stay with me,
as it is the practice everywhere else in the entire Holy Roman Empire
that widows who run a workshop with journeymen are allowed to
retain an apprentice until he has finished his training.'[15]

The individualized nature of widows' requests is not terribly
surprising, given the fact that there were very few women's guilds
or other corporate bodies in which women could develop a sense
of group work identity. In the few cases in which they did, their
objections to restrictions on their work are couched in corporate
terms. A group of unmarried veil weavers in Augsburg objected to
an ordinance which forbade them to continue weaving 'because
this is a fine and honourable female trade'.[16] Ceremonies which
celebrated women's work identity were very rare, in contrast to
the huge number of parades, banquets, drinking parties, and fest-
ivals in which men participated as members of a craft. In the few

13. Karl Bücher and Benno Schmidt, *Frankfurter Amts- und Zunfturkunden bis zum Jahre 1612* (Frankfurt: J. Baer, 1914), and numerous guild ordinances in city archives.
14. MU, Ratsitzungsprotokolle, 1461, fol. 39, 42; AMS 15, 1612, fol. 201, 1634, fol. 116, 127; FF, Bürgermeisterbücher 1580, fol. 189b; FF, Zünfte, C–54M (1640); Ugb. D3L (1588 & 1596), Ugb. C59, Gg; Memmingen Stadtarchiv (hereafter MM), Hutmachern 51, Nr. 3 (1613); Nuremberg Staatsarchiv (hereafter N), Ratsbücher, 2, fol. 282 & 318 (1479), 2, fol. 31 (1475), 11, fol. 324 (1520), 22, fol. 236 (1544).
15. FF, Zünfte, Ugb. C–32, R no. 1 (1663). Widows' supplications and requests can be found in many city archives.
16. Claus-Peter Clasen, *Die Augsburger Weber: Leistungen und Krisen des Textilgewerbes um 1600* (Augsburg: Verlag Hieronymus Mühlberger, 1981), pp. 130–2.

instances in which such ceremonies had been established, the women fervently defended their right to continue holding them. The Strasbourg midwives, for example, required each new midwife to provide all the others with a 'welcome meal' when she was taken on. The older midwives justified this ritual with the comment that the city council had a similar requirement for new council representatives and ambassadors, holders of offices which, they said, were certainly no more important or honourable than midwifery.[17] They recognized that such events were important in establishing work identity and publicly demonstrating group cohesion. Midwives in general seem to have had the strongest sense of work identity found among women, as they were always careful to mention their occupation when appearing in court, making an appeal, or acting in any legal or public capacity.

While journeymen and guild masters were fighting against widows' rights, professionalization and the formalization of training requirements worked against women's labour in several fields, most prominently in medicine. Until about 1500 there seems to have been little opposition to women practising medicine of all kinds. Women are listed as doctors in early tax lists and were even rewarded for special medical services.[18] Every housewife was expected to have some knowledge of herbs, salves, and ointments, and care of others was seen as an extension of household healing. A fourteenth-century law from Calabria even notes, 'It is better, out of consideration for morals and decency, for women rather than men to attend female patients.'[19]

Gradually, however, under pressure from barber-surgeons, physicians, and apothecaries, cities and territories began to pass regulations expressly forbidding 'women and other untrained persons' to practise medicine in any way.[20] These ordinances did not keep

17. AMS, 15, 1584, fol. 121.

18. Hess, *Die deutschen Frauenberufe des Mittelalters*, p. 101. Helmut Wachendorf, *Die Wirtschaftliche Stellung der Frau in den Deutschen Städten des Späteren Mittelalters* (Quackenbrück: C. Trute, 1934), pp. 23–6; Karl Bücher, *Die Berufe der Stadt Frankfurt a. M. im Mittelalter* (Leipzig: B.G. Teubner, 1914); Gerd Wunder, 'Die Bürgerschaft der Reichsstadt Hall von 1395–1600', *Württembergische Geschichtsquellen*, Vol. 25 (Stuttgart: W. Kohlhammer, 1956); FF, Bürgermeisterbücher 1436, fol. 17, 1446, fol. 47, 1491, fol. 96.

19. *Collectio Salernitana*, III, p. 338, quoted in *Not in God's Image: Women in History from the Greeks to the Victorians*, ed. Julia O'Faolain and Lauro Martines (New York: Harper and Row, 1973), p. 165.

20. Karl Weinhold, *Die Deutschen Frauen in dem Mittelalter* (Vienna: C. Gerold, 1851), 1:160; ST, Polizeiakten A–38, Württembergische Landesordnung; AB, Schätze, no. 282.

women from practising, however, nor prevent people from going to them if they felt they were skilful and effective. When male medical practitioners brought complaints, the women defended their activities with a strong sense of the value of what they were doing. Maria Marquardt, an Augsburg woman, noted that she had been working as a healer for thirty-three years, using 'the gift and skill which has been given to me by God'.[21] Elizabeth Heissin, a woman in Memmingen, when asked where she had learned her skill, answered that it came from 'God in Heaven who gave me soul and body, reason and understanding, for which I have to thank him daily'. She asked to be allowed to continue treating people, making the comment that such activities 'were done by honourable women not only here but also in other cities just as large and important as Memmingen. Such are fine things for women to do.'[22]

Occasionally women were even more forceful in their arguments, noting that in some cases women were better medical practitioners. Katharine Carberiner testified to the Munich city council:

> I use my feminine skills, given by the grace of God, only when someone entreats me earnestly, and never advertise myself, but only when someone has been left for lost, and they ask me many times. I do whatever I can possibly do out of Christian love and charity, using only simple and allowable means that should not be forbidden or proscribed in the least. Not one person who has come under my care has a complaint or grievance against me. If the doctors, apothecaries or barber-surgeons have claimed this, it is solely out of spite and jealousy.
>
> At all times, as is natural, women have more trust in other women to discover their secrets, problems and illnesses, than they have in men (as long as no unchristian means are used) – but perhaps this jealousy came from that. Undoubtedly as well, husbands who love and cherish their wives will seek any help and assistance they can, even that from women, if the wives have been given up (by the doctors) or otherwise come into great danger.
>
> Because I know that I can help in my own small way, I will do all I can, even, as according to the Gospel, we should help pull an ox out of the well it has fallen into on Sunday.[23]

Like the widows who asked to keep operating their shops, these women all argued their cases as individuals, stressing their practical

---

21. Handwerksakten Barbierer und Wundärzte, 21 Nov. 1571, quoted in Roper, 'Urban women', p. 17.
22. MM, Zünfte, 405, no. 12 (1603).
23. MU, Gewerbeamt, no. 9.

abilities and effectiveness, not their formal training or legal rights.
Though they occasionally mentioned that other women were also
practising, each pictured herself as blessed with extraordinary God-
given healing powers, for which she should be granted special dis-
pensation. The idea of divine favour as a justification for public
activity will appear again when we examine women who carried out
religious activities.

Another theme emerges from the requests of female medical
practitioners, however, and can be seen as well in women's requests
to work in other occupations. Women constantly stressed the fact
that others were dependent on them: their patients – 'especially
the poor and needy', their elderly parents, their invalid or ailing
husbands, their young children – 'my young and helpless child still
nursing at my breast'.[24] While this tactic may at first appear to be
simply a play on the authorities' sense of pity – and in some cases
it clearly was – recent studies of women's psychological and moral
development indicate that the approach may stem from something
deeper. Carol Gilligan, in *In a Different Voice: Psychological Theory and
Women's Development*, finds that women describe themselves in terms
of their relationships with others, relationships they see as a network rather than a hierarchy. When confronted with moral problems, women justify their solutions and the actions they take with
a value system based on responsibility in relationships and care,
rather than a value system based on rights and rules. 'The logic
underlying an ethic of care is a psychological logic of relationship,
which contrasts with the formal logic of fairness that informs the
justice approach.'[25] Because of this approach, women are much less
likely to base their decisions or actions on abstract principles or
absolutes, but instead to insist that each case must be seen in its
context.

Although the dangers of applying twentieth-century psychological theory to earlier periods are evident (as *Young Man Luther*
so clearly demonstrates), the parallels between the women Gilligan
studies and the Renaissance women making supplications about
their work are very striking. The Renaissance women also based
their appeals on their responsibility to others, to people who were
actually related to them or to people they cared about. They saw
themselves first as part of a network of relationships which included

24. AMS, 15, 1619, fol. 74 and 179; 1665, fol. 15–83 (*passim*); FF, Zünfte, Ugb. C–
32, R1 (1663); D–24, L4 (1698); Dübeck, *Købekoner og Konkurrence*, pp. 395–404.
25. Carol Gilligan, *In a Different Voice* (Cambridge, MA: Harvard University Press,
1982), p. 73.

family, relatives, friends, neighbours, and acquaintances, rather than as members of a hierarchical system such as a guild. They, too, rarely argued that they had a 'right' to do something because of precedent or regulations, but that the circumstances surrounding their cases might even warrant a break with the rules and the past. Though the appeals that were successful often involved the woman throwing herself on the mercy of the authorities 'as the protector and shield of poor widows and orphans', she may have done this not out of any feelings of her own helplessness, but out of feelings of her responsibility to others and a recognition that this kind of rhetoric might ultimately help her to live up to those responsibilities.[26] She recognized that male authorities thought of widows as a group deserving charity and pity, and saw that her request was more likely to be granted if they felt she was especially needy and would otherwise need public poor relief. Whether these women – who hired someone to write the supplication, provided the facts of the case, and appeared personally before city councils, ducal courts, and other bodies – were in fact as weak and pathetic as they attempted to appear is somewhat doubtful.

Trying to reconstruct women's thought patterns or determine which phrases were their own and which the notaries' in these supplications is very difficult and must always be done with reservations. An additional problem is that an ethic of care could – and did – lead some women to argue against their right to work. For example, if a woman had been an active participant in her husband's business, at his death she was required to pay back all debts. If these were high, it would be to her and her family's advantage to claim she had known nothing about, made no contribution to, and did not want to continue, the family business, for she could then retain her dowry and a share of the inheritance no matter how high the debts were. Because of her feelings of responsibility toward her family, she was thus forced into the curious position of denying her own competence and knowledge.[27]

Such occurrences were rare, however. A woman's assessment of her private responsibilities led much more often to a request for a public role, at least in the world of work. She asserted that she should be free to work because of, not despite, her private life. Thus in the realm of work as well as in financial decision-making,

26. FF, Ugb. D–24, L4, Bierbrauer (1698).
27. Ebel, *Forschungen*, pp. 110, 121; MU, 867, Schuldsachen (1598); AMS, Grosse Ratsbuch, no. 89 (1552); *Nürnberg Reformation 1564*, section 27:6; *Frankfurt Reformation* (Frankfurt, 1578), Part 3, Tit. 7, p. xii.

women stressed the connection, not the distinction, between public and private.

In a few instances, women's concern for their families went beyond matters of survival and support to matters of prestige. Jeanne Giunta, a book-publisher in Lyon, presented herself in a 1579 dedication as 'devoted to the typographical art, lest the honor that her father and Florentine ancestors won thereby be lost'.[28] She says:

> It is not new or unheard of for women to have such a trade, and one can find many of them who exercise not only the typographical art, but others more difficult and arduous, and who obtain thereby the highest of praise.[29]

Giunta's eloquence in praise of her family's honour sounds more like the voice of a Renaissance female writer than the voice of a typical Renaissance working woman. Perhaps this stems from the fact that the trade in which she was involved – printing – brought together individuals who were artisans, entrepreneurs, and scholars. She also came from a Florentine family, and so most likely had contact with the humanist tradition, a tradition that regarded public praise and honour as more important than political power, economic freedom, or legal rights. It is from women trained in this tradition, the learned women of the Renaissance, that we hear very different reasons for and a very different conception of a 'public role'.

Humanists since Petrarch had been concerned to choose between the 'vita activa' and the 'vita contemplativa', between public and private life, but had gradually opted for the active life. The best life, the one which earned oneself and one's family the most honour, was that which included not only scholarly activity, but also political and public service. Such a life was impossible for women, however, not only because of the realities of Renaissance politics, but also because for a woman, a public reputation was dishonourable, a sure sign of immorality and scandal.[30]

28. Quoted in Natalie Zemon Davis, 'Women in the *arts mécaniques* in sixteenth century Lyons', in *Lyon et l'Europe: Hommes et Sociétés* (Lyons: Presses Universitaires de Lyon, 1980), p. 155.

29. Ibid., p. 139.

30. Judith Brown, in an unpublished paper entitled 'A woman's place was in the home: women's work in Renaissance Tuscany', links this with patterns of employment in Renaissance Florence as well. She finds no women in occupations such as itinerant vendors, which did not require extensive training or capital investment and did have flexible hours (and thus would be possible for women with household chores), precisely because this was a publicly visible role. This is very different from the situation in northern Europe, in which no objection was made to female vendors

Male commentators linked women's educational achievements, if they were displayed in public, with unnatural sexuality; in the words of one, 'an eloquent woman is never chaste; and the behavior of many learned women confirms (this) truth'.[31] Thus educated women were caught in an internal conflict between humanist ideals and the traditional female role. They recognized that convention forced them to choose between these ideals; they could not be truly learned, or at least publicly learned, and still be ladies. Several female writers express this choice very clearly and often describe it in symbolic terms. Olympia Morata (1526–55), a Ferrarese Greek and Latin scholar who married a German physician and died at twenty-nine of the plague in Heidelberg, wrote, in Greek:

> I, a woman, have dropped the symbols of my sex,
> Yarn, shuttle, basket, thread.
> I love but the flowered Parnassus with the choirs of joy.
> Other women seek after what they choose.
> These only are my pride and my delight.[32]

or market-women on the grounds of their sex; they were frequently charged with hoarding, over-charging, making too much profit, selling spoiled food, or deceiving their customers, but so were male vendors. Brown finds particular opposition to women selling not only because they might be led into immoral behaviour, but because they might talk other women into buying something they didn't need – hadn't Eve talked Adam into something? – and thereby hurt their husbands. The exclusion of women from public life was so thorough that one commentator noted in 1610: 'In Florence women are more enclosed than in any other part of Italy; they see the world only from the small openings in their windows.' One is tempted to link this with the Florentine humanists' attempts to return to the values of classical Athens, where the cloistering of citizen women within the house was even more complete, though the humanist writers never specifically mention this. In comparing the Italian situation with that of northern Europe, one is struck by how much earlier a sharp division between public and private was made in Italy, and how much more often this division came about as a conscious move based on moral grounds – like protecting women's honour. In Northern Europe, the division was more gradual, and often came about as the unintentional result of something else – for example, the effort of Strasbourg to prevent the erosion of the city tax base, as noted above. At this point, I have not discovered any objections by Florentine women which would parallel those of the French and German women discussed above, although they probably exist somewhere. Brown does note the fact that opportunities for paid employment were increasing for Florentine women during the Renaissance as the silk industry expanded, which was work that could be carried out within the home. Thus their objections to restrictions in other fields may have been muted somewhat by the expanded opportunities in sericulture, silk-winding, and weaving.

31. From the text published by A. Segarizzi in his 'Niccolò Barbo, patrizio veneziano del secolo XV e le accuse contra Isotta Nogarola', *Giornale storico della letteratura italiana* 43 (1904): 53, quoted and translated by Margaret L. King, 'Thwarted ambitions: six learned women of the early Italian Renaissance', *Soundings* 76 (1976): 284.

32. *Carmina* in the *Opera* (Basel, 1570), quoted and translated by Roland H. Bainton in *Women of the Reformation in Germany and Italy* (Minneapolis: Augsburg Publishing House, 1971), p. 254. Similar sentiments are expressed by Madeleine des Roches

For most women the call of the spindle was too strong to resist. Even those who had been famous for their learning as girls gave up further study when they married and had families.[33] If they decided to write, they chose religious subject matter and often addressed their writings to their daughters or close female relatives. As Ruth Kelso and Ann Jones have pointed out, women's audiences and their themes were private.[34]

Those who chose the life of learning were generally forced to give up a normal family life. Most lived chaste lives of scholarly solitude in 'book-lined cells'. They chose celibacy because their desire for learning required it; their male admirers – and there were many – applauded that decision as they felt no woman could be both learned and sexually active. By becoming learned, she had penetrated a male preserve, which was only tolerable if she simultaneously rejected the world of women. As Margaret King has noted, 'Chastity was at once expressive . . . of the learned woman's defiance of the established natural order and of the learned man's attempt to constrain her energies by making her mind the prison for her body.'[35]

Both of these choices proved unacceptable to those searching for public honour and the opportunity to express themselves openly, as well as to those who wanted somehow to combine the two worlds. This latter ambivalence is best expressed in a poem by Catherine des Roches (1542–87), who, incidentally, chose never to marry and to remain with her mother until her death:

To my Spindle

My spindle and my care, I promise you and swear
To love you forever, and never to exchange
Your domestic honor for a good which is strange,
Which, inconstant, wanders, and tends its foolish snare.

With you at my side, dear, I feel much more secure
Than with paper and ink arrayed all around me

(1520–87), quoted in Tilde Sankovitch's essay, 'Inventing authority of origin: the difficult enterprise', in *Women in the Middle Ages and the Renaissance: Literary and Historical Perspectives*, ed. Mary Beth Rose (Syracuse, NY: Syracuse University Press, 1986), pp. 227–44.

33. King, 'Thwarted ambitions', *passim.*

34. Ruth Kelso, *Doctrine for the Lady of the Renaissance* (Urbana: University of Illinois Press, 1978), p. 25; and Ann Jones, 'City women and their audiences: Louise Labé and Veronica Franco', unpublished paper, p. 1.

35. Margaret L. King, 'Book-lined cells: women and humanism in the early Italian Renaissance', in *Beyond Their Sex: Learned Women of the European Past*, ed. Patricia H. Labalme (New York: New York University Press, 1980), p. 78.

For, if I needed defending, there you would be
To rebuff any danger, to help me endure.

But, spindle, my dearest, I do not believe
That, much as I love you, I will come to grief
If I do not quite let that good practice dwindle

Of writing sometimes, if I give you fair share,
If I write of your merit, my friend and my care,
And hold in my hand both my pen and my spindle.[36]

Public honour and expression were also justified eloquently by a variety of women. Many of these justifications ironically had a decidedly anti-female or at least anti-feminist bias. Most literary women, particularly those trained in Italy, accepted the male assessment of female inferiority and weakness as true for most women; they themselves, they felt, were simply exceptions. They often regretted being women because of 'the boundaries of my sex and mental powers' and sought to distance themselves from other 'babbling and chattering women'.[37] They recognized that they had a special gift, a love of learning aided by hard work, which could be available to any woman, but which only a few had the energy and will to develop. Laura Cereta, a fifteenth-century Brescian aristocrat, chided other women for their laziness: 'For knowledge is not given as a gift, but through study. . . . The free mind, not afraid of labour, presses on to attain the good.'[38] These women had accepted the Renaissance notion of the power of the individual will, which kept them from placing the responsibility for women's intellectual inferiority on anything but the women themselves. They argued that because they themselves had transcended this inferiority, they should have the right to claim public honour and gain a public reputation, in the same way that a few outstanding women had done throughout history.[39]

36. Translated and quoted in Sankovitch, 'Inventing authority of origin'. Catherine's ambivalence and the complex symbolism surrounding the pen and spindle – both may be identified with the penis, and the latter also with the female sexual organ in virginity as well as the mindless, female task of spinning – has been thoroughly analysed within the context of recent feminist literary criticism by Sankovitch in this paper.

37. Cassandra Fedele, *Epistolae et orationes* (Padua, 1636), p. 193, and Laura Cereta, *Epistolae* (Padua, 1640), p. 122, quoted and translated by King in 'Book-lined cells', pp. 71 and 73.

38. Cereta, *Epistolae*, p. 192, quoted and translated by King in 'Book-lined cells', p. 73.

39. As Hilda Smith has recently noted, sixteenth-century defences of women, written by both men and women, always include a list of 'women worthies', women who have transcended their sex and made important contributions. These were

There are a few women as early as the sixteenth century who recognized that the low intellectual status of their sex may not have been the responsibility of 'nature', or of the women themselves. Louise Labé (1520–66), a middle-class Lyonnaise poet who published her own poetry, was ambivalent about the matter, accusing both women and men. In 1555 she wrote:

> Since a time has come, Mademoiselle, when the severe laws of men no longer prevent women from applying themselves to the sciences and other disciplines, it seems to me that those of us who can should use this long-craved freedom to study and to let men see how greatly they wronged us when depriving us of its honor and advantages. And if any woman becomes so proficient as to be able to write down her thoughts, let her do so and not despise the honor but rather flaunt it instead of fine clothes, necklaces, and rings. For these may be considered ours only by use, whereas the honor of being educated is ours entirely . . . If the heavens had endowed me with sufficient wit to understand all I would have liked, I would serve in this as an example rather than an admonishment. But having devoted part of my youth to musical exercises, and finding the time left too short for the crudeness of my understanding, I am unable, in my own case, to achieve what I want for our sex, which is to see it outstrip men not only in beauty but in learning and virtue. All I can do is to beg our virtuous ladies to raise their minds somewhat above their distaffs and spindles and try to prove to the world that if we were not made to command, still we should not be disdained as companions in domestic and public matters by those who govern and command obedience. Apart from the good name that our sex will acquire thereby, we shall have caused men to devote more time and effort in the public good to virtuous studies for fear of seeing themselves left behind by those over whom they have always claimed superiority in practically everything. . . .[40]

It was not until the late seventeenth century, however, that women began to express publicly sentiments that might be labelled truly feminist, recognizing that women as a group suffered discrimination and should be given rights and privileges because of, not despite, their femaleness.[41]

---

implicitly anti-feminist, however, as they suggested that women could live up to male standards of accomplishment and action if only they tried hard enough. Hilda L. Smith, *Reason's Disciples: Seventeenth-Century English Feminists* (Urbana: University of Illinois Press, 1982), p. 7.

40. J. Aynard, ed., *Les Poètes Lyonnais Précurseurs de la Pléiade* (Paris: Bossard, 1924), pp. 157–9, quoted and translated in *Not in God's Image*, ed. O'Faolain/Martines, pp. 184–5.

41. Smith, *Reason's Disciples, passim.*

Learned women in northern Europe also felt the need to justify writing for a larger public than family and friends, and they too expressed their reasons in terms of possessing special gifts. These gifts could mean something as simple as being in the right place at the right time. Margaret Cavendish, the Duchess of Newcastle, introduces her biography of her husband with the comment:

> Nor is it inconsistent with my being a woman to write of wars, that was neither between Medes and Persians, Greeks and Trojans, Christians and Turks, but among my own countrymen, whose customs and inclinations, and most of the persons that held any considerable place in the armies was well known to me.[42]

A woman's gift could also be the inspiration provided by the life of another, a motivation for writing frequently expressed in dedicatory prefaces, for example, one by Aemilia (Bassano) Lanyer:

> To thee great Countess now will I applie
> My Pen, to write thy never dying fame;
> That when to Heav'n thy blessed Soule shall flie,
> These lines on earth record thy reverend name:
> And to this taske I meane my Muse to tie,
> Though wanting skill I shall but purchase blame:
> Pardon (deere Ladie) want of womans wit
> To pen thy praise, when few can equall it.[43]

This inspiration could even come to women who had received little formal education and could thus justify their writing. Mary Oxlie, a Scotswoman, began a poem in praise of the poet William Drummond:

> I Never rested on the Muses bed,
> Nor dipt my Quill in the Thessalian Fountaine,
> My rustick Muse was rudely fostered,
> And flies too low to reach the double mountaine.
>
> Then do not sparkes with your bright Suns compare,
> Perfection in a Womans worke is rare;
> From an untroubled mind should Verses flow;
> My discontents makes mine too muddy show;

42. Quoted in Natalie Zemon Davis, 'Gender and genre: women as historical writers, 1400–1820', in Labalme, *Beyond Their Sex*, p. 164.

43. *Salve Deux Rex Judaeorum . . .* (London: Valentine Simmes for Richard Bonian, 1611), quoted in Betty Travitsky, *The Paradise of Women: Writings by Englishwomen of the Renaissance* (Westport, CT: Greenwood Press, 1981), p. 98.

And hoarse encumbrances of household care
Where these remaine, the Muses ne're repaire.[44]

Gifts such as these could come to any woman, not only those who were particularly strong and energetic; as a result these writers did not see themselves as set apart from other women because of their writing. Rachel Speght, in her answer to a particularly vicious attack on women published in 1621, apologized for her writing and then noted: 'This my briefe Apologie (Right Honourable and Worshipfull) did I enterprise, not as thinking my selfe more fit then others to undertake such a taske, but as one, who ... did no whit dread to combate with our said malevolent adversarie. . . . This I alleage as a paradigmatical patterne for all women, noble and ignoble, to follow.'[45]

The most common reason women gave for writing was that they had received divine inspiration. Marie de France expressed this in the prologue to the *Lais*:

> Whoever has received knowledge
> and eloquence in speech from God
> should not be silent or conceal it,
> but demonstrate it willingly.[46]

Rachel Speght, in an allegorical poem entitled 'The Dream', argued:

> Both man and woman of three parts consist,
> Which *Paul* doth bodie, soule, and spirit call:
> And from this soule three faculties arise,
> The mind, the will, the power; then wherefore shall
> A woman have her intellect in vaine,
> Or not endevour *Knowledge* to attaine.
>
> The talent, God doth give, must be imploy'd
> His owne with vantage he must have againe:
> All parts and faculties were made for use;
> The God of *Knowledge* nothing gave in vaine.[47]

Anne Wheathill, a middle-class woman, thus introduced her volume of prayers and meditations:

44. *Poems by that most Famous Wit, William Drummond of Hawthornden* (London: R. Tomlins, 1656), in Travitsky, *The Paradise of Women*, pp. 139–40.

45. *A Mouzell for Malestomus* . . . (London: Nicholas Okes for Thomas Archer, 1617), in Travitsky, *The Paradise of Women*, p. 152.

46. Labalme, *Beyond their Sex*, pp. 27–8.

47. *Mortalities Memorandum with a Dreame Prefixed* (London: Edward Griffin for Jacob Bloome, 1621), in Travitsky, *The Paradise of Women*, p. 132.

Whereupon of the learned I may be judged grose and unwise; in presuming, without the counsell or helpe of anie, to take such an enterprise in hand; nevertheless, as GOD doth know, I have doone it with a good zeale, according to the weaknes of my knowledge and capacitie.[48]

Women used divine inspiration not only as a justification for writing literary works but also, of course, for writing or speaking about religion. Female mystics, anchoresses, abbesses, and even simple nuns throughout the Middle Ages had spoken and written on religious matters, asserting that God or the Holy Spirit had given them an insight which they were compelled to communicate to others. During the Reformation, women emerged both as supporters of the Protestants and defenders of the old faith, again stressing that the Spirit had given them understanding or was even forcing them to speak in public. When they were criticized for speaking out, a criticism usually supported by references to St Paul's admonitions against women speaking in church, they also defended their actions with biblical references, using both the Old and New Testaments.

Argula von Grumbach, a German noblewoman, wrote to the faculty of the University of Ingolstadt protesting the University's treatment of a young teacher accused of Lutheran leanings:

> I am not unacquainted with the word of Paul that women should be silent in church [1 Tim. 1:2] but, when no man will or can speak, I am driven by the word of the Lord when he said, 'He who confesses me on earth, him will I confess, and he who denies me, him will I deny' [Matt. 10, Luke 9] and I take comfort in the words of the prophet Isaiah [3:12, but not exact], 'I will send you children to be your princes and women to be your rulers.'[49]

A student at Ingolstadt responded to von Grumbach's protest with an anonymous satirical poem criticizing her actions:

> You forgot that you're a maid
> And are so fresh you're not afraid
> To assume the role of doctor
> and teach new faith to prince and proctor.
> By your stupidity inflated
> Ingolstadt is castigated.[50]

48. *A handfull of holesome (though homelie) hearbs* . . . (London: H. Denham, 1584), in Travitsky, *The Paradise of Women*, p. 146.

49. 'Wie ain Christliche Fraw des Adels . . . Sendtbrieffe/die Hohenschul zu Ingolstadt' (1523), quoted and translated in Bainton, *Germany and Italy*, pp. 97–8.

50. Th. Kolde, 'Arsacius Seehofer und Argula von Grumbach', *Beiträge zur Bayerischen Kirchengeschichte* XI (1905), quoted and translated in Bainton, *Germany and Italy*, p. 104.

To which she replied:

> I answer in the name of God
> To shut the mouth of this bold snob.
> Reproaches me with lack of shame
> When he is scared to give his name.
> A 'free student' at Ingolstadt,
> I will not give him tit for tat.
> If, as he boasts, he is so free
> Why not give his name to me?
> He tells me to mind my knitting.
> To obey my man indeed is fitting,
> But if he drives me from God's Word
> In Matthew ten it is declared
> Home and child we must forsake
> When God's honor is at stake.[51]

Sarah Fell, Margaret Fell Fox's daughter, used the example of Hannah to make a similar point:

> Hannah prayed, and Oh! the gracious words, and prayer, that pro-
> ceeded out of her mouth, by the powerful demonstration of the
> Eternall spirit, and the power of the almighty God in her . . . which
> all the adversaries and gainsayers against womens meetings, and
> womens speakings, is not able to gainsay, nor resist . . . the Lord hath
> regard unto and takes notice of the women, and despises them not.[52]

The Mary and Martha story was also mentioned frequently, as was the fact that the three women who discovered Christ's empty tomb were really the first preachers of the resurrection.

Women were most sharply criticized when they were writing or speaking on matters that involved theology or dogma rather than piety. As Roland Bainton has noted in his studies of women of the Reformation throughout Europe, women were more accepted and more active in any movement, from the *Alumbrados* in Spain to the Quakers in England, in which piety was more important than dogma, in which religious ideas were expressed in emotional terms rather than as systematic theology.[53] Women could not receive formal theological training in Europe, so any woman who did discuss theology stressed that the Spirit had given her understanding beyond that of most women, enabling her to write about such complicated

---

51. Ibid.
52. Milton D. Speizman and Jane C. Kronick, 'A seventeenth-century Quaker women's declaration', *Signs* 1, no. 1 (Autumn 1975): 237.
53. Roland Bainton, *Women of the Reformation: From Spain to Scandinavia* (Minneapolis: Augsburg Publishing House, 1977), pp. 10–11.

matters. Argula von Grumbach wrote: 'I send you not a woman's ranting, but the Word of God.'[54] Katharina Zell, the wife of Matthias Zell and a tireless worker for the Reformation in Strasbourg, wrote that she should be judged, 'not according to the standards of a woman, but according to the standards of one whom God has filled with the Holy Spirit'.[55]

Elizabeth Gottgabs, the abbess of Oberwesel convent, published a tract against the Lutherans in 1550 in which she noted:

> What can a poor woman do? What can she contribute as she has no arts or skill at arguing? If I am inexperienced and a child in such matters, so will my work be judged. But if it comes from the Spirit and is thus filled with the appropriate religious truth, then it will undoubtedly be noticed and accepted.[56]

These Northern European religious writers felt their inspiration set them apart from other women but did not make them superior. Unlike the women trained in the Italian humanist tradition, they downplayed their own merits and felt the Spirit could come to anyone. This attitude may have helped them maintain feelings of kinship with other women, but it created different problems. As Keith Thomas has noted:

> Appeal to divine inspiration was of very questionable value as a means of female emancipation. The whole emphasis was placed upon the omnipotence of God and the helplessness of his chosen handmaid should she be thrown upon her own resources. 'I am a very weak, and unworthy instrument,' wrote Mary Cary in the preface to one of her Fifth-Monarchy pamphlets, 'and [I] have not done this work by any strength of my own, but have been often made sensible, that I could do no more herein . . . of myself, than a pencil, or pen can do, when no hand guides it: being daily made sensible of my own insufficiency to do anything as of my self.' We should not overemphasize this objection: after all, Cromwell said the same sort of thing about his victories in battle without it noticeably diminishing their impact; but it does seem in this case that the language in which such writing

---

54. Bainton, *Germany and Italy*, p. 100.

55. Robert Stupperich, 'Die Frau in der Publizistik der Reformation', *Archiv für Kulturgeschichte* 37:226. Susan C. Karant-Nunn has also found that women preaching in Zwickau in the 1520s claimed to be divinely inspired. ('Continuity and change: some effects of the Reformation on the women of Zwickau', *The Sixteenth Century Journal* 13, no. 2 (Summer 1982): 37–8.

56. *Ein Christlicher bericht . . .* (Mainz, 1550), in 'Literarische Gegnerinnen Luthers', *Historisch-politische Blätter für das Katholische Deutschland* 139 (1907): 382. Teresa of Avila also expressed the same sentiments, as noted in Bainton, *Spain to Scandinavia*, p. 60.

was couched must have served to perpetuate the legend of women's inferiority.[57]

While female religious writers did stress female inferiority, both *vis-à-vis* God and *vis-à-vis* learned men, they also stressed, at least implicitly, the spiritual equality of all men and women. In the words of Anne Locke,

> But because great things by reason of my sexe, I may not doe, and that which I may, I ought to doe, I haue according to my duetie, brought my poore basket of stones to the strengthening of the wals of that Ierusalem, whereof (by Grace) we are all both Citizens and members.[58]

This recognition of spiritual equality did not lead women to demand political or social equality; there were no calls for woman's suffrage in the Renaissance. In this divided awareness they followed the thinking of most Catholic and main-line Protestant leaders, for whom spiritual equality was a private, internal matter and so was no justification for upsetting or opposing the established social order. The reaction against those who took the spiritual message to be a social, political, or economic one was sharp and swift, whether they were German peasants in 1525, English Diggers and Ranters in the 1640s, or Anabaptists throughout Europe in the sixteenth century.

Some women did feel, however, that spiritual equality or divine inspiration allowed them to speak or write about all matters concerning the church, including doctrine, church government, and finance. They were castigated for this approach, not only because they had no formal theological or legal training, but also because such matters were seen as public issues. Women were free to write and speak on religious matters as long as these were private and familial; prayer books, religious poetry, books of religious instructions for children, and devotional literature were perfectly acceptable. Sermons, exhortations, theological treatises, or doctrinal statements were not, however, both because they were more often presented publicly and because they concerned the church – any church, whether Protestant or Catholic – as a public institution.

Women challenged this division between private and public. They argued either that the Spirit had indeed given them the right to address public religious matters or else that there simply was no

57. Keith Thomas, 'Women and the Civil War sects', *Crisis in Europe, 1560–1660*, ed. Trevor Aston (Garden City, NY: Doubleday, 1967), p. 355.
58. *The Markes of the Children of God* (London, 1609), in Bainton, *Spain to Scandinavia*, p. 93.

basis for division between public and private in matters of religion. Argula von Grumbach based her argument on Matthew 10: 11–14, noting that cities, towns, and households are all held equally responsible for their 'worthiness' before God; thus the borders of concern and activity for the pious housewife were at least the town walls, if not beyond.[59] Katharina Zell agreed, noting: 'I have never mounted the pulpit, but I have done more than any minister in visiting those in misery. Is this disturbing the peace of the Church?'[60] Like the Strasbourg women opposing the imposition of guardians, these women saw a continuum from the household to the world beyond rather than a sharp split between public and private.

In a variety of realms of life, the Renaissance experienced the 'new division between public and private life' that Kelly describes, a division which continued to grow until it had expanded into a chasm by the nineteenth century. The period also saw opposition by women both to that division itself and to their being relegated to the private sphere. Widows, working women, writers, medical practitioners, midwives, and female religious thinkers all defined a 'public role' somewhat differently. For some, it was the ability to bring their own suits to court; for others, the right to keep operating a shop, to use skills they had mastered, or to support their families or defend their church; for still others, the opportunity to write something that would be remembered forever.

Women's arguments often involved setting themselves apart from other women because of their particular economic situation, strength of intellect, or contact with God, and thus they sound anti-feminist. As restrictions increased, however, these women also showed the beginnings of a recognition that their situation and circumstances resulted more from their sex than from their social status, economic class, or innate abilities; they showed, in other words, the beginnings of what we might call a feminist analysis of their situation. They usually presented their cases only in individualized terms, either because they felt this approach would be more effective, they really did perceive their circumstances as extraordinary, or they did not realize the larger implications of their arguments; however, a few spoke for all women: 'This is a fine and honourable female trade'; 'Women have more trust in other women'; 'What I want for

---

59. Stupperich, 'Die Frau', p. 223.
60. 'Ein Brief an die Genze Bürgerschaft der Stadt Strassburg...' in Bainton, *Germany and Italy*, p. 72.

our sex is to see it outstrip men'; 'The Lord hath regard unto and takes notice of women'; 'Such are fine things for women to do'. Thus one of the unforeseen results of the sharp public/private, male/female division was individual women's own realization that society viewed them, first of all, as women; and that any claim to a public role would have to be based on either a rejection of their female nature or on support for all women. Women since the Renaissance have faced the same choice.

PART ONE

Religion

Introductory essay

The history of religion in the early modern period, particularly in Germany but also elsewhere in Europe, has been dominated by the story of the Protestant and Catholic Reformations, and so has focused on theological ideas and intellectual currents, only rarely noting that the thinkers and leaders under study are all men. Within the last thirty years, some historians have moved away from a heavy emphasis on theology to examine the impact of the Reformation on the common people and their role in it, creating a social history of the Reformation. This Reformation, too, has generally been implicitly and occasionally even explicitly the story of the 'common man', with a focus on guilds, city councils, peasant armies, and other groups which did not include women. Thus the earliest work on women in the early modern period tended to be in realms other than religion, where researchers felt their ideas and insights were more welcome.

All of this is beginning to change, as witnessed by the publication in 1995 of the four-volume *Oxford Encyclopedia of the Reformation*, which, along with the expected articles on Martin Luther and John Calvin, transubstantiation and predestination, also has a large number of articles on topics that have been of concern to historians of women and gender: women, witchcraft, sexuality, family, marriage, weddings, prostitution. It also has biographical entries on twenty-five women, which may not seem like many compared to the roughly 500 men, but is assuredly many more than it would have been had this encyclopedia been prepared twenty years ago.

The entries in the *Encyclopedia of the Reformation* reflect how the historiography of women in early modern religion has developed. The first studies were largely biographical, focusing on queens and noblewomen who supported or hindered the Reformation in their territories, or the wives of prominent reformers, or the very few independent female religious leaders. Along with this came studies of male opinions about women and the family, which initially tended to view certain leaders either very positively or very negatively; only

recently have they begun to point out the nuances and contra-
dictions in their thoughts. Both of these types of studies generally
use well-known sources, but approach them with questions that have
never been asked before, and both continue today, particularly for
parts of Europe that have not been fully explored.

Along with biographical studies and analyses of male ideas,
recent research has examined how these ideas were communicated
through the use of plays, woodcuts, marriage and funeral sermons,
pamphlets, letters, and popular stories. Art historians are analysing
the paintings, woodcuts, and engravings that were produced to support both the Protestant and Catholic Reformations to find positive
and negative images of women, and to see how female characters
and attributes were used symbolically, such as the Pope being shown
as the Whore of Babylon in Protestant pamphlets.

Historians are also discovering new sources which provide evidence of women's lives. By combing archives and private family documents, social historians are discovering that the institutional and
political changes that accompanied the Reformation often affected
women's lives more than changes in religious ideas alone. The closing of the convents, secularization and centralization of public welfare and charitable institutions, changes in marriage and baptismal
ordinances, the possibility of divorce, clerical marriage, the closing
of public brothels, and the hardships created by the religious wars
– all these had a particular impact on women, and have recently
been the focus of local and regional studies.

Historians of women have also begun to explore women's responses to the Reformation, responses of both words and actions.
Women were not simply passive recipients of the Reformation message, but left convents, refused to leave convents, preached, proph-
esied, discussed religion with friends and family, converted their
husbands, left their husbands, wrote religious poems, hymns, and
polemics, and were martyred on all sides of the religious contro-
versy. Official sources, such as tax lists, city council minutes, and
court documents, reveal some of these actions, as do the published
and unpublished writings of women. Finding such sources can be
very difficult, for fewer women than men recorded their thoughts,
ideas, and reactions, and when they did, their writings were rarely
saved, for they were not regarded as valuable. Many of Luther's
letters to women, for instance, are still extant, though only a few
of theirs to him are. None of his wife's numerous letters to him
survive, though most of his to her do. Finding information about
women in official sources poses special problems, for sources are

arranged by male names, occupations, and places of residence, with women recorded only sporadically and then often only when widowed or single. Despite these difficulties, however, a picture of women's responses to the Reformation is slowing emerging, enabling us to compare these across class, regional, and denominational lines and to the more familiar responses of men. Men's experience as men has also been the focus of a few studies, with historians beginning to question, for example, what effects the Reformation had on notions of masculinity or ideas about real and symbolic fatherhood.

The essays which follow explore the lives of many women, some of whom may surprise you: mothers who were saints, Protestant nuns, women who published religious pamphlets. Women such as these have helped us to view the Reformation in a new way, to make a story that used to be one of pastors, princes, and peasants one which now includes both halves of the population.

CHAPTER TWO

From spiritual virginity to family as calling[1]

Sanctification of family life has long been seen as one of the most important social results of the Protestant Reformation. Recently, however, several scholars have pointed out the roots of this in pre-Reformation writers. John Yost notes that civic and Christian humanists also thought that 'God had established marriage and family life as the best means for providing spiritual and moral discipline in this world'.[2] Margaret Miles comments that this idea goes all the way back to Clement of Alexandria, who thought marriage might actually be better than celibacy as it trains the soul in patience.[3] Most medieval writers disagreed, and followed Jerome in favouring virginity over marriage, but they differed in their definition of virginity. As Clarissa Atkinson points out, some writers defined virginity as a physical state which, once lost, could not be recovered, and others, including Augustine, as a moral state, a 'purity of the mind which is not lost when the body is violated'.[4] The physical definition prevailed in the early Middle Ages, but by the later Middle Ages virginity was increasingly defined by psychological and moral qualities such as purity and holiness. This meant that individuals could achieve a state of spiritual virginity through an ascetic lifestyle or

1. The research for much of this paper was carried out in the Duke August Library in Wolfenbüttel, West Germany, and I would like to thank the American Council of Learned Societies and the Deutsche Akademische Austauschdienst for their support for this research. The paper was written while I was pregnant with my son Kai, whom I wish to thank for making the words of these long-dead women resonate so clearly.
2. John Yost, 'Changing attitudes toward married life in civic and Christian humanism', *American Society for Reformation Research* 1 (December 1977): 164.
3. Margaret Miles, *Fullness of Life: Historical Foundations for a New Asceticism* (Philadelphia, 1981), p. 45.
4. Clarissa Atkinson, ' "Precious balsam in a fragile glass": the ideology of virginity in the later Middle Ages', *Journal of Family History* 8 (Summer 1983): 134.

mystical visions, even if they were married and had families. This change was particularly important for women, for whom virginity had always been the crucial factor in achieving a reputation for holiness. In contrast to the early Middle Ages, when almost all female saints were physically virgins, in the late Middle Ages there were a number of saints who were also wives and mothers.

Late medieval women opting for spiritual virginity occasionally left their families, viewing them as a hindrance to their religious vocation, but more often forced their husbands to accept vows of chastity and continued living with them in a spiritual marriage. They thus continued on in their maternal and familial responsibilities, abstaining only from a physical spousal relationship. The change brought by the Protestant Reformation, then, was not so much a sanctification of *family* life, but a sanctification of the spousal sexual relationship. Late medieval Catholic women could become spiritual virgins *after* having had sexual relations, but Protestant women could be spiritually pure while still having sex, or, in the eyes of some Protestant writers, *through* having sex. As Wolfgang Capito wrote to Zwingli on the latter's marriage, Anna Reinhart 'had taken him as if he were Christ to be her husband'.[5] In the more famous words of Luther:

> What better and more useful thing can be taught in the church than the example of a godly mother of the household who prays, sighs, cries out, gives thanks, rules the house, performs the functions of sex and desires offspring with the greatest chastity, grace and godliness: What more should she do?[6]

Male opinions about the relative virtues of marriage and virginity are fairly well known, so what I would like to do is explore some of the less well known female opinions. I will start with a few pre-Reformation saints and holy women from several parts of Europe to give an idea of their attitudes towards virginity and the family. The bulk of my discussion will examine post-Reformation women, both those who accepted and those who rejected or modified Protestant ideas about the family as a woman's calling. In this I will limit my discussion to Germany, as there are numerous examples from that area alone.

The pattern of women renouncing the world and their husbands to live a spiritual life begins with Mary of Oignies (d. 1213), who convinced her husband that they should live together as brother

---

5. Quoted in Alice Zimmerli-Witschi, 'Frauen in der Reformationszeit' (Ph.D. Thesis, University of Zurich, 1981), p. 178.

6. *D. Martin Luthers Werke. Kritische Gesamtausgabe* (Weimar, 1883–), Vol. xx, p. 149.

and sister, and Elizabeth of Hungary (d. 1231), who refused to remarry after her husband died on a pilgrimage and devoted her life to charity.[7] It continues with Angela of Foligno (d. 1309) whose mother, husband and sons all died within a short time of each other, leaving her free to lead a religious life and leading Angela to comment: 'I received a great consolation from their death.'[8] The fifteenth century provides the example of Catherine of Genoa (d. 1510), the mystical theologian, who, after ten years of marriage, convinced her husband to live with her in a life of perpetual continence.[9] All of these women rejected the sexual aspect of marriage, but neither they nor their biographers (nor the Catholic Church itself, as they all later became saints) were concerned about their physical status. They never comment on the fact that they are not virgins, or that they had been wives and mothers.

This lack of concern about physical status was not shared by one of the most famous late medieval married saints, Bridget of Sweden (d. 1373). Bridget was married and had eight children, but after her husband's death began to see visions, travelled to Rome, and pushed for the return of the papacy to Rome. She apparently accepted the idea that one could become a 'spiritual virgin' through widowhood or marital chastity, for her visions never mention spousal relations, nor does she see herself as a 'bride of Christ', a frequent self-description of actual or spiritual virgins. Motherhood still troubled her, however, and her visions show a very ambivalent attitude toward giving birth. She often sees giving birth as evil, as in this vision of a mother speaking to her daughter:

> Listen, O my snaky and poisonous daughter; woe to me that I have been your mother . . . you, daughter, resemble the tail of a cow as it walks in muddy places; every time the cow moves its tail, it stains and splatters those that are approaching. You, daughter, are like a cow, because you do not have divine wisdom and you function according to the workings and movements of your body. Therefore, O my daughter, why are you proud of your progeny? There will never be any honour or virtue with you, for the filth of my viscera was your couch. My shameful member was your entrance into the world, and the filth of my blood your vestment when you were born.[10]

7. Atkinson, ' "Precious balsam" ': 139–40.
8. Ibid., p. 140.
9. Donald Christopher Nugent, 'Mystic of pure love: Saint Catherine of Genoa', in Katharina M. Wilson, ed., *Women Writers of the Renaissance and Reformation* (Athens, GA, 1987), p. 68.
10. *Revelationes* 6.52, quoted in Barbara Obrist, 'The Swedish visionary: Saint Bridget', in Katharina M. Wilson, ed., *Medieval Women Writers* (Athens, GA, 1984), p. 242.

Mary appears frequently to Bridget to ease her doubts about maternity, and to remind her that she, too, was a mother. She does this by sharing the most graphic details of birth, as in the following vision:

> After this the Virgin Mary appeared to me again, in the same place, and said: it has been a long time since in Rome I promised you that I would show you here in Bethlehem how my offspring had been born. And although in Naples I showed you something of it, that is to say the way I was standing when I gave birth to my son, you still should know for sure that I stood and gave birth such as you have seen it now – my knees were bent and I was alone in the stable, praying; I gave birth to him with such exultation and joy of my soul that I had no difficulties when he got out of my body or any pain. Then I wrapped him in swaddling clothes that I had prepared long ago. When Joseph saw this he was astonished, and full of joy and happiness, because I had given birth without any help.[11]

It is hard to imagine someone who was not a mother having a vision like this, and clear that Bridget needed to be reassured that physical motherhood was perfectly compatible with holiness. Virginity was something that could be defined morally and had always been somewhat ambivalent physically (Augustine, for example, discusses the issue of whether a woman whose hymen had been broken by something other than intercourse was still a physical virgin), but motherhood was an inescapable biological fact. Mary thus provides Bridget with the example of holy maternity she needs. Mary performs the same function for Margery Kempe, the fifteenth-century English mystic, who, when despairing about being pregnant again, hears Christ say: 'Forasmuch as thou art a maiden in thy soul, I shall take thee by the one hand, and my Mother by the other hand, and so shalt thou dance in Heaven with other maidens and virgins.'[12]

Though motherhood was troubling to late medieval female saints and mystics, it could also be a source of power. Mother-saints were often very closely identified with the Madonna, and depicted with the infant Jesus. Though this may seem to be a familial image, it is not, because, of course, there is no father in the picture. With the Madonna, the presence of the father is simply understood, but when a human woman, the mother of human children, is depicted with a more than human infant, the question of paternity becomes problematic. The mother-saint, like Mary in Bridget's vision, appears

11. *Revelationes* 7.22 in ibid., p. 245.
12. *The Book of Margery Kempe*, ed. William Butler-Bowdon (New York, 1944), p. 42.

to have given birth by herself, with a father playing a very minor role, in the same way that Joseph appears afterwards in Bridget's vision. Thus the maternal image subverts, rather than complements, a familial image.

This subversion has been demonstrated best in a study of Saint Francesca of Rome (d. 1440) by Guy Boanes and Lyndal Roper, who note that her cult provided strong maternal images, but her actions proved detrimental to family values.[13] Her feelings of responsibility extended beyond her immediate family to include the poor, and she frequently gave away grain from family stores during times of famine. She actually worked in the hospital her marital family had established, and begged in the streets, to the great embarrassment of all her relatives. Even the miracles attributed to her tended to be anti-family, for many of them involved getting a husband to allow his wife to enter a convent.

Though she helped other married women who wished to renounce family life and join a convent, Francesca herself did not enter a convent until after her husband died, nor did she attempt a spiritual marriage. She recognized that although her husband and family may have hindered her sense of religious duty somewhat, they also allowed her to fulfil it, providing wealth with which she could help the poor and establish a convent. Her family also gave her a social position from which she could critique aristocratic Roman society much more effectively than if she had been lower or middle class.

Thus by the end of the Middle Ages physical motherhood was not an impossible obstacle on the road to sanctity, and spiritual motherhood, expressed through helping others, could speed one along that road. What happened when motherhood became the only road to the sanctified life? How did Protestant women view virginity and maternity? How did they conceptualize their family and their family responsibilities?

I would like to begin with women who accepted the Protestant ideas, who attacked virginity or viewed the family as their calling. Generally, those who attacked virginity had very little to say about the family, as they seemed to model themselves on Luther's more polemical anti-celibacy pieces. In 1524, Ursula Weyda published a treatise against the abbot of Pegau, in which she attacks monastic vows and tells monks and nuns to leave their monasteries:

13. Guy Boanes and Lyndal Roper, 'Feminine piety in fifteenth-century Rome: Santa Francesca Romana', in Jim Obelkevich, Lyndal Roper, and Raphael Samuel, eds, *Disciplines of Faith: Studies in Religion, Politics and Patriarchy* (London, 1987), pp. 177–93.

Help, help! It is time to escape God's anger before it suddenly descends upon us ... Leave the old church and return to your baptismal vows, for in baptism we all vow to believe his word and follow it ... Break the bonds of your monastic tonsure and take off your habits with free and certain conscience, even if you have taken a thousand oaths.[14]

Ursula of Münsterberg, a noblewoman who left a convent in Saxony and took refuge with the Luthers in Wittenberg, compared good works, including vows of celibacy, to adultery. In a letter explaining why she had left the convent, she comments: 'we are bound to Christ in marriage through baptism and belief ... but we had come out of our chaste marriage to Christ ... by committing adultery with another, that is with our feigned good works'.[15] It is interesting that Ursula cannot give up the Bride of Christ imagery that was so prevalent in convent spirituality, but instead extends it to include all baptized believers. This means that in her opinion all Christians were expected to be spiritual virgins, though this did not imply a change in their physical status. By comparing convent life to adultery, Ursula is in fact turning the idea of spiritual virginity on its head, stating that only those who do not renounce the world are spiritual virgins, for only they can be true to their vows to Christ.

Ursula Weyda and Ursula of Münsterberg thus agree that virginity is no guarantee of higher spiritual status, but they make no mention of marriage as the better road to salvation. I have looked through a number of works published by German women in the sixteenth and seventeenth centuries, and not one of them praises marriage in and of itself, nor discusses their duties toward their husbands. Many of them *do* see the family as their calling and proper sphere of activity, but they define that family in terms of motherhood, grandmotherhood, and, interestingly enough, daughterhood.

Noblewomen wrote advice manuals for their sons, who would be rulers, and their daughters, who might become regents.[16] The most common printed works by women in early modern Germany

---

14. Quoted in Paul A. Russell, *Lay Theology in the Reformation: Popular Pamphleteers in Southwest Germany 1521–1525* (Cambridge, 1986), pp. 202–3.

15. Ludwig Rabus, *Der heiligen auserwählten Gotteszeugen ... wahrhafte Historien* (Strasbourg, 1572), fol. 478v.

16. E.g. Elizabeth of Brandenburg, *Unterrichtung und Ordnung ... so Wir aus ganz mütterliche Wohlmeinung und getreuem Herzen ... unserm freundlichen, herzlieben Söhne ...* (1535), reprinted in Friedrich Karl von Strombeck, ed., *Deutscher Fürstenspiegel aus dem 16. Jahrhundert* (Braunschweig, 1824), pp. 57–130; Benigna Solms-Laubach, *Immer Grünendes Klee-Blatt Mütterlicher Vermahnungen* (Frankfurt, 1717).

were collections of hymns, prayers, and sayings designed for private devotional purposes. These often include a preface explaining why the author felt it necessary to break convention and publish, with the most usual justification being duty as a mother. Anna von Schleebusch, a German noblewoman, extended this to include her duty as a grandmother, comparing herself to Jacob who blessed not only his own children but his son Joseph's children.[17]

Sibylla Schwarz was also concerned about her duty as a daughter, translating the following poem out of Dutch for her readers:

A Daughter Nurses her Mother

O mother, with so many heavy bands
You lie here bound both feet and hands
Driven to such need by hunger and thirst
That only death these bands will burst.
What should I do for you? You who have raised me
I'll do the same now for you who have suckled me
Come, take bread and wine, nurse now from me
We'll both be daughters, both mothers be.[18]

Women also wrote poems to commemorate the deaths of their fathers and mothers, some of which were later published along with the pastoral funeral sermon.[19] In the large Stolberg collection of funeral sermons at the Herzog August Bibliothek in Wolfenbüttel, I found no poetry by women commemorating their husbands, nor is any mentioned in the recent lexicon of German women writers by Woods and Furstenwald or Paullini's eighteenth-century list of learned women.[20] At least in terms of sentiments they were willing to express publicly, early modern German women saw their family vocation as primarily maternal and filial, rather than spousal.

Like St Francesca of Rome, some German women also interpreted their maternal responsibilities more broadly, to include mothering their subjects, if they were rulers, or helping other women and families. Elisabeth of Brunswick and Emilie-Juliana of Schwarzburg-Rudolstadt both wrote advice books for their subjects, in Emilie's

17. Anna Elisabeth von Schleebusch, *Anmuthiger Seel-erquickender Wurtz-garten oder auserlesenes Gebet-Buch . . .* (Leipzig, 1702), Vorrede.

18. Sibylla Schwarz, *Deutsche Poetische Gedichte* (Danzig, 1650), unpaginated (my translation).

19. E.g. Duke August Library, Wolfenbüttel, Stolberg Leichenpredigtesammlung, nos. 7335, 13113, 15418.

20. Jean M. Woods and Maria Furstenwald, *Schriftstellerinnen, Kunstlerinnen und gelehrte Frauen des deutschen Barock* (Stuttgart, 1984); C.F. Paullini, *Hoch und Wohl-gelahrtes Teutches Frauenzimmer* (Frankfurt and Leipzig: Johann Michael Funcke, 1712).

words 'out of our sovereign motherly heart and hand for the strengthening edification of our subjects' (Lands-*kinder* in German).[21] Her
book consists of prayers and hymns written especially for families,
to help them through difficult times such as the death of children.
It includes special prayers for midwives and pregnant women to say
which ask God to provide physical strength and wisdom, and to make
the delivery quick and uncomplicated. This was very different from
similar prayer books written by pastors, which tell women to leave
everything passively up to God and to remember that their labour
pains are divinely ordained.[22]

While authors such as these appear to accept the Protestant
notion of the family as the woman's proper avenue to spirituality,
their very writing, or at least publication of their writings, subverts
this, as it gives them an audience beyond the family. This can be
seen more clearly in authors who view family responsibilities as only
one small part of a woman's calling as a Christian. Katherina Zell,
for example, saw herself as in some ways a spiritual mother to many,
yet the advice she gave was as anti-family as any of the actions of
St Francesca. She wrote consoling the wives of men who had been
banished for religious reasons from the small town of Kentzingen,
but does not advise patience or joining their husbands in exile (as
many city councils would suggest to the wives of religious refugees),
but 'taking on a manly Abraham-like spirit'. She notes that Christ
clearly said that only those willing to leave father and mother, husband, wife, and child would be worthy to follow him.[23] Though in
this case the split between husband and wife did not occur because
the spouses chose different faiths, Katherine's words indicate what
her opinion in a situation like that would be. That opinion was
shared by Argula von Grumbach, the most famous female supporter
of Luther, who refused to be silent even though her husband did
not agree with her and was removed from his official position because of her writings.[24] Both of these women use maternal imagery
(Argula at one point describes herself as a mother lion defending
her young) and a sense of responsibility toward their actual family
or the family of Christians to justify disobedience of or at least

21. Emilie Juliana von Schwarzburg-Rudolstadt, *Geistliches Weiber-Aqua-Vit* . . .
(Rudolstadt, 1683), title page.

22. Johann Hugo, *Tröstlicher und kurtzer bericht/wes sich alle Gottsforchtige schwangere
Ehefrauwen/ vor und in kindnoten zu trösten haben* (Frankfurt, 1563).

23. Katherina Schutzin [Zell], *Den leydenden Christgläubigen weybern der gemain zu
Kentzingen* . . . (Augsburg, 1524).

24. Rabus, *Heiligen Gotteszeugen*, fols. 103–29.

lack of concern for a spouse. They thus sharply disagree with every magisterial Protestant reformer, who view a woman's duty of obedience toward her husband as taking precedence over her religious beliefs.[25] Zell and von Grumbach view the family not as the limit of a woman's religious vocation but, like St Francesca, as the source for her religious authority in the larger community.

There were other Protestant female writers who not only subverted ideas about the family as the proper sphere for women's religious activity, but directly opposed them. Anna von Medum published a long tract trying to convince Jews to convert to Christianity and Christians to act better so that Jews would convert. She includes a discussion of her family's opposition to her writing and to her preaching to the Jews, justifying her actions by explaining that God 'called' her to do this. She uses the word 'calling' (*Beruf*) throughout, and comments that true callings are internal and have nothing to do with one's external or official calling as a pastor or similar religious authority. Like Katherina Zell and Anna von Schleebusch, she goes back to the Old Testament for models, noting that women not only preached, but also circumcised their sons, performing a ritual central to the Jewish tradition though they did not have any official priestly office.[26] For Anna von Medum, her 'calling' had no limits, and was totally unrelated to her family.

This was also true for Protestant women who supported virginity. Though most Protestant writers viewed marriage as the proper state for all women, Luther in his early writings had suggested the possibility of a truly Christian celibate life, and a few later writers expanded on this. Conrad Porta, a pastor in Eisleben, wrote one of the first 'virgin's mirrors' in 1580, telling women who are virgins not to despair, for their state was also blessed by God.[27] His approval of virginity was ambivalent at best, for he consoles them that they would probably eventually find a man, with the aid of their parents and God. Protestants could not reject virginity totally, of course, because it was still a necessary precondition to marriage, but just made it a temporary virtue. 'Virgin's mirrors' written by Protestant pastors became a common genre in the late sixteenth century,

25. *D. Martin Luthers Sämmtliche Werke* (Erlangen and Frankfurt, 1826–57), Vol. li, p. 428; John H. Bratt, 'The role and status of women in the writings of John Calvin', in Peter de Klerk, ed., *Renaissance, Reformation, Resurgence* (Grand Rapids, MI, 1976), p. 9.

26. Anna von Medum, *Geistlicher Judischer Wundbalsam* . . . (Amsterdam, 1646), pp. 39–49.

27. Conrad Porta, *Jungfrawenspiegel, Aus Gottes Wort und D. M. Lutheri Schrifften* . . . (Eisleben, 1580).

perhaps motivated by the realities of early modern marriage patterns, and most of them adopt a similar consolatory tone.[28]

Women who supported virginity did not view it as an unfortu-
nate necessity, however, nor as a temporary state to be abandoned
whenever the first man became available, but as a positive good.
Anna Sophia of Hesse-Darmstadt was the abbess of the Protestant
convent of Quedlinburg, which survived as an independent institution until the eighteenth century. In her collection of devotional
poetry and songs, she notes that David had specifically required
virgins to sing God's praises in the Psalms, as had Augustine.[29]
She compares the women in her convent to the vestal virgins, commenting that they also had the tasks of watching, guarding against
sacrilege, and making offerings. Not content to rely on ancient
examples, she also quotes Anna Maria von Schurman, her contemporary, on the value of education to women and their duty to
honour God on their own. As the abbess of a powerful convent,
Anna Sophia had a source of religious authority totally independent of a family which brought with it a strong sense of vocation.
Though abbesses were often compared to mothers, she nowhere
uses maternal imagery to strengthen or describe her position, but
relies solely on the image of God calling each Christian.

Most Protestant women writers *did* see their religious calling in
terms of motherhood, however, but interpreted that motherhood
in spiritual as well as physical terms and used it as a springboard
for activities beyond the family sphere. In this they had powerful
pre-Reformation models of motherhood to guide them: not only
Mary but also the late medieval mother-saints provided them with
examples of sanctified motherhood that they could adapt to their
own purposes.

Women were not as willing to accept Protestant ideas of sanctified spousehood, and in many cases their sense of maternal duty led
them to oppose and contradict their husbands publicly. Unlike Capito
in his comment to Zwingli, they clearly did not view their husbands
as if they were Christ. This can be seen not only in words but also
in actions: many widows who were easily still of marriageable age
chose not to remarry, though this might mean financial hardship.[30]

28. Georg Draudius, *Bibliotheca Librorum Germanicorum Classica* . . . (Frankfurt, 1611),
and Frankfurt Book Fair catalogues from 1560 to 1700, now found in the Duke
August Library, Wolfenbüttel.

29. Anna Sophia, *Der treue Seelenfreund Christus Jesus* . . . (Jena, 1658), Zuschrift.

30. Barbara J. Todd, 'The remarrying widow: a stereotype reconsidered', in Mary
Prior, ed., *Women in English Society 1500–1800* (London, 1985), pp. 54–92.

I can only speculate as to the reasons for this, for no female writer discusses spousehood or wifely duties directly. One reason might be the lack of pre-Reformation models for sanctified spousehood, another women's recognition that substituting duty to husband for duty to Christ was no gain. A third might be women's taking the notion of the priesthood of all believers literally.

Whatever the reasons for women's lack of interest in their spousal duties, it disturbed both Protestant and Catholic male authors. Protestants in Germany and elsewhere emphasized wifely obedience much more than maternal duties. The Counter-Reformation Catholic Church encouraged the cult of Joseph, stressing that even in this most unusual of families, the mother and child were under the care and guidance not only of a heavenly, but also an earthly, father. Even Mary was no longer to gain her strength only from God, as she had in Bridget's vision, a clear lesson for ordinary women.

Judging by the women who wrote in early modern Germany, the lesson was not learned exactly as the religious authorities wished it to be. Protestant women writers in early modern Germany used the notion of the family as their religious calling when it suited their purposes, and rejected it when it did not. Sanctified motherhood, which was supposed to be a complement to family unity, had instead turned out to subvert it. Sanctified spousehood or, as Milton put it, 'she for God in him', was rejected, disregarded, or ignored.

CHAPTER THREE

Ideology meets the Empire: reformed convents and the Reformation

In December 1564, Stephan Mollitor, a Wittenberg-trained pastor, chose a rather strange text for the funeral sermon of the abbess of Gernrode: 'Woe to you, O land, when your king is a child' (Ecclesiastes 10:16). He then used the text not only to criticize the fact that the new abbess was only fifteen years old but also to rail against female rulership in general.[1] Mollitor was not alone in his disparagement of female rule, of course; John Knox's *First Blast of the Trumpet Against the Monstrous Regiment of Women* had appeared only six years earlier. Among those joining their voices were François Hotman, Michel de Montaigne, Thomas Becon, and George Buchanan. These attacks led others, including John Aylmer, John Case, Torquato Tasso, and John Leslie, to defend female monarchy.[2] The debate over gynaecocracy hinged on questions about what we would now call the social construction of gender: How could a queen exhibit the manly qualities necessary for ruling while still remaining a woman? If her private moral virtues came into conflict with her political duties, which should take precedence? How could a married queen be a monarch over her own husband at some times, yet a wife to him at others?

Most of those involved in the debate over female rule lived in western Europe, where the issue was not simply a theoretical one in the century of Mary and Elizabeth Tudor, Mary Stuart, and

1. Dr Franke, 'Elisabeth von Weide und Wildenfels: Aebtissin des freien weltlichen Stiftes Gernrode 1504–1532', *Mitteilungen des Vereins für Anhaltische Geschichte und Altertumskunde* 8 (1899): 328; Hans K. Schulze, *Das Stift Gernrode* (Cologne: Böhlau, 1965), p. 51.
2. Summaries of the debate over female rule may be found in Paula Louise Scaling, 'The scepter or the distaff: the question of female sovereignty, 1515–1607', *The Historian* 41, no. 1 (1978): 59–75; Ian MacLean, *The Renaissance Notion of Woman* (Cambridge: Cambridge University Press, 1980).

Catherine de Medicis. Knox had been inspired to write his attack by the dreadful (in his eyes) spectacle of two Catholic queens on one island – Mary Tudor and Mary Stuart. Stephan Mollitor was also speaking from personal experience, for forty years earlier he had been called to Gernrode when the abbess of the free imperial abbey there decided to become Lutheran, and, like any good Lutheran prince, hired Protestant preachers to convert her territory.[3] Mollitor had thus spent his entire pastoral career under the jurisdiction of not only women but abbesses, women whose very existence seemed to contradict Lutheran teachings. No wonder the poor man was upset.

Although 'Lutheran abbess' may sound like an oxymoron, it is not. During the sixteenth century, a number of convents and abbeys transformed themselves into Protestant establishments, in some cases with surprisingly little loss of power or independence for the abbess. Most of these were located in several areas of central Germany that became Protestant, particularly the duchies of Lüneburg and Brunswick/Calenburg and the bishoprics of Magdeburg and Halberstadt. These same areas of the Holy Roman Empire also saw some convents which successfully resisted all attempts by Protestant secular nobles to close them or to force them to give up their Catholicism; these convents remained as Catholic institutions within Protestant territories, in some cases until the nineteenth century. The abbesses of many of these Lutheran or Catholic convents continued to play an active political, religious, and cultural role in the Empire, despite attacks on female rule and grave doubts on the part of their fellow Lutherans about the possibility of a truly Christian (that is, Lutheran) convent life. I would like to explore the story of these convents – Quedlinburg, Gandersheim, Heiningen, Gernrode, Lüne, Meyerdorf, Althaldensleben, Marienborn, Barsinghausen, Mariensee, Wennigsen, Wülfinghausen, Ebstorf, Isenhagen, Medingen, Walsrode, and Wienhausen – in an attempt to understand what factors allowed the abbesses apparently to overcome both gender and religious ideology.

Medieval historians have, of course, long recognized the tremendous power wielded by abbesses. Three of the abbeys under consideration – Gandersheim, Quedlinburg and Gernrode – were free imperial abbeys, whose abbesses were the most powerful women in the Empire. Free imperial abbeys were institutions whose only overlord was the emperor; the abbess had jurisdiction not only over the abbey itself, but also over the land and villages belonging to it,

---

3. Franke, 'Elisabeth von Weide', p. 328; Schulze, *Das Stift Gernrode*, p. 64.

which made her a *Landesherr* (territorial ruler). These three abbeys were not convents in the technical sense of the term inasmuch as their residents had never taken formal vows or been strictly cloistered. They were generally termed secular endowments (*weltliche Stifte*), and the residents could leave if they chose or if family circumstances required it. They belonged to no order and were only vaguely under the jurisdiction of a bishop.[4] Each of them had been established in the ninth or tenth century and had a long tradition of learning and cultural activity; Quedlinburg and Gandersheim in particular had European-wide reputations. Their ties to the emperors were extremely close, as they had either been founded by one of the Ottonians or received imperial privileges shortly after their founding. All of the abbesses and most of the residents were from the nobility, and their families had frequently made large bequests to the abbeys. Thus, by the time of the Reformation, the abbeys had received centuries of imperial and noble patronage, with their rights and privileges confirmed by both pope and emperor.

These three abbeys were not only recipients of patronage, however, but also sources of it. Long before the Reformation, the abbesses had received the right to name most church officials in their territories. (Matilda, the sister of Otto II and the abbess of Quedlinburg in the tenth century, was even called 'metropolitana' – overseer of bishops – by her biographer).[5] Each abbess also appointed secular officials such as toll collectors, bailiffs, and legal personnel. She had the right to mint money or to grant minting privileges, and many of the coins bear portraits of the abbess herself or her family's coat of arms.[6] Except for the emperor, she was the ultimate legal authority in her territory, and apparently, because she was not cloistered, she did hear some cases herself. As a free imperial ruler, she sent a representative to the imperial diet, and she frequently brought specific cases to the emperor if she felt her rights were being infringed upon. The abbess was also a source of artistic patronage, hiring builders, sculptors, painters, and musicians; and of social patronage, supporting hospitals, orphanages,

4. They may thus be compared with Fontevrault and the Paraclete in France, which also had close ties to the French royal house. Penny Schine Gold, *The Lady and the Virgin: Image, Attitude and Experience in Twelfth-Century France* (Chicago: University of Chicago Press, 1985).

5. Suzanne Wemple, 'Sanctity and power: the dual pursuit of early medieval women', in *Becoming Visible: Women in European History*, ed. Renate Bridenthal, Claudia Koonz, and Susan Stuard, 2nd edn (Boston: Houghton Mifflin, 1987), p. 148.

6. Alan M. Stahl, 'Monastic minting in the Middle Ages', in *The Medieval Monastery*, ed. Andrew MacLeish (St Cloud, MN: North Star Press, 1985), pp. 65–7.

and occasionally schools. The noble residents of the abbey did not do any manual labour themselves, so the abbey hired local women and men to cook, clean, and tend the gardens.

The other convents were not independent in the way these three abbeys were but were under the control of regional nobles. This did not mean that their abbesses were not powerful figures, however. Because the convents were landowners, they had control over the residents on that land and the same sort of patronage that free imperial abbesses had, though on a smaller scale. The other convents were also allied with noble houses, for most of their residents were noble; in some cases they were also allied with a religious order, to which, at least in theory, they could turn for support or assistance.

The political and intellectual high point for many of these convents was the eleventh century, before the Gregorian reforms ordered strict cloistering for women and the universities emerged to provide advanced education for men only. Most of them were not moribund in the later Middle Ages, however, as evidenced by their involvement in pre-Reformation reform movements designed to return convent life to its original standards of religious observance. Particularly after the Council of Constance, many convents passed stricter rules, and nuns travelled from one reformed convent to another to help others restore discipline. In the 1440s, for example, three nuns from the reformed convent at Heiningen near Goslar stayed for three years at the convent at Neuwerk, helping the nuns there to make similar reforms.[7]

Some convents enthusiastically accepted reform, but others were less willing, particularly if the impetus for reform came from outside the convent and the nuns could see that other than spiritual factors were involved. In many areas of Germany, bishops used reforms to try to curtail the power of prominent abbesses and take over convent property; in other areas secular rulers were the instigators. For example, in 1469 the convent of Wienhausen was forcibly reformed by Duke Otto of Lüneburg, who removed all objects of value from the premises, noting that poverty was part of the strict rule of St Benedict. The abbess, Katherine von Hoya, violently objected, and all the nuns agreed with her, telling Otto that obedience to the abbess was an even more important part of Benedictine life. Otto then carted the abbess and most of her assistants off to

---

7. Lina Eckenstein, *Women Under Monasticism* (New York: Russell and Russell, 1963 [1896]), p. 418.

one of his castles and placed Wienhausen under the authority of the abbess from a nearby convent who had been more amenable to his reform moves. Under continual pressure from the duke and from high officials of the Benedictine order, the nuns at Wienhausen agreed to elect a new abbess, but only if the old one were allowed to return to the convent and live out the rest of her days in peace. The new abbess and the nuns had to agree to Otto's reforms, but they immediately began encouraging local noblewomen to give gifts of money and goods to replace the confiscated (or, more accurately, stolen) property.[8]

The reform at Wienhausen predated the Protestant Reformation by more than half a century, but in many ways it prefigured later attempts by Protestant rulers to introduce Lutheran teachings. Indeed, the later chroniclers at Wienhausen, who were nuns, date all further events at the convent from this reform, not from the Lutheran one, indicating which event was more significant in the minds of the nuns themselves. Though such reforms could be financially disastrous for convents, they did bring back high standards of spirituality.

Long traditions of power, independence, and prestige combined with a reinvigorated spiritual life to make reformed convents the most vocal and resolute opponents of the Protestant Reformation. Duke Ernst of Brunswick, who had been trained at the University of Wittenberg, began to introduce the Reformation in his territories in the 1520s. Almost all of the male monasteries agreed with very little pressure to disband and give their property to the duke, but all of the female convents in his territories refused even to listen to Protestant preachers. In Walsrode and Medingen, the nuns locked the convent doors and took refuge in the choir of the chapel; Duke Ernst first pleaded with them personally, then ordered the gates forcibly opened and a hole bashed in the choir for his Protestant preacher to speak through.[9] In Lüne, the nuns lit old felt slippers to drive out the preacher with smoke, sang during his sermons, and when ordered to be quiet did their rosaries. They were forbidden to hold public mass, and so they held it in their private quarters or the convent granary.[10] The nuns in Heiningen

8. *Chronik und Totenbuch des Klosters Wienhausen* (Wienhausen: Kloster Wienhausen, 1986), fols. 19–41.

9. Adolph Wrede, *Die Einführung der Reformation im Lüneburgischen durch Herzog Ernst den Bekenner* (Göttingen: Dietrich, 1887), pp. 127, 217.

10. Ulrich Faust, ed., *Die Frauenklöster in Niedersachsen, Schleswig-Holstein und Bremen*, Germania Benedictina, Vol. 11: Norddeutschland (St Ottilien: EOS-Verlag, 1984), p. 384.

refused to give any food to the Protestant preachers sent to the convent, hiding whatever they had, and none gave in to ducal pressure to leave, despite promises of a 20-gulden dowry.[11]

The prioress and the convent residents at Ebstorf answered ducal threats with a letter stating that though they had no wish to oppose his wishes, they knew their only salvation lay with the Catholic Church. Though they were 'poor uneducated women', they knew the church fathers approved of convent life, and they had read praises of virginity in the Bible; so how could they listen to someone who preached against convents? Both the duke and his chief reformer Urbanus Rhegius were very upset by this letter, replying that it was unseemly for a woman to address a prince on matters of theology. Rhegius went on to comment that if it was proper for a father to discipline his children, why should not the duke, as the father of his country, force them to hear about the true religion?[12] He also noted that the letter could not possibly have been written by the prioress herself as its grasp of theology and church tradition was impossible for a woman.

The prioress of Ebstorf was not the only woman to show a clear understanding of theology, however. The visitations accompanying the Reformation in the bishoprics of Magdeburg and Halberstadt found many nuns able to argue very skilfully in favour of their Catholic beliefs. The abbess at Althaldensleben, for example, pointed out that if she had accepted the first Protestant teachings introduced into the convent, she would now be branded a Philipist and have to change her beliefs again. As she was uncertain what further changes the Protestants might make, she preferred to stay with the old Catholic teachings.[13]

Convents in other parts of Germany also opposed the Reformation with similar tactics, but what makes these central German convents different is the fact that the nuns were often successful.[14] Of the twenty-two female convents in Magdeburg and Halberstadt,

11. Gerhard Taddy, *Das Kloster Heiningen von der Grundung bis zur Aufhebung,* Veröffentlichungen des Max-Planck Instituts für Geschichte 14 (Göttingen: Vandenhoeck and Ruprecht, 1966), pp. 120, 122.

12. Wrede, *Die Einführung der Reformation,* p. 218.

13. Franz Schrader, *Ringen, Untergang und Überleben der katholischen Klöster in den Hochstiften Magdeburg und Halberstadt von der Reformation bis zum Westfalischen-Frieden,* Katholisches Leben und Kirchenreform im Zeitalter der Glaubensspaltung 37 (Münster: Aschendorff, 1977), p. 43.

14. For the situation in two other areas of Germany see Franz Binder, *Charitas Pirckheimer: Aebtissen von St. Clara zu Nürnberg* (Freiburg: Herder'sche Verlagshandlung, 1878); Lorna Jane Abray, *The People's Reformation: Magistrates, Clergy and Commons in Strasbourg 1500–1598* (Ithaca, NY: Cornell University Press, 1985); and Francis

eleven were still in existence and still Catholic in 1648, despite having been plundered repeatedly in both the sixteenth-century wars of religion and the Thirty Years War. None of them, I might add, owed its Catholic status to the Edict of Restitution. This rate of survival is much higher than that of male monasteries, of which six out of twenty-nine survived to 1648. That any convents or monasteries survived in Protestant areas is of course somewhat unusual, and Franz Schrader attributes this to their strong spiritual life, economic independence, and banding together, combined with differences in opinion among Protestant authorities about how they should be handled.[15] Schrader makes no attempt to explain the gender difference, however, though it is rather striking and was commented upon by both Protestant and Catholic contemporaries. In the sixteenth century, Bishop Heinrich Julius, who became Lutheran, noted, for example, that the continuation of Catholicism in the convents was 'the result of the resoluteness of the nuns. . . . The monks, though, are very lukewarm in the practice of their Catholic religion.'[16] In 1625, a Catholic missionary reported back to the papal nuncio in Cologne that 'the four women's convents [in Magdeburg] have remained truer to their beliefs and vows than the men's monasteries, who have almost all fallen away'.[17]

The convents in Brunswick and Lüneburg were not successful in their struggle to remain Catholic, but by becoming Protestant they were able to survive the Reformation as religious institutions for women. Most of them fought theological change as long as they could, but they finally put independence and spiritual practices above mere theology and agreed to accept Lutheran doctrines as long as their lives were not radically changed. Indeed, it is often difficult to tell exactly what religion a convent followed at any particular point, as Catholic and Protestant women lived together and their observances and rules were a mixture of both. Lüne, for instance, was forced to accept a Protestant ordinance in 1555, which declared that the convent was now an educational centre (*Ausbildungsstätte*) for women; but the women wore Benedictine habits and described themselves as belonging to the Benedictine

---

Rapp, 'Zur Spiritualität im Elsässischen Frauenkloster am Ende des Mittelalters', in *Frauenmystik im Mittelalter*, ed. Peter Dinzelbacher and Dieter R. Bauer (Ostfildern: Schwabenverlag, 1985). Rapp notes that some Strasbourg convents also survived into the seventeenth century, which would make Alsace an interesting case for comparative purposes.

15. Schrader, *Ringen, Untergang, und Überleben*, p. 86.
16. Quoted in ibid., p. 54.
17. Quoted in ibid., p. 74.

order until 1610.[18] In 1573, Duke August passed a new convent ordinance that allowed all residents to leave whenever they wished, but later a nun in Heiningen who did not wish to leave and marry was punished and had all her goods confiscated.[19] The first Lutheran pastor was sent to Wienhausen in 1529, and the duke later took away much of the convent's land and all its prayer books. Church services were not switched from Latin to German until 1602, however, and until the 1640s residents who died provided in their wills for candles to be lit perpetually for the repose of their souls. The first woman willingly left the convent to marry only in 1651.[20]

Free imperial abbeys could hold out longer against military and political pressure than those under the control of nobles, as we can see in the case of Gandersheim, which fought the Reformation for decades. The abbey was surrounded by the territory of the dukes of Brunswick, some of whom were vigorous Lutherans who wanted abbey lands for the support of their new university. Duke Julius (ruled 1568–89) attempted to have his own candidates installed as abbesses, and during much of his reign there were actually two abbesses, one elected by the residents and one chosen by the duke. Both attempted to collect taxes and tolls, and the elected abbess continually received imperial letters of protection, which were of little practical use in asserting her rights. Finally, in 1588, the elected abbess was allowed to return and assume her rightful place after the body of a newborn child was found in the abbey's cellar and the duke's appointee admitted that she had borne the child, which had died soon thereafter.[21] Despite the confession, there have always been doubts about whether the child was actually hers or whether the abbey residents had pressured her into confession; she was, in any case, imprisoned for the rest of her life.

In political terms, the abbey won, for the duke gave up his claims to abbey land and agreed that it would remain a free imperial endowment. Later abbesses continued to receive imperial recognition and to send representatives to the diet. In religious terms, the duke won, for the abbess elected in 1589 and all those who followed her were Protestant, no longer requesting papal recognition. Anna Erika, elected in 1589, clearly placed politics and abbey traditions over religion, however; she had backed the elected abbess

18. Faust, *Die Frauenklöster*, p. 385.
19. Taddy, *Das Kloster Heiningen*, p. 138.
20. *Chronik Wienhausen*, fols. 70, 82, 88, 89.
21. Kurt Kronenberg, *Die Äbtissinnen der Reichsstifts Gandersheim* (Bad Gandersheim: Gandersheim Kreisblatt, 1981), pp. 103–6.

who preceded her in a long dispute with the duke, despite the fact that the two women differed in religion.[22]

Outside pressure was not always responsible for an abbey's accepting the Reformation. In Gernrode and Quedlinburg the abbesses themselves accepted the new theology and energetically introduced it into their territories. They took to heart Luther's early teachings on the possibility of a truly Christian convent life, which were also expressed in statements of faith such as the Wittenberg Articles of 1536: 'If certain persons of outstanding character, capable of living a life under a rule, feel a desire to pass their lives in the cloister, we do not wish to forbid them, so long as their doctrine and worship remain pure.'[23] They chose to ignore his more negative opinions, most fully expressed in *De votis monasticis* (1522).[24]

Elisabeth of Weide and Wildenfels was elected abbess of Gernrode in 1504, the first free imperial abbess to open her abbey to Lutheran teachings. She sent a representative to the Diet of Worms in 1521, in part to ask for the emperor's assistance in getting land she felt was the abbey's back from local nobles who had confiscated it, but also to get a firsthand report about what Luther was saying. Five years later she began to reform her territories, bringing in the later so ungrateful Stephan Mollitor, and appointing Lutheran pastors in the villages under her rule. One of these was soon driven from his post by Johann von Anhalt, a local nobleman who had long had designs on abbey land and who argued that the abbess had no right to appoint married Lutheran clergy. The abbess appealed to the emperor, who valued imperial tradition more than religion in this case and ordered Anhalt to allow the pastor to resume his duties. Elisabeth also appealed to both the pope and the emperor in 1527 to force local bishops to stop taxing her subjects; despite her Lutheran appointments, both pope and emperor took her side against the bishops.[25] Gernrode continued to receive imperial privileges at least until 1577.[26]

Anna von Stolberg, abbess of Quedlinburg from 1515 to 1574, controlled nine churches, a hospital, and two male monasteries.

22. Ibid., pp. 109–11.
23. 'Wittenberger Artikel, 1536', *Quellenschriften zur Geschichte des Protestantismus* 2 (Leipzig: A. Deichert, 1905), p. 75.
24. For a discussion of Luther's changing ideas on the possibility of chaste convent life, see Bernhard Löhse, *Mönchtum und Reformation – Luthers Auseinandersetzung mit dem Mönchsideal des Mittelalters. Forschungen zur Kirchen und Dogmengeschichte* 12 (Göttingen: Vandenhoeck and Ruprecht, 1963).
25. Franke, 'Elisabeth von Weide', p. 319.
26. Schulze, *Das Stift Gernrode*, p. 10.

She accepted the Protestant Reformation in the 1540s, started a consistory, made all priests swear to the Augsburg Confession, and set the salaries for both church and school officials. Despite vehement objections from the order, she turned her Franciscan monastery into a city school for both girls and boys, an interesting gender reversal of the usual pattern of male authorities transforming convents into schools or using convent property to fund scholars at universities. Though these actions gave clear proof of her religious ideas, when she asked for a coadjutor abbess to help her in her later years, she received both imperial and papal confirmation of the woman she chose. Seventeenth-century abbesses were confirmed by the emperor alone but continued to exert both secular and spiritual authority. In 1680 the abbess Anna Sophia issued a new baptismal ordinance, and in 1700 the abbess Anna Dorothea gave out an 'edict against the separatists'.[27]

Given Lutheran ideas about the power of secular authorities in matters of religion and the near impossibility of a truly Christian convent, these abbesses might appear naive at best. Indeed, what happened later at Gernrode would seem to bear this out. By 1532, the princes of Anhalt were putting pressure on the nuns to elect an abbess of their choice, and by 1541 they ordered the abbess to report to them on the state of religion in her churches. After 1564, all the abbesses were members of the house of Anhalt and were chosen as children, remaining in the convent only until they married.[28] The pattern was repeated in several other convents, leading some historians to dismiss all post-Reformation convents as simply residences and finishing schools for noble daughters.[29] The problem with this is that not all convents came under strict princely control. In Quedlinburg and Gandersheim, the abbesses retained their secular independence and their religious authority. The Lutheran convents in Brunswick and Lüneburg and the Catholic convents in Magdeburg and Halberstadt also continued to recruit new members, maintain schools, and control land and population. What accounts for their endurance?

The easiest explanation for the abbeys' survival lies in the networks of patronage in which they were enmeshed. In the case of the free imperial abbeys, the Habsburg emperors were not willing

27. Friedrich Ernst Kettner, *Kirchen und Reformations Historie des Kayserl. Freyen Weltichen Stiffts Quedlinburg* (Quedlinburg: Theodore Schwan, 1710), pp. 123–64.

28. Schulze, *Das Stift Gernrode*, pp. 50–1, 66.

29. Cf. Erhard Stiller, *Die Unabhängigkeit des Klosters Loccum von Staat und Kirche nach der Reformation* (Göttingen: Vandenhoeck and Ruprecht, 1966), p. 71.

to move against or even reprimand institutions where female members of their own family had resided and whose connections to former emperors were stronger than their own. The free imperial abbeys represented Habsburg ideas of what the Empire should be in an era of increasingly strong secular territorial rulers, a fact not lost on the abbesses. Elisabeth von Weide, for example, played on imperial pride when she commented that bishops taxing her subjects were attempting to limit imperial power.[30] In other convents, noble residents used their family connections and ties to religious orders to put pressure on secular rulers. The abbesses in Brunswick, for example, sent both their male relatives and local clergy to the emperor to request a letter of protection; the letter was issued, though it was not of much use against Duke Ernst's drastic measures.[31]

In the case of convents controlled by local nobles, regional peculiarities provide part of the answer to the question of longevity. The duchies of Brunswick and Lüneburg were unusual in that the holdings and income from the convents never became simply part of the ducal treasury. They were administered by ducal officials, but as a separate fund, which exists to this day.[32] This has been dismissed as simply a bureaucratic distinction, but it did give convent residents officials who were specifically responsible for their interests and to whom they could go with complaints, which they did.[33] The decision to leave convent income as a separate fund was first made by Duchess Elisabeth of Brunswick, who ruled during the minority of her son. Elisabeth wrote a long advice manual to her son about how to be a good ruler, in which she specifically noted that all convent income was to be used for charitable, educational, and religious purposes; she said that no nuns should be ordered out of convents or convents left without lands or income because 'to leave them just like that would be un-Christian and unloving'.[34] Though her son paid no attention to the rest of her advice, he, and his successors, followed her on this point. Protestant rulers

---

30. Franke, 'Elisabeth von Weide', p. 319.
31. Wrede, *Die Einführung der Reformation*, pp. 131, 224.
32. 'Klosterfonds und Klosterkammer Hannover', *Niedersachsen, Zeitschrift für Heimat und Kultur* 82 (March 1982): 21.
33. Taddy, *Das Kloster Heiningen*, p. 146.
34. 'Unterrichtung und Ordnung . . .', in *Deutscher Fürstenspiegel aus dem 16. Jahrhundert*, ed. Friedrich Karl von Strombeck (Braunschweig: Friedrich Vieweg, 1824), pp. 57–130. (It is tempting to make a connection between her action and the fact that all the monastic establishments that survived in her territories were for women, though this would probably be pushing the evidence a bit far.)

throughout much of Germany used economic pressure to force convents and monasteries to close, confiscating their lands and holdings, and this small difference in Brunswick may have been more
significant than it initially appears to be.

Political factors also entered in in both Brunswick and the
bishoprics. In the sixteenth century, Brunswick was divided politically between two branches of the same ruling house. The convents
were often caught in power struggles between the two branches, as
well as among the emperor, pope, and both the Protestant and
Catholic dukes. The initial efforts through plunder and destruction
of the Protestant dukes to force the convents to convert had not
worked; the second round of efforts, begun under Duke Julius in
1538, were more moderate and more concerned with securing the
outward allegiance of the convents than their theological change.[35]
Because territories flopped back and forth between Protestantism
and Catholicism, depending on the whims of the current duke and
the military situation, it worked to everyone's advantage to obscure
the exact religious affiliation of a convent; that way, depending
on the outcome, Catholic orders and authorities did not have to
admit ever losing control, and Protestant authorities could claim
an early date of conversion.[36] The situation in the bishoprics was
somewhat similar, with episcopal and other church authorities dis-
agreeing on how convents should be handled.[37]

The convents' role as a source of patronage was also instru-
mental in their survival. Positions as officials were often handed
down within the same family for generations, a source of income
that would be lost if the abbey were dissolved. The convents continued to absorb poorer women as support staff, making lower-class
families more willing to accept a convent in their midst. I have not
found a single example of popular protest against any of these
convents after the initial wave of convent storming in the 1520s.
In May 1525, Elisabeth von Weide was, in fact, able to convince a
group of peasants intent on storming Gernrode to return home by
reminding them of all she had done for them; though her words
were very patronizing, the fact that she neither took any revenge on
the leaders nor allowed her brother to do so is certainly partly
responsible for the fact that the abbey was left alone after that.[38]

35. Taddy, *Das Kloster Heiningen*, p. 128.
36. Stiller, *Die Unabhängigkeit*, p. 14.
37. Schrader, *Ringen, Untergang, und Überleben*, p. 86.
38. Franke, 'Elisabeth von Weide', pp. 326–7.

Patronage and political circumstances alone are not enough to explain the abbeys' continuation as Lutheran institutions. After all, male monasteries were also linked to the emperor and noble houses and provided services to local populations. To my knowledge, only one male monastery, the Augustinian house of Möllenbeck, near Rinteln on the Weser River, accepted Lutheran theology, yet continued as a monastic establishment, and then only until 1675.[39] As mentioned above, many fewer male monasteries put up a fight against the Reformation, and those that did capitulated much faster than female houses. In the ability of the four abbeys to survive, gender played as important a role as political connections.

Why were women's religious institutions more successful in their efforts to remain in existence? The answer to this question involves both external and internal factors. To look first at external factors: after initial attempts to convert or disband them, women's religious establishments were allowed to survive because they were not viewed to be as great a threat as monasteries. The residents were, after all, women. Gender stereotypes about female weakness may have provoked opposition to female rule, but they also enabled men to take actual examples of that rule less seriously, at least at the local level. We can see this in the language of documents such as the Peace of Augsburg: in the clause termed the 'Ecclesiastical Reservation', church officials who gave up Catholicism after 1552 were to lose their positions. Though the framers were certainly aware of the existence of female-headed abbeys, the language was completely male-specific.[40] Abbesses were simply not as significant in practical terms as abbots or bishops. (Sixteenth-century writers did not generally use the generic male, as evidenced by the frequency with which 'male and female' or 'he and she' show up in documents.)

Though noble and upper-bourgeois families hungered for abbey lands, they were also unwilling to bear all the consequences of closing the abbeys. What would they do with their daughters if the abbeys were closed? The cost of dowries was rising in early modern Germany, and even wealthy families could often not afford to marry off all their daughters; they wanted an honourable place to send those daughters for whom they could not find an appropriate marriage partner. The problem was particularly acute in the case of the free imperial abbeys, for all the residents were noble. As six

39. François Biot, *The Rise of Protestant Monasticism* (Baltimore: Helicon, 1963), pp. 65–7.
40. 'Augsburger Reichstags abschiede', in *Geschichte in Quellen*, ed. F. Dickmann, Renaissance, Glaubenskämpfe, Absolutismus 3 (Munich: Beck, 1966), pp. 204–10.

noblemen wrote to Duke Heinrich of Brunswick when he first spoke of suppressing all monasteries, including Gandersheim: 'What would happen to our sisters' and relatives' honour (*Ehre*) and our reputation (*Rumes*) if they are forced to marry renegade monks, cobblers, and tailors?'[41] The lack of available marriage partners among the nobility was certainly understood by the abbey residents as well: studies of convents and other *Stifte* that admitted both bourgeois and noble women have found that noble women tended to stay until death in convents that were forbidden to admit new members, while the bourgeois residents left.[42] Convent life for daughters was more integrated into noble than middle-class family patterns, and so it was harder for both the residents and their families to give up these foundations.

There were also internal factors that contributed to the continuation of the convents. Most of these convents were institutions with long-established traditions of political power and cultural importance. The residents were very aware of their position and fought any attempt, whether theologically motivated or not, to restrict their independence. They realized, too, that as women they had no position in the Lutheran church outside the abbey, and so they were more adamant than their monastic brothers about keeping the convents flourishing.[43] Former monks could become pastors in the Protestant churches, but for former nuns the only role available was that of pastor's wife, an unthinkable decrease in status for a woman of noble or patrician birth.

That the firmness of the nuns resulted from loyalty to their own traditions, and not simply loyalty to Catholicism, can be seen by their reaction to Counter-Reformation moves, particularly those proposed by the Jesuit order. When with the Edict of Restitution Heiningen was returned to Catholicism, the Jesuits wanted to take over part of the convent's income, but the nuns adamantly refused. The Jesuits tried again in 1644 by sending two representatives, but the nuns

41. Johann Karl Seidemann, *Dr. Jacob Schenck, der vermeintlicher Antinomer, Freibergs Reformator* (Leipzig: C. Hinrichs'sche, 1875), Anhang 7, p. 193.

42. Christina Vanja, *Besitz- und Sozialgeschichte der Zisterzienserinnenklöster Caldern und Georgenberg und des Prämonstratenserinnenstiftes Hachborn in Hessen im späten Mittelalter*, Quellen und Forschungen zur hessischen Geschichte 45 (Darmstadt: Historische Kommission für Hessen, 1984), p. 195.

43. The same gender difference was found in France during the Revolution, when nuns were much more likely than monks to stay in their communities. (Olwen Hufton and Frank Tallett, 'Communities of women, the religious life, and public service in eighteenth-century France', in *Connecting Spheres: Women in the Western World, 1500 to the Present*, ed. Marilyn Boxer and Jean Quataert (New York: Oxford University Press, 1987), p. 76.)

would not let them in the door.[44] The Counter-Reformation church was appalled to learn that the convents in Magdeburg and Halberstadt allowed anyone in to hear mass, which it regarded as a flagrant violation of cloister regulations. It ordered the nuns to stop, but they paid no attention.[45]

Abbesses clearly recognized their special status and reflected it in their writings as well as actions. Anna Sophia of Quedlinburg, for example, published a number of hymns and a book of meditations entitled *Der treue Seelenfreund Christus Jesus*.[46] Her book included a long introduction and afterword discussing the special duties that virgins had to praise God, and comparing the women in her convent to both the vestal virgins and biblical women such as Deborah, Hannah, Judith, and Mary. She quoted Augustine about virgins praising Christ and mentioned Anna Maria von Schurman's recent book advocating women's education, which had been published in Utrecht in 1641 in Latin.[47] Her work was regarded as theologically suspect by some Lutheran theologians, who thought that she stressed the ubiquity of Christ's presence too strongly in her comment that women could feel this presence equally with men. The book of meditations was later judged acceptable, however, and was reprinted several times.[48] Anna Sophia made no general statements about the capabilities of all women, but she did stress those of her noble co-residents; she clearly recognized that identification with her class would take her further than identification with her gender.

Although in practice the continuation of convents was rarely challenged after the mid-sixteenth century, there were still theoretical doubts about the abbesses' spiritual and temporal powers, particularly among Lutherans. Even those Lutheran commentators who chose to praise the abbesses felt it necessary to justify and explain their power. Friedrich Kettner, who wrote a long history of Quedlinburg that was published in 1710, included a long discussion about why the titles 'abbess', 'prioress', and 'canoness' could legitimately be maintained, using examples from the New Testament and early church to show that these were not later popish inventions. He also gave a wonderfully convoluted argument about why the authority of a woman should not be the curse it is deemed

---

44. Taddy, *Das Kloster Heiningen*, p. 184.
45. Schrader, *Ringen, Untergang, und Überleben*, p. 58.
46. Published by Georg Sengenwald, Jena, 1658.
47. Una Birch, *Anna von Schurman: Artist, Scholar, Saint* (London: Longmans, 1909), p. 188.
48. Ibid., p. 130.

to be in Isaiah 3:12 ('I will give you children to be your oppressors and women to be your rulers...'). It seems that Isaiah was not talking about the female sex here but about those of feminine temperament (*Gemuth*), according to Kettner, who then included a long list of ancient and contemporary female rulers.[49]

The abbesses' temporal authority was questioned in that most theoretical milieu, the university law school. The early seventeenth century saw frequent debates in schools such as Rostock and Ingolstadt about whether women could succeed to feudal holdings, debates which included the case of abbesses.[50] Their case was also taken up in discussion about the temporal power of the clergy in general.[51]

In the long run, at least until 1807, doubts and debates did not matter. Patronage networks combined with ambivalence about gender and religious ideology to allow abbesses a wide range of powers. Class proved itself more important than either gender or religion, a fact which we might view as demonstrating once again the 'backward' nature of the Holy Roman Empire. I choose to see matters slightly differently. Heinz Schilling has recently rightfully stressed the political and cultural triumph of the nobility in Germany after the Thirty Years War.[52] From this perspective, we can view these abbesses as harbingers rather than as throwbacks.

49. Ibid.
50. MacLean, *The Renaissance Notion*, pp. 74–5.
51. Ibid., p. 75.
52. *Aufbruch und Krise: Deutschland 1517–1648* (Frankfurt: Siedler, 1988). Carolyn Lougee has pointed out that, at least in France, seventeenth-century noble culture was in many ways dominated by women (*Le Paradis des Femmes: Women, Salons, and Social Stratification in Seventeenth-Century France* (Princeton: Princeton University Press, 1976)). This was also true in the Holy Roman Empire, where women were secular rulers as well as abbesses. Hostility toward the nobility and clergy in France was of course indirectly responsible for the end of the abbesses' power and independence, for the abbeys in the empire were secularized and their lands confiscated following Napoleon's conquests, conquests which had their roots in the French Revolution. Recent analysis of the Revolution and of the thinkers who contributed to it, especially Rousseau, has pointed out the gendered content of the critique of the nobility: Rousseau, Diderot, and others regarded the prominence of women among the nobility as a sign of that class's decadence. (See several of the essays in Samia Spencer, ed., *French Women and the Age of Enlightenment*, Bloomington: Indiana University Press, 1985; Susan Miller Okin, *Women in Western Political Thought*, Princeton: Princeton University Press, 1979; and Joel Schwartz, *The Sexual Politics of Jean-Jacques Rousseau*, Chicago: University of Chicago Press, 1985.) In the democratic ideology of the Revolution, gender differences far outweighed those of class, in the same way that they did in the republican ideology of Renaissance Florence (see Diane Owen Hughes, 'Invisible Madonnas? The Italian historiographical tradition and the women of medieval Italy', in *Women in Medieval History and Historiography*, ed. Susan Mosher Stuard (Philadelphia: University of Pennsylvania Press, 1987)). Though we may criticize the abbesses for being elitist, membership in and identification with the aristocracy was the only road to political power available to women in the early modern period.

CHAPTER FOUR

The Reformation of the women

'Since it were very pernicious that the opinions of men, although good and holy, should be put in the place of the commandment of God, I desire that this matter may be cleared up for the well-being and the concord of the churches.' These are words spoken by Charlotte de Mornay, a French noblewoman and Calvinist Protestant, in 1584, to the consistory of Montauban, where she was residing. The matter in question was the consistory's excommunication of her and her entire household because she wore her hair in curls. Such matters, de Mornay continued, were no grounds for the exclusion of someone from church ceremonies and services, and she as a noblewoman was certainly not going to obey the middle-class pastors on an issue that had nothing to do with her or anyone else's salvation.[1]

This conflict and de Mornay's comments about it highlight many of the issues involving women's religious life in the Reformation period. First, though we may view the arrangement of women's hair as trivial, it had tremendous social and symbolic importance. Immediately upon marriage, women covered their hair, for long flowing hair was the mark of someone who was sexually available, either as a virgin or prostitute. Protestant woodcuts often contrast pious women listening to sermons with their hair carefully covered with women buying indulgences whose heads only bear a few feathers or ribbons. Both the New Testament and church fathers such as Tertullian had ordered women to cover their heads, not simply as a gesture of respect but also specifically to lessen their sexual attractiveness.[2]

1. Quoted in James Anderson, *Ladies of the Reformation: In Germany, France and Spain* (London: Blackie and Sons, 1857), p. 466.
2. Margaret Miles, *Carnal Knowing: Female Nakedness and Religious Meaning in the Christian West* (Boston: Beacon Press, 1989), pp. 48–51.

Thus the pastors claimed biblical authority for their position, and at the heart of the issue was the control of female sexuality and the maintenance of a moral order in which women were subservient. These factors will emerge in nearly all the religious conflicts involving women in the Reformation period, even when the participants did not articulate them.

Second, the key question for women was often the conflict between the authorities de Mornay mentions: the opinions of men and the commandment of God. Women had to choose between what male political and religious authorities, and sometimes even their fathers and husbands, told them to do, and what they perceived as God's plan for their lives. Third, de Mornay's confidence in challenging the pastors, and the source of some of her irritation, came from her status as a noblewoman; the women whose religious choices had the most impact in early modern Europe were usually noblewomen or rulers, whose actions affected their subjects as well as themselves and their families. (Thus the placement of our discussion about women under the more general rubric of 'the common people' is in many ways misleading. It reinforces the notion, so well expressed by a colleague of mine, that in using the nearly obligatory trinity of race, class, and gender as a tool of historical analysis, women always seem to have more gender, blacks more race, and men more class.)

Finally, this incident nicely captures the ambiguities of the title of this session, the Reformation *of* the women, an ambiguity fortuitously present in the German 'die Reformation der Frauen' as well. By her actions, de Mornay transformed the consistory's attempts to reform *her* into a more far-reaching theological discussion in which *she* played a role. She was not alone in this, for the Reformation period saw Protestant and Catholic women throughout Europe doing the same thing, taking new or traditional ideas about their place and role expressed by men and using these as a call to action. Most studies of women and the Reformation (my own included) have focused on either one or the other sense of 'of' – i.e., either Luther's or Calvin's or Bullinger's or some other man's ideas about women, marriage, and the family and the legal and social changes that resulted from these, or women's actions in support of or opposition to the Reformation. Here I would like to highlight some examples from both the Protestant and Catholic Reformations where the two senses of 'of' are in tension, where moves to 'reform' women were suddenly faced with 'reformed' or 'reforming' women who often had very different ideas about the type of reforms necessary.

My first example is also the best studied, women who took the Protestant notion of a priesthood of all believers literally and preached or published polemical religious literature explaining their own ideas. Women's preaching or publishing religious material stood in direct opposition to the words ascribed to St Paul (1 Timothy 2: 11–15) which ordered women not to teach or preach, so that all women who published felt it necessary to justify their actions. The boldest, such as Argula von Grumbach, a German noblewoman who published a defence of a teacher accused of Lutheran leanings, commented that the situation was so serious that Paul's words should simply be disregarded: 'I am not unfamiliar with Paul's words that women should be silent in church but when I see that no man will or can speak, I am driven by the word of God when he said, He who confesses me on earth, him will I confess and he who denies me, him will I deny' (Matthew 10, Luke 9).[3] Ursula Weyda, a middle-class German woman who attacked the abbot of Pegau in a 1524 pamphlet, agreed: 'If all women were forbidden to speak, how could daughters prophesy as Joel predicted? Although St Paul forbade women to preach in churches and instructed them to obey their husbands, what if the churches were full of liars?'[4] Marie Dentière, a former abbess who left her convent to help the cause of the Reformation in Geneva, published a letter to Queen Marguerite of Navarre in 1539 defending some of the reformers exiled from that city, in which she gives ringing support to this view: 'I ask, didn't Jesus die just as much for the poor illiterates and the idiots as for the shaven, tonsured, and mighty lords? Did he only say, "Go, preach my Gospel to the wise lords and grand doctors?" Did he not say, "To all?" Do we have two Gospels, one for men and the other for women? . . . For we ought not, any more than men, hide and bury within the earth that which God has . . . revealed to us women?'[5] Katherina Zell, the wife of one of Strasbourg's reformers and a tireless worker for the Reformation, supported Dentière in this, asking that her writings be judged, 'not according to the standards of a woman, but according to the standards of one whom God has filled with the Holy Spirit'.[6]

3. Ludwig Rabus, *Historien der heyligen Außerwolten Gottes Zeugen, Bekennern und Martyrern* (n. p. 1557), fol. 41.

4. Quoted in Paul A. Russell, *Lay Theology in the Reformation: Popular Pamphleteers in Southwest Germany 1521–1525* (Cambridge: Cambridge University Press, 1986), p. 203.

5. Quoted in Thomas Head, 'Marie Dentière: a propagandist for the reform', in Katharina M. Wilson, ed., *Women Writers of the Renaissance and Reformation* (Athens: University of Georgia Press, 1987), p. 260.

6. Robert Stupperich, 'Die Frau in der Publizistik der Reformation', *Archiv für Kulturgeschichte* 37 (1927): 226.

Zell's wish was never granted, and women's writings were always judged first on the basis of gender. Argula von Grumbach's husband was ordered to force her to stop writing, and Marie Dentière's pamphlets were confiscated by the very religious authorities she was defending. Once Protestant churches were institutionalized, polemical writings by women supporting magisterial churches largely stopped. The reformation of women (their being made Protestant) was not to become a reformation which included female voices, other than those singing (and very occasionally writing) hymns.

A second example is provided by women whose religious convictions came to disagree with those of their husbands. Should a woman whose own faith had been reformed (either Protestant or Catholic) be encouraged to reform that of others within her household, including her husband? This issue was tackled in theory by both Protestant and Catholic authors, with Catholics and English Puritans generally encouraging active domestic missionary work on the part of women, and continental Protestants prayer and forbearance. Jesuits encouraged the students at their seminaries to urge their mothers to return to confession and begin Catholic practices in the home, and other Catholic writers approved of daughters inspiring their parents as well: 'Young girls will reform their families, their families will reform their provinces, their provinces will reform the world.'[7] There are several well-known examples among noble families of women whose domestic missionary activities were quite successful. It is difficult to gain objective evidence about middle- and lower-class women, but at least their opponents took their actions seriously. Richard Hooker, an Anglican, commented that the Puritans made special efforts to convert women because they were 'diligent in drawing away their husbands, children, servants, friends and allies in the same way'.[8] English judges and the Privy Council frequently complained about the influence recusant women had on their husbands, children, and servants.[9] Evidence from Venice indicates that husbands recognized that a

7. R. Po-Chia Hsia, *Society and Religion in Münster, 1535–1618* (New Haven: Yale University Press, 1984), p. 67; Elizabeth Rapley, *The Dévotes: Women and Church in Seventeenth-Century France* (Montreal and Kingston: McGill-Queen's University Press, 1990), p. 157.

8. Quoted in Patrick Collinson, 'The role of women in the English Reformation illustrated by the life and friendships of Anne Locke', in *Studies in Church History*, Vol. 2, ed. G.J. Cuming (London: Thomas Nelson, 1975), p. 259.

9. Diane Willen, 'Women and religion in early modern England', in Sherrin Marshall, ed., *Women in Reformation and Counter-Reformation Europe: Public and Private Worlds* (Bloomington: Indiana University Press, 1989), p. 154.

priest hearing confessions could provide wives with an alternative source of male authority, for men charged with heresy often beat their wives after the women came home from confession.[10]

Should a woman's religious convictions provide just grounds for her leaving her spouse? In terms of general principles, neither Catholic nor magisterial Protestants recommended that wives leave husbands with whom they disagreed; a few Anabaptists did, but they expected the women to remarry quickly and thus come under the control of a male believer. In practice, Catholic political authorities put fewer blocks in the path of a woman who did. Protestant city councils in Germany were suspicious of any woman who asked to be admitted to citizenship independently and questioned her intently about her marital status. Catholic cities such as Munich were more concerned about whether the woman who wanted to immigrate had always been a good Catholic than whether or not she was married, particularly if she wanted to enter a convent.[11] Protestant reformers were actually more willing to praise or accept individual women who had left their husbands than Protestant political authorities were, because they did not have to translate this into policy. Elisabeth of Brandenburg, the wife of Joachim I, lived for a while in the Luther household after leaving her Catholic husband, and even John Knox, hardly a friend of independent women, accepted English married women without their husbands in his entourage in Geneva.[12] Economic and social realities meant that leaving a spouse for religious reasons remained within the realm of theory for most women, anyway, making it easier to view the few who did as exceptions to the rule. For most women, any religious reformation which she experienced would remain a private matter.

The one exception to this provides our third example, the case of women rulers, those women for whom the reformation *of* the women led most clearly and least problematically (in the eyes of male reformers) to a reformation *by* women. Though none of the reformers differentiated between noblewomen and commoners in their public advice or writings, in private they recognized that noblewomen had a great deal of power and made special attempts to win them over. Luther corresponded regularly with a number

10. John Martin, 'Out of the shadow: heretical and Catholic women in Renaissance Venice', *Journal of Family History* 10 (1985): 27.

11. Munich, Stadtarchiv, Ratsitzungsprotokolle, 1598, fol. 171; 1601, fol. 24.

12. Collinson, 'Role'; A. Daniel Frankforter, 'Elizabeth Bowes and John Knox: a woman and Reformation theology', *Church History* 56 (1987).

of prominent noblewomen, and Calvin was even more assiduous at 'courting ladies in high places'.[13] Their efforts met with results, for female rulers frequently converted their territories to Protestantism or influenced their male relatives to do so. In Germany, Elisabeth of Brunswick-Calenberg brought in Protestant preachers and established a new church structure; in France, Marguerite of Navarre and her daughter Jeanne d'Albret supported Calvinism through patronage and political influence; in Norway, Lady Inger of Austraat, a powerful and wealthy noblewoman, led the opposition to the Norwegian archbishop who remained loyal to Catholicism.[14] In all of these cases political and dynastic concerns mixed with religious convictions, in the same way they did for male rulers and nobles.

A female ruler's ability to transform her private religious convictions into the official religion of her territory *was* problematic in the case of one special type of female ruler, the abbess. Abbesses, particularly those of free imperial convents, provide a fourth and especially instructive example of women who transformed efforts to reform them into efforts to carry out reforms. Many free imperial convents, and also those established by regional ruling houses, had undergone reforms in the fifteenth century to bring them back to high standards of spiritual observance. These reforms were sometimes introduced by bishops or male leaders of the order to which a convent was affiliated, but the ones that were most successful were those which gained the enthusiastic support of the abbess. Some abbesses made careers of travelling from house to house carrying out reforms, and at times their zeal for strict observance far surpassed that of the male members of their order.

Reformed convents proved to be the most vocal and resolute opponents of the Protestant Reformation. This was recognized by their contemporaries: Bishop Heinrich Julius of Halberstadt, who was Lutheran, noted that the continuation of Catholicism in the convents was 'the result of the resoluteness of the nuns ... the monks, though, are very lukewarm in the practice of their religion'.[15] A papal nuncio reported that 'the four women's convents

13. Charmarie Blaisdell, 'Calvin's letters to women: the courting of ladies in high places', *Sixteenth Century Journal* 12 (1982).

14. Nancy Lyman Roelker, 'The role of noblewomen in the French Reformation', *Archiv für Reformationsgeschichte* 63 (1972); K.E. Christopherson, 'Lady Inger and her family: Norway's exemplar of mixed motives in the Reformation', *Church History* 55 (1986).

15. Quoted in Franz Schrader, *Ringen, Untergang und Überleben der Katholischen Klöster in den Hochstiften Magdeburg und Halberstadt von der Reformation bis zum Westfälischen Frieden.* Katholisches Leben und Kirchenreform im Zeitalter der Glaubensspaltung, 37 (Münster: Aschendorff, 1977), p. 54.

[in Magdeburg] have remained truer to their beliefs and vows than the men's monasteries, who have almost all fallen away'.[16] Nuns were often subjected to verbal abuse, denied confessors, required to hear Protestant sermons daily, forcibly removed from convents because of the will of their families or even had their convents physically dismantled around them. They were the only adults treated in this manner, in part because territories could not expel them the way they could monks who rejected Protestant teachings; cloistered nuns were generally members of prominent local noble and patrician families whereas monks were more socially diverse and often came from another part of Germany. In many areas, political authorities simply stopped trying to convert the nuns and instead confiscated their lands and refused to allow new novices. In other areas, political authorities gave up completely, and the converts survived as Catholic institutions within Protestant territories until the nineteenth-century secularization of all church lands. The 'reformation' that mattered to them was that of the fifteenth century.

Not all convents and abbesses fought Lutheran teachings, however; some accepted the new theology and energetically introduced it into their territories. Anna von Stolberg, for example, was the abbess of the free imperial abbey of Quedlinburg, and so governed a sizable territory including nine churches, a hospital and two male monasteries. She accepted the Protestant Reformation in the 1540s, and carried out a number of moves that were standard for Protestant authorities, including closing the monasteries, requiring clergy to swear to the Augsburg Confession, and setting up a primary school. Though her actions gave clear proof of her religious ideas, she continued to receive both imperial and papal privileges, for Catholic authorities were unwilling to cut off support from what was, at any rate, still a *convent*.[17]

Protestant authorities were ambivalent about Lutheran convents, and class and gender both worked to aid the abbeys' ability to survive. Gender stereotypes about female weakness may have provoked opposition to female rule in theory, but they also enabled men to take actual examples of that rule less seriously, at least at the local level. These abbeys were not viewed as as great a threat as male monasteries because their residents were, after all, women. Most of the residents were also noble or patrician, whose families not only resented any insult to their female members, but were also

16. Quoted in Schrader, *Ringen*, p. 74.
17. Friedrich Ernst Kettner, *Kirchen und Reformations Historie/des Kayserl. Freyen Weltlichen Stifts Quedlingburg* (Quedlinburg: Theodore Schwan, 1710), pp. 123–64.

unwilling to bear the consequences of closing the abbeys. Dowries were getting larger, and even wealthy families were often not able to find appropriate partners for all of their daughters. As six noble-men writing to one of the Dukes of Brunswick when he was con-templating closing the convents in his territory put it, 'What would happen to our sisters' and relatives' honour and our reputation if they are forced to marry renegade monks, cobblers, and tailors?'[18] These, by the way, were Lutheran nobles. The women's class status not only gave them support from beyond the convent walls, but pro-vided a large part of their internal motivation and self-conception as well, in the same way it did for Charlotte de Mornay. They real-ized that there was no place for female leadership within the new Protestant churches unless they kept abbeys open. Former monks could become pastors, but for former nuns the only role was a pastor's wife, an unthinkable decrease in status for a woman of noble standing. Anna Sophia, a later abbess of Quedlinburg, wrote a book of meditations which included a long introduction and afterword discussing the special duties which virgins had to praise God and comparing the women in her convent both to the vestal virgins and to biblical women such as Deborah, Hannah, Judith and Mary.[19] She makes no statements about the capabilities of all women the way the middle-class Ursula Weyda and Marie Dentière did, but does stress those of her noble co-residents; she clearly recognized that identification with her class would take her further than identification with her gender.

Though I have discovered no actual moves against Lutheran abbeys on the part of political authorities, some Protestant theorists were troubled by these institutions both because of Luther's and others' critique of monastic life and the fact that they were places where women held power directly and passed it on to other women, rather than simply ruling in the absence or during the minority of a man, as was the case with female secular rulers.[20] Some Lutheran writers chose a legalistic way out, noting that many of these abbeys were not convents in the technical sense of the word, but secu-lar endowments (*Stifte*) in which the women took no final vows; therefore they weren't *really* monastic establishments. Others used even more convoluted reasoning, commenting that though Isaiah

18. Quoted in Johann Karl Seidemann, *Dr Jacob Schenk, der vermeintliche Antinomer, Freibergs Reformator* (Leipzig: C. Hinrichs'sche, 1875), Anhang 7, p. 193.

19. *Der Treue Seelenfreund Christus Jesus* (Jena: Georg Sengenwald, 1658).

20. Lyndal Roper, *The Holy Household: Women and Morals in Reformation Augsburg* (Oxford: Clarendon Press, 1989), p. 221.

appears to view female rulership as a curse (Isaish 3: 12, 'I will give you children to be your oppressors and women to be your rulers'), he was talking not about the female sex here, but about those of the feminine temperament (*Gemuth*) which did not include such brave and virile abbesses.[21] The most common way for both Catholic and Protestant theorists to resolve the issue of Lutheran abbesses was simply to ignore them; in the Ecclesiastical Reservation of the Peace of Augsburg, for example, the language is completely male-specific.[22] This avoidance is firmly entrenched in both Protestant and Catholic historiography of the Reformation, so that female religious are viewed as willing recipients (à la Katherine von Bora) or heroic opponents (à la Charitas Pirckheimer) of a reforming message they in no way shaped. The residents of the Lutheran abbeys which still exist in Germany today would no doubt be surprised to learn that their forbears are described as so passive.

So far I have been talking largely about women who responded to Protestant ideas with their own writings or actions, but the same thing happened in the Catholic Reformation. A fifth example of women who transformed efforts to reform them into efforts to carry out reforms is provided by the numerous women in Europe who felt God had called them to oppose Protestants directly through missionary work, or to carry out the type of active service to the world in schools and hospitals that the friars and the new orders were making increasingly popular with men. For example, Angela Merici founded the Company of St Ursula in Brescia, Italy. The Company was a group of lay single women and widows dedicated to serving the poor, the ill, orphans, and war victims, earning their own living through teaching or weaving. Merici received papal approval in 1535, for the Pope saw this as a counterpart to the large number of men's lay confraternities and societies being founded at that point.[23]

Similar groups of lay women dedicated to charitable service began to spring up in other cities of Italy, Spain, and France, and in 1541, Isabel Roser decided to go one step further and ask for papal approval for an order of religious women with a similar mission. Roser had been an associate of Loyola's in Barcelona and saw her group as a female order of Jesuits which would also not be cut off

21. Kettner, *Kirchen*, p. 130.
22. 'Augsburger Reichstagabschiede' in *Geschichte in Quellen*, Vol. 3, ed. F. Dickmann (Munich: Beck, 1966), p. 205.
23. Dorothy L. Latz, 'Feminine lay evangelism in Northern Italy: St Angela Merici and others', unpublished paper.

from the world but would devote itself to education, care of the sick and assistance to the poor, and in so doing win converts back to Catholicism. This was going too far, however. Loyola was horrified at the thought of religious women in constant contact with lay people and Pope Paul III refused to grant his approval. Despite this, her group continued to grow in Rome and the Netherlands, where they spread Loyola's teaching through the use of the Jesuit catechism.[24]

The Council of Trent responded to these efforts and to Protestant critiques of convent life with the same move that had been part of church reforms since the Gregorian – compulsory claustration for all women's religious communities. Enforcement of this decree came slowly, however, for several reasons. First, women's communities themselves fought it or ignored it. Followers of Isabel Roser, for example, were still active into the seventeenth century, for in 1630 Pope Urban VIII published a Bull to suppress them, and reported that they were building convents and choosing abbesses and rectors. Second, church officials themselves recognized the value of the services performed by such communities, particularly in the area of girls' education and care of the sick. Well after Trent, Charles Borromeo invited members of the Company of St Ursula to Milan, and transformed the group from one of lay women into one of religious who lived communally, though they still were not cloistered and did not take solemn vows; in terms of their status, they were much like the secular endowments of Germany.[25] From Milan, the Ursulines spread throughout the rest of Italy and into France, and began to focus completely on the education of girls. They became so popular that noble families began to send their daughters to Ursuline houses for an education, and girls from wealthy families became Ursulines themselves.

The very success of the Ursulines led to the enforcement of claustration, however, as well as other Tridentine decrees regulating women religious. Secular endowments were not a tradition in France the way they were in Germany, and wealthy families were uncomfortable with the fact that because Ursulines did not take solemn vows, their daughters who had joined communities could theoretically leave at any time and make a claim on family

24. Ruth Liebowitz, 'Virgins in the service of Christ: the dispute over an active apostolate for women during the Counter-Reformation', in R.R. Reuther, ed., *Women of Spirit* (New York: Simon and Schuster, 1979), pp. 132–52; Johann Henry Feustking, *Gynaeceum Haeretico Fanaticum* (Frankfurt and Leipzig: Christian Gerdes, 1704), p. 533.
25. Rapley, *Dévotes*, p. 50.

inheritance. (Solemn vows bound one permanently to a religious establishment, and made an individual legally dead in the secular world.) Gradually the Ursuline houses in France and Italy were ordered to accept claustration, take solemn vows, and put themselves under the authority of their local bishop, thus preventing any movement or cooperation between houses.[26] They were still allowed to teach girls, but now only within the confines of a convent. Class and family interests had worked in favour of women's independent religious actions for convents in Protestant Germany, but against them in Catholic France.

Extraordinary circumstances occasionally led church leadership to relax its restrictions, but only to a point. The situation of English Catholics under Protestant rulers was viewed as a special case, and a few women gained approval to go on their own as missionaries there. One of these was Luisa de Carvajal y Mendoza, a Spanish noblewoman who opposed her family's wishes and neither married nor entered a convent. She was quite effective at converting non-Catholics and bolstering the faith of her co-religionists, and later commented that being a woman helped her, as the English never suspected a woman could be a missionary.[27] Paul V, pope from 1605 to 1621, was relatively open to female initiatives and in 1616 granted Mary Ward, who had run a school for English Catholic girls in exile in the Spanish Netherlands, provisional approval for her Institute of the Blessed Virgin Mary. She wanted women in her Institute to return to England as missionaries, for 'it seems that the female sex also in its own measure, should and can . . . undertake something more than ordinary in this great common spiritual undertaking'.[28] She openly modelled the Institute on the Jesuits and began to minister to the poor and sick in London, visiting Catholic prisoners and teaching in private homes. The reports of her successes proved too much for church leadership, and she was ordered to stop all missionary work, for 'it was never heard in the Church that women should discharge the Apostolic Office'.[29] Undaunted, Ward shifted her emphasis, and the Institute began to open houses in many cities throughout Europe in which women who took no formal vows operated free schools for both boys and girls, teaching them

26. Ibid., pp. 54–61.
27. Milagros Ortega Costa, 'Spanish women in the Reformation', in Sherrin Marshall, ed., *Women in Reformation and Counter-Reformation Europe: Public and Private Worlds* (Bloomington: Indiana University Press, 1989), p. 108.
28. Rapley, *Dévotes*, p. 29.
29. Ibid., p. 31.

reading, writing, and a trade. The Institute needed constant donations, for which Ward and her associates travelled extensively and
corresponded with secular and church authorities. Ward recognized
that this public solicitation of funds was necessary in order for her
schools to flourish, and so asked that the Institute never be under
the control of a bishop, but report directly to the Pope. She also
realized that this sort of public role for women was something new
in Catholicism, in her words 'a course never thought of before', but
she stressed that there 'is no such difference between men and
women that women may not do great things as we have seen by the
example of many saints'.[30] Her popularity and independence proved
too much for the church hierarchy, however, and the year after the
Bull was published against Roser Ward's schools, most of her houses
were ordered closed, and Ward herself imprisoned by the Inquisi-
tion in Munich. 'Jesuitesses', as Ward's Institute was termed by her
enemies, were not to be tolerated, and similar other uncloistered
communities of women, such as the Visitation, started by Jeanne de
Chantal and Francis de Sales, to serve the poor, were ordered to
accept claustration or be closed.[31]

Female religious were thus blocked in all of their efforts to create a community of women dedicated to reforming the world, but
beginning in the seventeenth century, lay women in some parts
of Europe were slowly able to create just that. The first example of
this was the Daughters of Charity begun by Vincent de Paul and
Madame de Gras; though both founders privately thought of the
group as a religious community, they realized that outwardly maintaining secular status was the only thing that allowed them to serve
the poor and ill. The Daughters took no public vows and did not
wear religious habits, and constantly stressed that they would work
only where invited by a bishop or priest. This subversion of the rules
was successful, for the Daughters of Charity received papal approval
and served as the model for other women's communities which
emphasized educating the poor or girls; by 1700 numerous teaching and charitable 'congregations' were found throughout Catholic
Europe. They explicitly used the Virgin Mary as their model, stressing that she, too, had served as a missionary during the Visitation.
The congregations were often backed by larger women's religious
confraternities, in which elite women supported a congregation

30. Marie B. Rowlands, 'Recusant women 1560–1640', in Mary Prior, ed., *Women
in English Society 1500–1800* (London: Methuen, 1985), p. 173.
31. Rapley, *Dévotes*, pp. 32–41.

financially or engaged in charitable works themselves. The choice which the Council of Trent had attempted to impose on women, 'maritus aut murus' (a husband or a cloister), had finally been replaced by a range of options.[32] These intermediate groups provided lay women with companionship, devotional practices, and an outlet for their energies beyond the household, and may partly be responsible for women's greater loyalty to the church with the growing secularism of the eighteenth century.[33]

For female religious in Catholic Europe, however, the only way they could act as reformers was by instructing girls, and that only within the convent. No nuns were sent to the foreign missions for any public duties, though once colonies were established in the New World and Asia cloistered convents quickly followed. The exclusion of women from what were judged the most exciting and important parts of the Catholic Reformation – countering Protestants and winning new converts – is reflected in the relative lack of women from the sixteenth century who were made saints. Luisa de Carvajal was raised to the status of Venerable, the first rung on the ladder to sanctity, but only 18.1 per cent of those who reached the top of the ladder from the sixteenth century were women, whereas 27.7 per cent of those from the fifteenth century had been female.[34] Most of the women who did achieve sainthood followed a very different path, one of mysticism or of reforming existing orders, a path in some ways set by my sixth and final example, the most famous religious woman of the sixteenth century, Teresa of Avila. If any woman made a reformation of her own, it was Teresa.

Teresa took her vows as a Carmelite at twenty, and then spent the next twenty-five years in relative obscurity in her convent at Avila. During this time of external inaction, she went through great spiritual turmoil, extremes of exaltation and melancholy, and suffered physical effects such as illness, trances, and paralysis. The mystical path which she created during these adversities was one of union with God not through mortification of the flesh, but through prayer, purification of the spirit, and assistance to the women of her convent. Teresa's confessors ordered her not only to describe her mystical experiences in writing, but to reflect on them and try

32. Ibid., pp. 74–141.

33. Kathryn Norberg, 'The Counter-Reformation and women religious and lay', in John W. O'Malley, S.J., ed., *Catholicism in Early Modern History: A Guide to Research* (St Louis, MO: Center for Reformation Research, 1988), p. 142.

34. Rudolph M. Bell and Donald Weinstein, *Saints and Society: The Two Worlds of Western Christendom, 1000–1700* (Chicago: University of Chicago Press, 1982), p. 220.

to explain why she thought these were happening to her. Though Teresa complained about having to do this, she also clearly developed a sense of passion about her writing, for she edited and refined her work, transforming it into a full spiritual autobiography. Writing had been imposed on her as a way of demonstrating she was not tainted with Alumbrado, Lutheran, or other heretical ideas, but her autobiography became a document designed to keep others from heresy or convert those already lapsed.

Like Angela Merici and Mary Ward, Teresa also yearned for some kind of active ministry, and explicitly chafed at the restrictions on her because of her sex: 'Nor did you, Lord, when You walked in the world, despise women; rather, You always, with great compassion, helped [or favoured] them. And You found as much love and more faith in them than You did in men. Is it not enough, Lord, that the world has intimidated us . . . so that we may not do anything worthwhile for You in public?'[35] In part she solved this by interpreting her prayers and those of other nuns as public actions: 'we shall be fighting for Him [God] even though we are very cloistered'.[36] When she was fifty-two, she also began to reform her Carmelite order, attempting to return it to its original standards of spirituality and poverty. To do this, she travelled all around Spain, founding new convents, writing meditations, instructions for monastic administrators, and hundreds of letters, provoking the wrath or annoyance of some church authorities; a papal nuncio called her a 'fidgety, restless, disobedient and obstinate woman, who under the guise of devotion invents evil doctrine and breaks cloister'.[37]

Teresa's success in reforming the Carmelites won her more supporters than critics within the church, however, for, unlike Angela Merici and Mary Ward, she did not advocate institutionalized roles for women outside the convent. Her frustration at men's alterations of Christ's view of women did not lead her to break with the male church hierarchy, and the words I just quoted which expressed that frustration were expunged from her works by church censors. In the same way that Lutheran convents disappeared from German Reformation history, the version of Teresa which was presented for her canonization proceedings, held very shortly after her death, was one which avoided inconsistencies and embarrassments. She was fitted into the acceptable model of woman mystic and reformer,

35. *The Way of Perfection* 3,7, quoted in Jodi Bilinkoff, 'Private prayer, public apostolate: the mission of Teresa of Avila', unpublished paper, p. 5.
36. *The Way of Perfection* 3,5, quoted in ibid., p. 8.
37. Quoted in ibid., p. 9.

assuming a public role only when ordered to do so by her confessor or superior; only recently have we begun to understand that Teresa thought of herself as a Counter-Reformation fighter, viewing the new religious houses she established as answers to the Protestant takeover of Catholic churches elsewhere in Europe.

What conclusions can we draw from these six rather disparate examples – Protestant polemicists, wives who disagreed with their husbands, reforming rulers, abbesses, Catholic activists, and Teresa?

In many ways, they sound exactly like their male counterparts. Protestants find biblical examples of great women or use Paul's words in one place to argue against those in another, while Catholics build traditions, using the life of Mary to serve as an example for activism. Rulers and abbesses took their right to make political decisions for their territories as the self-evident privilege of their class, and only spoke about their gender when others made an issue of it. Both men and women agreed that women are morally and mentally weaker, and that female religious authority is possible only in times of extra-ordinary need. As long as women worked within (or subverted, depending on how you look at it) male-defined limits, they received some support for their acting in support of a Reformation.

In other ways, however, these women approach things very differently. In our terminology, male religious and political authorities thought of women as a sex, while the women who have left us their thoughts thought of women as a gender. The 'Reformation of the women' in the intellectual and institutional constructs of men – marriage and funeral sermons, treatises on celibacy, laws regarding prostitution, adultery, marriage, inheritance, and morals, the *Hausvater*- and much smaller *Hausmutterliteratur* – not only was one imposed on women, but one which largely concerned their physical and sexual status. Both sexes were urged by Protestants to give up the monastic life, but for women this was automatically expected to lead to marriage; the claustration of women ordered by Trent explicitly aimed at preventing all sexual contacts; the ultimate critiques of Teresa, Mary Ward, Marie Dentière, and others like them were always sexual, not theological – 'they undertook and exercised many other works unsuitable to their sex and their capacity, their feminine modesty and, above all, their virginal shame'.[38] Sixteenth-century male religious reformers, like nineteenth-century male social reformers, thought of women as 'the sex'.

---

38. Papal Bull of Suppression of Mary Ward's Institute of the Blessed Virgin Mary, 1631, quoted in Rapley, *Dévotes*, p. 33.

Reformation women, however, view their own situation in ways that might be understandable to a contemporary post-structural deconstructionist. They saw being a woman as not simply a matter of biology and sexuality, but of traditions, laws, customs, political systems, economic relations and emotional linkages – in other words, though they would never have expressed it this way, they saw gender as socially constructed. They saw themselves (and sometimes other women) as less determined by their biology and sexual status and more by their intellectual capacities, spiritual gifts, and, among noblewomen, social class. Because they thought that such things could to a degree overcome or make irrelevant their gender, they felt driven not simply to *be* reformed, but to *do* reforms. Current research, much of it still at the dissertation stage, is recovering the actions of such women.

I have concentrated here too much, perhaps, on the second sense of the 'Reformation of the women'. Current research also suggests that if any Reformation was successful in the sixteenth century, it was that 'of the women' in the first sense, a restriction of women's sphere of independent actions and an increase in the power of male heads of household, both temporal and spiritual.[39] Women did, in a sense, have more gender, despite what they argued, because that was always a more important determinant of their experience than it was for men of their class. A concentration on the first sense alone, however, negates the subjectivity and historical agency of women, making the Reformation yet another example of the oppression of women. There are plenty of examples of that, so I have chosen to examine some women who made the Reformation their own. For Argula von Grumbach, Anna von Stolberg, Marie Dentière, Teresa of Avila, and even Charlotte de Mornay, it was a Reformation in which female voices were more than a supporting chorus.

39. Roper, *Holy Household*; Nathalie Davis, 'City women and religious change' and 'Women on top', in her *Society and Culture in Early Modern France* (Stanford University Press, 1975); Dagmar Lorenz, 'Vom Kloster zur Küche: Die Frau vor und nach der Reformation Dr. Martin Luthers', in Barbara Becker-Cantarino, ed., *Die Frau von der Reformation zur Romantik: Die Situation der Frau vor dem Hintergrund der Literatur und Sozialgeschichte* (Bonn: Bouvier Verlag Herbert Grundmann, 1980), pp. 7–35; Susan Karant-Nunn, 'Continuity and change: some effects of the Reformation on the women of Zwickau', *Sixteenth Century Journal* 13/2 (1982); Barbara Becker-Cantarino, *Der Lange Weg zur Mündigkeit: Frau und Literatur (1500–1800)* (Stuttgart: J.B. Metzlersche Verlag, 1987), pp. 40–4.

PART TWO

Law

Introductory essay

Legal history has always been a significant part of historical scholarship, and because so much law revolves around issues such as marriage and inheritance, which have a direct impact on women, women's experience was not excluded from legal history the way it was from many other areas of historical investigation. Most legal codes have made clear and explicit distinctions between the rights and duties of men and those of women, so that it has also been difficult to subsume women under the notion of a generic 'man'.

Beginning in the late nineteenth century, historians and jurists investigated many aspects of the history of private and criminal law throughout the many territories of the Holy Roman Empire; each territory generally issued its own law codes and ordinances, so that this was a rich topic both for those looking at a specific locality and those who undertook more general studies. These early works tended to focus on law codes alone – they were usually printed, and one could easily trace change over time in their various versions – a focus which has continued in some scholarship until today, particularly that done by scholars associated with faculties of law. Historians working within law schools have also been interested in the development of legal theory itself, using as their sources the treatises written by civil, criminal, and canon lawyers as well as related works in political philosophy and government.

Studies of women's theoretical legal position in both Germany and elsewhere in the early modern period have noted a slow tendency toward primogeniture and an increasing unwillingness to let even unmarried adult women handle their legal affairs. Many legal codes, including common law in England and the codes in many of the territories of the Empire, gave both daughters and widows rights to specific portions of family property, but these were gradually eroded in favour of a more patrilineal and primogenitive inheritance structure. This did not happen everywhere in Germany, however, so that some studies have also focused on specific villages and localities where inheritance remained partible, and asked about the reasons for the continuation of this alternative pattern.

Many institutional and political historians have become less interested in simply investigating legal theory and prescriptive law codes and have turned instead to looking at how laws were actually implemented and enforced; for this they use official government records produced by courts, councils, and rulers. They have pointed out the ways in which differences of opinion among authorities and officials often led to wide variation in the actual enforcement of laws – even within one territory – and traced the ways in which problems associated with implementing laws shaped the subsequent development of legal theory. It is clear from these investigations that the links between theory and practice went both directions, that is, that the drafting of law codes was not simply influenced by theory but also by how well specific laws actually worked to shape society.

Studies of the actual enforcement of law codes have demonstrated that women were often able to use ambiguities in the legal system to obtain and retain property, secure their inheritances, and gain advantages both for and within their families. Notions about women's frailty, irrationality, and weakness could actually work to women's advantage, as judges and officials were more likely to allow them to slip through the cracks than they were men. This looseness also resulted from ambivalence in official attitudes toward certain aspects of women's legal position, or from conflicting aims within the laws: widows, for example, could not be rendered totally powerless despite strong patriarchal tendencies because this would disadvantage their children; prostitutes, for another example, were to be both punished and protected, though the balance between these changed over time.

Studies of the actual impact of legal change have also been carried out by social historians over the last several decades, as they have explored the law from the bottom up, that is, the individuals and groups caught up in the legal system rather than the institutions and ideas that structured it. This social history of the law has traced the criminalization of certain behaviours, for the early modern period primarily those which were viewed as disruptive of morality, social discipline, and public order, such as prostitution, vagrancy, begging, and homosexuality. This places law codes and cases in a broader ideological and cultural context than earlier scholarship did, tying law to literature, state-building, religious change, and economic trends.

In terms of women, this broadening of the history of law has led on the one hand to intensive investigations of individuals – a servant accused of infanticide, a daughter who defied her parents and married against their wishes, a woman who cross-dressed in order to work as a sailor, a wife who screamed at her husband in public – which use personal and family documents along with more traditional legal sources. On the other hand it has led to considerations of the entire social construction of gender, as law joins with other structures to shape the power relationships among men and women. The legal history of women is no longer simply the story of codes, courts, and treatises, but also of bodies, communities, and consciousness.

CHAPTER FIVE

Frail, weak, and helpless: women's legal position in theory and reality

The sixteenth century in Germany saw several major changes in law codes and legal structures. Humanist lawyers encouraged the introduction of Roman law, favouring it over Germanic law because it was systematic and comprehensive: it gradually replaced or augmented older Germanic law codes in civil matters. The *Carolina Constitutio Criminalis*, a standardized code of criminal procedure drawn up for Charles V, was gradually adopted in most of the territories of the Empire. The Reformation ended the power of canon law, forcing Protestant areas to devise new ordinances in regard to marriage and morals, and to establish new courts to replace Catholic church courts, or expand the jurisdiction of existing courts. There was also change in Catholic areas, for the decrees of the Council of Trent – particularly the decree Tametsi – cleared up many ambiguities in canon law regarding marriage.

All of these changes in civil, criminal, and church law had an impact on the legal position of women in Germany. Civil codes established their rights to buy, sell, and trade property, act in legal capacities without guardians, control their children, inherit and will cash and goods, and carry out other financial transactions. Criminal procedures determined how female suspects would be treated, and what sort of punishments would be meted out. Church law largely determined their rights to marry and divorce, and set penalties for sexual crimes and deviance.

In the first half of this essay I wish to discuss how women's theoretical legal status changed during the sixteenth century. The second half will turn from theory to reality, examining women's actions in courts and other legal bodies to assess the actual impact of these changes.

The realm of legal theory in regard to women may itself be divided into two levels. The first is the level of pure theory, the discussion among jurists of 'woman' in the abstract. This was provoked by a gloss on the Roman law of homicide by the French humanist jurist Jacques Cujas in which he asserted – perhaps flippantly – that a woman (*mulier*) is not a human being (*homo*).[1] Though he was using this to satirize the inflexible scholastic approach to language, other jurists, as well as theologians, took him seriously and set out to prove that women are human.[2] No one argued, however, that this shared humanity should imply legal equality.

Academic jurists found justification in both Roman and German law for excluding women from a wide variety of legal functions. Roman law stressed women's alleged physical and mental weakness, her *levitas, fragilitas, infirmitas et imbecilitas*, and held women, along with peasants and the simple-minded, as not fully responsible for their own actions. Germanic law based women's secondary status on their inability to perform vassal service and duty to obey their husbands: the age of this tradition was alone grounds for its acceptance among jurists, who regarded *mores* and *consuetudo* (traditions and institutions) as adequate grounds for most laws. Academic jurisprudence thus made clear distinctions between men and women, and further subdivided women according to their relationship to a man; a woman's legal status was determined by her marital status as maiden/wife/widow, and occasionally also by her physiological status as virgin/pregnant/nursing mother/ mother.

The second level of legal theory is made up of codes which transformed these ideas into actual laws and regulations. During the late fifteenth and sixteenth centuries most areas of Germany revised their civil codes to include procedures and principles drawn from Roman law. This had less of an impact on women than one might expect, however, for, of all branches of law, family law was the most resistant to change. Jurists began to use Roman terms for such things as a woman's dowry (*dos*), but did not give women the absolute rights to their dowry that they possessed under traditional Roman law. Such dowry rights meant that a woman had a claim to part of her husband's income, and rights *vis-à-vis* his creditors,

1. Ian MacLean, *The Renaissance Notion of Woman* (Cambridge: Cambridge University Press, 1980), p. 70.

2. Ibid., pp. 71–81; Manfred P. Fleischer, 'Are women human? The debate of 1595 between Valens Acidalius and Simon Geddicus', *The Sixteenth Century Journal* 12 no. 2 (1981): 107–21.

both of which were perceived as un-German.[3] Only in a few parts of Germany did a widow have absolute right to a certain part of her husband's estate, as she did to her 'widow's third' under English common law.[4]

Roman law did have an impact in the area of guardianship. The oldest Germanic codes had required that every woman have a male legal guardian because she was not capable of bearing arms; this gender-based guardianship gradually died out in the later Middle Ages as court proceedings replaced trial by combat and trial by ordeal. Women everywhere in Germany were regarded as legally capable of holding land and appearing in court on their own behalf. In the sixteenth century, gender-based guardianship reappeared, now based on Roman ideas of women's mental weakness and *fragilitas*. Though Roman law itself did not have gender-based guardianship, its rules for the guardianship of children were carried over to the guardianship of women.[5] Roman ideas about guardianship also affected mothers' rights to their children. Early German codes had known only fatherly authority, but the idea of joint parental authority over children had grown gradually in the Middle Ages. This died again with the reception of Roman law, with its concept of *patria potestas*.[6]

These trends were common throughout Germany, but there were variations because each territory of the Empire devised its own code, combining Roman and traditional law as it deemed appropriate. Thus to explore women's legal position in detail it is necessary to look at a specific political entity. I have chosen the free imperial city of Nuremberg, which served as a model for other cities and princely territories.

Nuremberg revised its civil law code in 1484 and 1564, and in marriage and family matters there is little difference between the two 'reformations', as such revisions are termed. Both recognize two types of marriage, which, with minor variations, were found throughout Germany. The first and much more common type involved communal ownership of all property (*Gütergemeinschaft*); in the words of the code, 'man and wife marry their goods together

3. Marianne Weber, *Ehefrau und Mutter in der Rechtsentwicklung* (Tübingen: J.C.B. Mohr, 1907), pp. 237–41; Rudolf Huebner, *A History of Germanic Private Law*, tr. Francis S. Philbrick (Boston: Little, Brown, 1918), p. 633.

4. Hans Thieme, 'Die Rechtstellung der Frau in Deutschland', *Recueils de la Société Jean Bodin* 12 no. 2 (1962): 372.

5. Huebner, *History of Germanic Private Law*, p. 67.

6. Ibid., p. 365.

as well'.[7] Theoretically the wife's approval was necessary for any transaction which concerned family property, for she was co-owner of all movables and immovables. In actuality, during the sixteenth century husbands were gradually given more rights to act alone or for their wives in all financial matters. Though women remained co-owners, they were no longer considered co-administrators.[8] The Nuremberg city council recognized that women had often lost their say in family financial matters, and in the 1564 code required widows to pay off only half of their husband's debts.[9] It also did not leave a woman totally at the mercy of her husband's whims while he was alive. If a wife could prove that her husband was *in Abfall* (going to waste), losing money through gambling, drink, unwise investments, or simply bad luck, she had the right to take over 'the value of her dowry and his matching payment from his property and goods into her own management'.[10] The council was not only protecting widows and other women with these provisions, of course, but also keeping them from requiring public support – a fortunate conjuncture of its paternalism and fiscal conservatism.

In the second type of marriage, only part of the property of each spouse was considered marital property (*Heyratsgüter*).[11] This limited community of goods was termed *Güterverbindung*, and was more common for landed families who wished to maintain family ownership of certain pieces of property. It was originally less favourable for women than a marriage with total communal ownership, for everything the couple earned during the course of the marriage belonged solely to the husband, who also had the *usufruct* of all his wife's property during the course of the marriage. In actuality, it became more favourable for women, for they retained the right to co-administer their own property. By the late sixteenth century, *Güterverbindung* was termed *das Gesetz für die Weiber* (the law for women) in Nuremberg.[12]

In both types of marriage, a woman theoretically lost the ability to carry out financial transactions without the approval of her husband. The guiding force behind these restrictions was the concept of *weibliche Freiheit*, 'female freedom' in exact translation. Basically

7. *Der Verneurte Reformation der Stadt Nürnberg 1564* (Nuremberg, 1564), Sec. 28: 1.
8. Weber, *Ehefrau und Mutter*, p. 230.
9. *Reformation 1564*, Sec. 33: 9.
10. Ibid., Sec. 28: 5.
11. Ibid., Sec. 27: 2.
12. Bertha Kipfmuller, *Die Frau im Rechte der freien Reichsstadt Nürnberg* (Dillingen: Schwäbische Verlagsdruckerei, 1929), p. 35.

this meant that women had the 'freedom' to declare their signatures invalid on contracts and agreements, saying they had been pressured or misled or had not understood what they were doing. Authorities justified *weibliche Freiheit* by noting it protected women, though it was actually greater protection for their husbands, of course. The Nuremberg city council recognized that some married women were in occupations which required that they buy and sell goods or loan and borrow money. It specifically exempted 'female tailors, shopkeepers, hotel-keepers, and market-women' from any restrictions, exceptions which were also made in other cities.[13] Unmarried women and widows over the age of eighteen who owned their own property could make contracts, borrow, and lend without a man as co-signer; not until the seventeenth century was gender-based guardianship made law in Nuremberg.[14]

Women could appear in court as witnesses in civil cases, if no male witnesses were available, but could not be used as witnesses for a will. Pregnant women were given special rights as witnesses; along with other 'dangerously ill' people, they were allowed to give their testimony before a case had been officially opened, in case they were no longer available once it had been opened.[15] A woman could freely make her own will, and had the right to a certain share of her parents' estate (*Legitima*). Despite the Lutheran insistence on parental approval for marriage, a daughter could not be disinherited for marrying against her parents' will if it could be shown that the parents had not found her a husband before she was twenty-two; sons could be disinherited for this at any time.[16] Because children were viewed as tangible property belonging to their father's family, a married woman had less legal control of her own children than did her husband's father. If she remarried, she lost all control of her children by her first husband, which was not the case with a man who remarried.[17]

13. Andreas Baader, ed., *Nürnberger Polizeiordnungen aus der 13. bis 15. Jahrhundert.* Vol. 63 of Bibliothek des literarische Verein Stuttgart (Stuttgart: Literarische Verein, 1862), p. 30.

14. *Reformation 1564*, Sec. 19: 5.

15. Otto Reiser, 'Beweis und Beweisverfahren im Zivilprozess der freien Reichsstadt Nürnberg' (Juristische Dissertation, Erlangen, 1955), pp. 45, 74.

16. Albrecht Purucker, 'Das Testamentrecht der Nürnberger Reformation' (Jur. Diss., Erlangen, 1948), p. 7.

17. This was actually more liberal than in other cities which accepted Roman law more completely, in which a widow had no rights over her own children, whether she remarried or not. In Nuremberg, only if a mother did not properly care for her children's affairs was her guardianship lifted. (Dieter Beck, 'Die Rechtstellung der Minderjährige nach Nürnberger Stadtrecht' (Jur. Diss., Erlangen, 1950), p. 52).

Though women were clearly unequal in terms of civil legal rights, they were most definitely equal in terms of civil responsibilities. Female heads of household – about 12 per cent of the total number of households in both 1497 and 1561 – were responsible for paying taxes and providing soldiers for the city's defence.[18] If a female citizen moved out of Nuremberg, she was required to pay the same tax that men were for giving up citizenship rights. Noncitizen women, including domestic servants, who wanted to live in the city had to apply annually for permission.[19]

Women were also equal to men in terms of their liability in criminal cases: *weibliche Freiheit* applied only to civil law. Nuremberg did not have a uniform code of criminal law, but after 1532 used the *Carolina* to systematize procedure. The *Carolina* was heavily influenced by Roman law, which required a confession or absolute proof in capital cases, and saw punishment as a matter of state concern and not simply up to the discretion of the injured party. Though the requirement of a confession or eye-witnesses appears to be a humane and just one, in actuality it sanctioned judicial torture, particularly in cases where proof was difficult to obtain, such as witchcraft or infanticide.[20] Pregnant women and nursing mothers were to be handled more mildly than other suspects, but women who pretended to be pregnant in order to get preferential treatment were to be dealt with more harshly once this was discovered. Women who were to be executed were generally buried alive until 1515, when the council decided to switch to drowning 'in consideration of what a horrible death being buried alive is for women and that such punishments are no longer being carried out in many imperial areas'.[21] They were drowned from 1515 to 1558, when the city executioner recommended that they be beheaded because the Pegnitz river which flowed through the city had been frozen several times when he was supposed to carry out an execution. The council accepted his reasoning and also came to the conclusion

18. Otto Puchner, 'Das Register des Gemeinen Pfennigs (1497) der Reichsstadt Nürnberg als bevölkerungsgeschichtliche Quelle', *Jahrbuch für fränkische Landesforschung* 34/35 (1974/75), p. 936; Rudolf Endres, 'Zur Einwohnerzahl und Bevölkerungsstruktur Nürnbergs im 15/16. Jahrhunderts', *Mitteilungen des Verein für Geschichte der Stadt Nürnberg* 57 (1970): 263.

19. Gunther Düll, 'Das Bürgerrecht der freien Reichsstadt Nürnberg vom Ende des 13. Jahrhunderts bis Anfang des 16. Jahrhunderts' (Jur. Diss., Erlangen, 1954), p. 122.

20. Carl Ludwig von Bar, *A History of Continental Criminal Law*, tr. Thomas S. Bell (Boston: Little, Brown, 1916), p. 220.

21. Hermann Knapp, *Das Lochgefängnis, Tortur und Richtung im Alt-Nürnberg* (Nuremberg: Heerdegen-Barbeck, 1907), p. 73.

that a beheading had more shock value than a drowning, when no one could see the actual death.[22] Men were generally beheaded, or hung if they had committed a 'dishonourable' crime like theft. For lesser crimes, corporal punishment, mutilation, and banishment were prescribed for both women and men, though a wife was generally included in her husband's banishment – including that for adultery! – while the opposite was not the case.[23]

In theory, the most dramatic legal change in sixteenth-century Nuremberg was the ending of the jurisdiction of the Catholic church in marriage and morals cases. By January 1525, marriage cases were no longer going to the bishop's court at Bamberg, and the city council asked for an official opinion (*Gutachten*) from the city's jurists and theologians about what should be done.[24] Though Andreas Osiander, the Lutheran pastor in the city's main church, wanted to establish a consistory, the council decided instead to turn over jurisdiction in marriage cases to the regular city civil court. The court's name was changed from *Stadtgericht* to *Stadt- und Ehegericht*, and it was also to handle morals cases like blasphemy and non-attendance at church.[25] As in all Protestant areas, marriage was no longer considered a sacrament, but a legally binding marriage now required the presence of a pastor and witnesses. Clandestine marriages were strictly forbidden, and parental approval was stressed as highly desirable, though, as we have seen, not absolutely necessary in the case of daughters. Luther recommended that fathers be given the right to annul marriages which their children had entered into without their approval, even if they had been consummated, but Nuremberg followed the more moderate ideas of Melanchthon and the Wittenberg jurists on the matter.[26]

Turning now from theory to reality, the changes in the sixteenth century are less dramatic than one might expect, and may best be seen as long-term trends which continue on into the seventeenth and eighteenth centuries. The number of women who bought and sold property independently gradually decreased. In the fifty-year

---

22. Ibid., p. 71; *Meister Franntz Schmidts Scharfrichters in Nürnberg all sein Richten*, ed. Albrecht Keller (Leipzig: Wilhelm Heims, 1913).

23. Düll, 'Das Bürgerrecht', p. 71.

24. Nuremberg Staatsarchiv, Rep. 51, Ratschlagbücher, Vol. 4, fol. 190 (17 January 1525).

25. Judith Harvey, 'The influence of the Reformation on Nuremberg marriage laws: 1520–1535' (Ph.D. diss., Ohio State University, 1972).

26. George Howard Joyce, *Christian Marriage: An Historical and Doctrinal Study* (London: Streed and Ward, 1948), p. 118.

period from 1484 to 1534, 23 per cent of those buying or selling houses or land were women; from 1534 to 1584, 18 per cent; and from 1584 to 1624, 16 per cent.[27] Most of the sales which involve widows or single women (*Jungfrau*) from the first half of the six-teenth century make no mention of guardians at all, and some specifically state that the woman herself appeared before the court. In the last half of the century, widows more often appeared with male advisors, either their sons, brothers, or guardians (*Vormunder, Advocaten, Curatores*), or else the men brought the case alone on behalf of the women. Because wives were co-owners of marital prop-erty, their names always appear on contracts, but the number of married women who bought and sold property on their own declined. In addition, by the end of the sixteenth century a spe-cific explanation was always given when a married woman appeared alone in court – her husband was ill, away fighting, gone on a busi-ness venture – whereas in the early part of the century this was not deemed necessary. These trends are the result of ideas about female *fragilitas* and *imbecilitas*, and also of the growing profession-alization of the legal system. As more formal legal language was required in supplications and arguments, those without university training, which included all women, could no longer argue their own cases.

A similar trend is apparent in wills. Women often used their wills to express religious convictions, by endowing funds for preachers and teachers, and also to assist other women, with donations for poor expectant mothers or funds for trousseaus for poor girls.[28] During the sixteenth century, wills made jointly by husbands and wives became more common, with donations to specifically female charities decreasing.[29]

Most of the changes in criminal procedure applied equally to women and men, but women were often the only ones to suffer punishment in cases of fornication, for they alone bore the proof of their actions. Punishments for moral crimes increased in severity

27. Nuremberg Stadtarchiv, Rep. B7/I, II, III, Grundverbriefungsbücher (Libri Litterarum), Vols. 2–132.
28. J.C. Siebenkees, *Nachrichten von Armenstiftungen in Nürnberg* (Nuremberg: Schneider, 1792), passim; idem, *Nachrichten von der Nürnbergischen Armenschulen und Schulstiftungen* (Nuremberg: Schneider, 1793), p. 71. For a discussion of women's and joint wills elsewhere in Germany, see R. Po-Chia Hsia, 'Civic wills as sources for the study of piety in Münster, 1530–1618', *The Sixteenth Century Journal* 14 no. 3 (1983): 321–48.
29. Purucket, 'Das Testamentrecht', p. 52.

throughout the sixteenth century, and even setting out a foundling was criminalized.[30] It is not surprising that the most common capital crime among women was infanticide, and that almost all of these women were unmarried.[31] Women were more likely than men to be put up to public ridicule, forced to wear a stone collar (*Lasterstein*) or sit in the stocks for fighting in public, blasphemy, or scolding, all particularly 'unfeminine' activities. The wives of wealthier citizens could also be forbidden to wear a *Schurz*, a type of veil which indicated their social standing, if the council felt their conduct had been in some way unseemly. Rarely were women fined, because that would have penalized their husbands as well.

The municipal marriage court made no immediate break with tradition in cases of divorce and remarriage. It did allow divorce in cases of adultery, but initially continued to prohibit the remarriage of either party. Gradually it began to allow the innocent party to remarry, but still preferred that he or she leave the area or at least donate something 'ad pias causas'.[32] There was no relaxation in the canonical impediments to marriage, despite Osiander's arguments to the contrary. In general, though marriage had become a matter for temporal authorities, the city council was unwilling to break sharply with Catholic practice because it was attempting to keep peace with the emperor at all costs.

In terms of both theory and reality, women's legal position clearly deteriorated in the sixteenth century. The parts of Roman law which placed women in a dependent or secondary position were incorporated into traditional codes, while those which gave them specific independent rights were not. Governments came to view law as a tool for shaping society, expanding their civil, criminal, and church codes to make them more systematic and comprehensive, and more vigorously prosecuting those who violated these codes. This had a particular impact on women, who had often slipped through the cracks of the older, looser codes, or whose infractions were simply ignored. Governments gradually became less willing to make exceptions in the case of women, for they felt any laxness might disrupt public order. Thus Nuremberg began to insist that all women moving

---

30. Karl Roetzer, *Die Delikte des Abtreibung, Kindstötung sowie Kindsaussetzungen und ihre Bestrafung in der Reichsstadt Nürnberg* (Jur. Diss., Erlangen, 1957), p. 86.

31. Ibid., p. 103; *Meister Franntz*, passim.

32. Kipfmuller, *Die Frau im Rechte*, p. 18. For Protestant reluctance to allow divorce elsewhere in Germany, see Thomas Max Safley, *Let No Man Put Asunder: The Control of Marriage in the German Southwest* (Kirksville, MO: Sixteenth Century Journal Publishers, 1984), p. 131.

away formally renounce their citizenship; all women who conducted business apply formally for the right to do so; all widows have a male city official write their will and take their inventory; all couples marry in the approved manner.[33] The reality of women's inferior legal status lagged somewhat behind the theory, but by the seventeenth century women throughout Germany found it increasingly difficult to act as independent legal persons in the way their grandmothers had. They were human beings, but not persons.

33. Nuremberg Staatsarchiv, Rep. 52b, Amts- und Standbücher, no. 303, fols. 206–7; Rep. 78, Nürnberger Testamenten, no. 1253 (1562–82); Nuremberg Stadtarchiv, Inventarbücher, nos. 1–4, 16–17 (1529–84); Rep. D15/I, Heiliggeistspital Inventarbücher, nos. 4021–6771 (1563–1600); Emil Sehling, ed., *Die evangelische Kirchenordnungen des XVI. Jahrhunderts*, Vol. 11: *Bayern*, part 1; *Franken* (Tübingen, 1962), pp. 140–305.

CHAPTER SIX

*Paternalism in practice:
the control of servants and prostitutes
in early modern German cities*[1]

Throughout the Middle Ages, city governments attempted to oversee and prescribe everything that went on in their town down to
the smallest detail, from the length of men's doublets to the ingre-
dients in bread. These moves were always justified as contributing to
the 'public good', by promoting economic growth, improving the
town's physical security, assuring consumers of fair weights and measures, or protecting the residents' health. They demonstrate clearly
the paternalistic nature of city governments, the sentiment on the
part of authorities that they could best identify and implement what
served the good of the community as a whole.

During the early modern period, city governments became
increasingly concerned with maintaining morality and order along
with economic and physical security. This concern, evident in Catholic, Lutheran, and Reformed cities, led to two trends in municipal
legislation. The first was the extension of regulation into the household, and the second, the exclusion of certain groups from considerations of the 'public good'. The first development may be traced
by an examination of the regulations regarding domestic servants,
and the second by the ordinances restricting and eventually closing
public brothels. Such prescriptive sources do not reveal much about
the actual experience of domestic servants or prostitutes and nothing about their thoughts and desires. They do reveal the ideals and
attitudes of urban political leaders and describe their strategies for

1. The research for this article was supported by grants from the American Council
of Learned Societies, the Deutscher Akademischer Austauschdienst, and the Regents
of the University of Wisconsin. Some of the material has also been included in my
book *Working Women in Renaissance Germany* (New Brunswick, NJ, 1987) and is included
here with the permission of Rutgers University Press. All translations are my own
unless otherwise noted.

putting these ideals into practice. They are thus useful in assessing how far a political elite was willing to carry considerations of the communal good, and how it determined where the margins of the 'community' would be set.

Domestic service

City governments first regulated the public aspects of domestic service. They set up systems of employment agents, to whom girls or boys coming in from the countryside could go if they had no relatives or personal contacts in the city. The earliest mention of such agents is in Nuremberg in 1421, when both men and women are listed; but, by the sixteenth century, domestic service was strictly a female occupation. The wording of the appointment of employment agents in the Nuremberg city council minutes is exactly the same as that for a master craftsman or minor city official. They first received a comprehensive ordinance in Nuremberg in 1521, in Strasbourg in 1557, and in Munich in 1580, although it is clear in all of these cities that the system was already in operation before the ordinance was drafted. The ordinances were usually issued to clear up disagreements and solve problems that the city councils saw in the agents' handling of servants. They are all somewhat different in that they respond to particular problems in each city, but many of the clauses are the same in all of them.[2]

The number of official employment agents was limited: to eight in Nuremberg and Munich, and to five in Strasbourg. All were to hang out signs in front of their houses so that people coming in from the countryside would know where to locate them. Servants were to be sent out to all households, rich and poor, without favouritism, unless the agent knew the employer had a history of mistreating servants.

City councils felt that servants were changing positions much too frequently and so ordered the agents to refuse to find a new position for anyone who had not worked at least six months. Indeed, any servant who left a household without just cause, like the death of an employer, was suspect and was to be investigated before being sent to a new position. In Munich and Strasbourg two special days,

2. Nuremberg Staatsarchiv (hereafter NB) Amts- und Standbücher, no. 101, fols. 558–67; Munich Stadtarchiv (hereafter MU) Gewerbeamt, no. 1569 (1580); Strasbourg, Archives Municipales (hereafter AMS), Statuten, Vol. 18, fols. 30–34 (1557).

six months apart, were set as the only times during which servants could change jobs; in Nuremberg, servants were to change positions only once a year.[3] Ann Kussmaul, in a recent study of servants in husbandry in early modern England, notes that specific dates for changing positions were necessary in rural areas, where households were far apart; hiring fairs where servants and employers could find each other were organized on these days in many counties.[4] The urban practice may be partly a continuation of this rural pattern, but it was also motivated by a desire to limit mobility among domestic servants. Individuals in cities did not have to travel the long distances to find prospective employers that they did in rural areas and could easily have changed positions frequently had the law allowed it.

The agents were paid for placements by both the employer and the servant, with the employer paying about twice as much as the servant. The amount a servant paid varied according to his or her rank, with cooks and other higher level servants paying two to three times as much as a children's maid or stable boy. The rates that the agents could charge were set in the ordinances, although they could charge an extra fee for extra work, for 'much running back and forth'. They were always forbidden to accept any presents, with a stiff fine and possible loss of office if they did.

Employment agents were not to keep the trunks or goods of any servants, first because this would enable the servants to leave a place of employment more easily, and second because the trunk could contain stolen goods. In fact, Strasbourg specifically ordered its employment agents not to be a part of any stealing ring or accept any goods they felt might have been stolen 'because they as the holder give the stealer the opportunity and cause to do such a deed'.[5]

These early ordinances reflect many of the same aims as other municipal market regulations – control of wages and prices, limitation of the numbers of individuals in any occupation, public transaction of all exchanges, prevention of theft, and orderly transfer of goods, which in this case happened to be people. Clauses that were added later have a different tone and do not stem from economic considerations. Employment agents were to reinforce the distinction between master and servant, not praising or denigrating any

3. Ibid.
4. Ann Kussmaul, *Servants in Husbandry in Early Modern England* (Cambridge, 1981).
5. AMS, Statuten, Vol. 10, 1628 Gesindeordnung.

master in front of any servant. They were not to offer new jobs to any servants, 'because no one can keep servants these days – who would otherwise gladly stay – as the agents run after them with promises of a better position'.[6] Most importantly, they were not to house any servants and to report anyone who was housing servants, for, the city governments asserted, this allowed servants to 'walk up and down freely whenever they want to, and is a source of great annoyance'.[7] Thus, along with facilitating the hiring of servants, employment agents were expected to assist city authorities in enforcing standards of conduct among the servants they had placed.

The emphasis on order and decorum led many city governments to begin regulating the activities of the servants themselves. In 1499 in Nuremberg, maids were not allowed into any dances at the city hall without their mistresses; they were always to be seated behind their mistresses if they did attend, for the council felt the maids' conduct did not always show the proper deference. Later, an attempt was made to forbid them attendance altogether, but enough wealthy women complained and the maids were again allowed to accompany their mistresses, although they had to stay in a separate locked room until they were needed. If a woman wanted her maid, she could send for her.[8] The conduct of maids at dances was also seen as a problem in Frankfurt, where the city council discussed cancelling all dances 'because maids seduce other servants, and cause them not only to do questionable acts, but also to stay away from their work longer than is proper'.[9]

During the middle of the sixteenth century, a number of city councils passed ordinances for servants, mainly because they felt that wages were too high. Strasbourg limited the wages a normal servant could be paid to 6 gulden a year, 'although one may certainly pay less'; employers were not responsible to pay servants anything if they found them unsuitable or if the servants left without cause. The following year, a second, sterner, notice was issued because the council heard that servants were even demanding gifts of their employers and were, in general, behaving in a 'disobedient, contrary, untrue, and otherwise inappropriate manner'.[10] In addition to their regular salary, only servants who had served 'obediently,

---

6. AMS, Akten der XV, 1587, fol. 168b.
7. AMS, Grosse Ratsbuch, Vol. 1, no. 150; a similar clause is in MU, Zimilien no. 29, Eidbuch 1688.
8. NB, Ratsbuch 6, fol. 59 (1499); NB, Ratsbuch 9, fol. 48 (1508).
9. Frankfurt Stadtarchiv (hereafter FF), Bürgermeisterbücher, 1604, fol. 29.
10. AMS Statuten, Vol. 18, fols. 30–35.

truly, and industriously' for a long time were to be rewarded with anything extra, and this was to be done only once. Servants who did not own at least 100 gulden worth of property themselves were not allowed to wear silk or satin, a property limit which probably excluded all servants. The council stated that this was to prevent extravagant expenditure on the part of servants. But, as this restriction even applied to clothing they had inherited or been given by a generous employer, it is clear the council was also attempting to maintain social distinctions.[11]

An ordinance passed at the same time in the Duchy of Württemberg was even stricter than that in Strasbourg. Servants were specifically charged with causing the general inflation, as they demanded a salary along with their room and board, so that salary was to be strictly limited.[12] No one was to be taken on as a servant without proof of her or his conduct and honourable dismissal from the last position.

The Munich ordinance from 1580 sees a great amount of distrust between employer and servant. Servants were not to leave the house for any reason without the knowledge of their employers. They were to take no food out of the house at any time and had to open their chests and trunks if their employers suspected them of having taken anything. If they pretended to be ill to get out of work, the servants were to be banished. If they really were ill and the employer didn't want them around, they could go to some unspecified 'honourable place' until they were healthy again. Servants who spoke against their masters were to be strictly punished. Hostility between servants was also to be avoided; upper-level servants were specifically ordered not to treat those under them too harshly.[13]

Recognizing that the problems they perceived in regard to servants could not be dealt with by restrictions on servants alone, city councils began to regulate the conduct of employers as well. In Strasbourg, as long as the first master provided well enough, no

---

11. Dress that obscured or confused status distinctions was viewed as very threatening in early modern society, as a clear sign of social disorder. The author of the English pamphlet *Hic Mulier* (1620) criticized women who dressed like men not only because they broke down gender distinctions but, even more, because class distinctions among women were lost when they all dressed in similar men's clothing. See Mary Beth Rose, 'Women in men's clothing: apparel and social stability in *The Roaring Girl*', *English Literary Renaissance* 14 no. 3 (Autumn 1984): 367–91.

12. Stuttgart, Württembergische Haupstaatsarchiv (hereafter ST), Generalreskripta, A–39, Bu. 3 (1562).

13. MU, Gewerbeamt, no. 1569 (1580).

one was to coax a servant away from a master with 'more pay, tips, beer, money, or other devices', under penalty of a fine of 10 gulden. Promises of marriage were not to be used with female servants, unless they were legitimate and did not first involve a period of employment in the future husband's home.[14] In the Duchy of Württemberg, no employer was to give a servant more than one glass of wine a day, even on festive occasions.[15] In Munich, masters found to be 'entirely too strict and harsh' were to be punished.[16] Municipal oversight of domestic servants thus extended to what went on within a household as well as in the public marketplace.

In some ways this was no different than guild or municipal regulations pertaining to apprentices, journeymen, and masters; all of them restricted activities in a household workshop, and guild regulations were motivated by moral as well as economic considerations. Guild leaders were caught up in the increased concern with propriety and decorum in the same way that municipal authorities were; in many cities, of course, guild leaders were the municipal authorities.

Cities' attempts to control servants extended not only into the household but into the family as well. Parents were forbidden to give their children shelter or aid if they had left a position without notice, or to take their children out of one place of employment and put them in another. The 1665 Strasbourg ordinance went much further than that:

> Numerous complaints have been made that some widows living here have two, three, or more daughters living with them at their expense. These girls go into service during the winter, but during the summer return to their mothers partly because they want to wear more expensive clothes than servants are normally allowed to, and partly because they want to have more freedom to walk around, to saunter back and forth whenever they want to. It is our experience that this causes nothing but shame, immodesty, wantonness, and immorality, so that a watchful eye should be kept on this, and if it is discovered, the parents as well as the daughters should be punished with a fine, a jail sentence, or even banishment from the city in order to serve as an example to others.[17]

Young women were thus to be prevented from living with their own mothers if they were not needed in the household, as the

14. AMS, Statuten, Vol. 18, fol. 30.
15. ST, Generalreskripta, A–39, Bu. 3 (1562).
16. MU, Gewerbeamt, no. 1569 (1580).
17. AMS, Statuten, Vol. 33, no. 61 (1665).

council felt the mothers could not control them as well as an employer could. Even the family itself was not as important as propriety and decorum in the city, at least in this case.

The 'freedom to walk around' mentioned in the Strasbourg ordinance was particularly disturbing to civic authorities. The Munich ordinance from 1580 forbade anyone to coax servants away from their masters, not only with promises of gifts or money, but also with promises of 'more freedom'.[18] This was expected to lead to 'shame, immodesty, wantonness, and immorality', and also might make servants more resentful of all control by their employers, causing them to leave domestic service and search for employment elsewhere. This was unthinkable, in the view of city authorities, because it would remove young single people, and particularly young single women, from the control of respectable, and generally male, heads of household.[19] Cities responded to the threat by forbidding all city residents to rent rooms to single men or women who were not in service somewhere, or to keep their trunks or possessions. Any unmarried man or woman servant who would not take a position but tried to live on his or her own as a day labourer was to be banished, as were the people who housed them, even if they were public innkeepers.[20]

In the case of women, this included those who had a trade with which they had formerly supported themselves. Unmarried spinners in Augsburg, for example, were ordered to live with a weaver and not independently, so that their living arrangements were analogous to domestic service, even though their actual work continued to be thread production.[21] Servants who married and set up their own households but were then not able to find enough work to support themselves and their families were also to be banished, 'so that such young people will first think over how they will support themselves and their children before they get married'.[22]

18. MU, Gewerbeamt, no. 1569 (1580).

19. Gordon Schochet has discovered these same opinions among authorities in England. See *Patriarchalism in Political Thought: The Authoritarian Family and Political Speculations and Attitudes Especially in Seventeenth-Century England* (Oxford, 1975).

20. Grethe Jacobsen has discovered similar legislation in Malmø, Denmark, in a city ordinance that 'demanded that all self-supporting maidens should take work as servants or be exiled from town'. See 'Women, marriage, and magisterial reformation: the case of Malmø, Denmark', in *Pietas et Societas: New Trends in Reformation Social History, Essays in Memory of Harold Grimm*, ed. Kyle C. Sessions and Phillip N. Bebb (Kirksville, MO, 1985), p. 76.

21. Claus-Peter Clasen, *Die Augsburger Weber um 1600: Leistung und Krisen eines Textilgewerbes* (Augsburg, 1983), pp. 130–3.

22. MU, Gewerbeamt, no. 1569 (1580).

By the end of the sixteenth century, the regulations regarding domestic service served three distinct purposes. The first was economic. In this period of inflation, city authorities attempted to control wages and prices. They could regulate the prices of most things only to a degree: those of foodstuffs and raw materials were largely outside their control, though they tried fiercely to limit them. The wages of servants and day labourers could be held down more easily, though the frequency with which such regulations were repeated indicates that the limits were often being broken.

The second was social. City governments wanted social distinctions clearly observed, even if this meant forbidding upper-class employers to give gifts to their servants or bring their maids along to private parties. This was also the period of the hardening of sumptuary clothing laws, which made the distinction between master and servant immediately visible because of fabric colour and quality, or style of apron and headgear.[23]

The third was both social and ideological. City governments viewed male-headed households as the best instrument of social control and strengthening them the best means to assure order, decorum, morality, and stability. Whenever possible, all unmarried individuals, especially unmarried women, were to be placed under the control of a male-headed household. This even applied to women who had long supported themselves independently, though city governments often justified such moves with a note of paternalistic concern for these women's well-being. It also applied to unmarried women who were living with their own mothers, if the conduct of the young woman was deemed to be unacceptable.

Cities achieved greater control of domestic servants and attempted to achieve greater control of all unmarried individuals by broadening their concepts of what the public good demanded. Servants themselves continued to be considered as part of that 'public', however, for even the harshest restrictions allowed a servant to leave a violent master and allowed employment agents to refuse to send servants to such individuals. As long as servants were safely within orderly households, they fitted into city authorities' vision of the ideal community and thus deserved protection.

23. *Frankfurt um 1600: Alltagsleben in der Stadt.* Kleine Schriften des Historische Museums, Vol. 7 (Frankfurt, 1976); Ingeborg Köhler, 'Bestimmungen des Rates der Reichsstadt Nürnberg über die Kleidung seiner Bürgerinnen' (Zulassungsarbeit, University of Munich, 1953); Kent Greenfield, *Sumptuary Law in Nuremberg,* Johns Hopkins University Studies in History and Political Science, Vol. 36 (Baltimore, 1918).

Public brothels

The relationship between prostitution and the 'public good' was an ambiguous one for city authorities. During the medieval period, prostitution had been viewed by both church and secular authorities as, at worst, a necessary evil or, at best, as an Ulm ordinance put it, as 'enhancing the good piety, and honour of the whole community'.[24] This changed during the sixteenth century, and brothels were closed with justifications couched in exactly the same language as this Ulm ordinance. This involved a change in attitude about the city's responsibility to provide outlets for male sexuality, and about the role of prostitutes, displacing them from the margins of the community to a position totally outside it.

The first step in regulating prostitution was opening an official municipal brothel (*Frauenhaus*). Although the founding of the brothel was not usually announced publicly, by the fifteenth century nearly every major city in Germany and most of the smaller ones had an official house of prostitution.[25] All prostitutes were ordered to either move into the brothel or leave the city. Many of these houses, such as one in Frankfurt and one in Mainz, actually belonged to bishops or religious houses; the bishop of Mainz complained at one point that the house was not getting enough business.[26]

Ordinances were passed to ensure that the brothels would serve the community as planned, but inadvertently they also protected the prostitutes against excessive exploitation. Though the prostitutes' status in the community was marginal, their health and safety were regarded as important. Because the brothel was frequently visited by foreign dignitaries and merchants, a dilapidated building, undernourished or ill-dressed prostitutes, and violent brawls all reflected badly on the city. The brothel was a very visible municipal institution and thus warranted and received close attention. Beginning in the fifteenth century, lengthy brothel ordinances were passed in many German cities.

Some clauses in the ordinances were designed to reflect the prostitutes' marginality. No daughter of a citizen was to live in the brothel, and only women who had been prostitutes elsewhere were supposed

24. Quoted in Lyndal Roper, 'Discipline and respectability: prostitution and the Reformation in Augsburg', *History Workshop* 19 (Spring 1985): 4.
25. Iwan Bloch, *Die Prostitution* (Berlin, 1912), pp. 740–5.
26. Max Bauer, *Liebesleben in deutscher Vergangenheit* (Berlin, 1924), p. 148.

to be taken in, a rule that was obviously not always followed as then no woman would have been eligible. In 1548 in Nuremberg, a citizen's daughter was found working as a prostitute; the brothel manager was given a light fine, but the poor woman was held in the city jail for five years.[27]

Their distinction from 'honourable women' was reinforced by the requirement that prostitutes wear special clothing. Prostitutes in Strasbourg were to wear a shorter coat than was customary, with a yellow band of cloth somewhere on their clothing.[28] Yellow bands or veils were a common way of identifying prostitutes. They could not wear any elaborate jewelry, have silk or fur trim on anything, or leave their hair uncovered in the fashion of other young, unmarried women. They were often forbidden to have a maid servant accompany them when they went out; if two prostitutes went somewhere together, they were ordered to walk side by side, not one behind the other, lest people even think one were a maid.[29]

The location of the brothel (or brothels) also reflected the prostitutes' marginal status. Often they were set up just inside one of the city's gates, on a small street away from the general flow of traffic, so that people were not constantly reminded of their presence. In 1469 in Strasbourg, prostitutes were found to be living throughout the city, to the dismay of 'decent and honourable people'; the council gave them a week to move into the section of the city in which 'women such as these have always lived'. It also took a survey of the women, finding eight to be living in the official brothel with the manager, and fourteen others 'living alone' or 'living with two, three, or four others', which makes one suspect that these were women who ran small, unofficial houses. In addition, there is a list of sixteen names with the note 'these do not want to be considered public prostitutes [*offen huren*]'. Several members of the city council were sent to examine the houses where these women were living, to make sure they were 'appropriate for such use', and reported that at least twenty-five or thirty houses in the approved area could be used by prostitutes, along with the official brothel.[30] Apparently this still was not enough, or at any rate the women did not want to move into these houses, for the council repeated its warning that they were not to live among 'honourable

---

27. NB, Ratsbuch 24, fol. 128 (1548); Ratsbuch 26, fol. 356 (1553).
28. AMS, Statuten, Vol. 2, fols. 75, 78.
29. Ibid., fol. 130; Vol. 29, fol. 154; Werner Danckert, *Unehrliche Leute: Die verfemte Berufe* (Bern/Munich, 1963), p. 150.
30. AMS, Statuten, Vol. 2, fol. 70; Vol. 29, fol. 34 (1469).

people', but only in one area of the city. It increased the fines and threats of punishment in 1471, 1493, 1496, 1501, and on into the sixteenth century.

The Strasbourg city council was also troubled by women who made their living in a 'dishonourable' way, yet claimed they were not really prostitutes but had another occupation or craft. These women as well were to move to the approved area of the city 'and not protect themselves with the argument that they do not carry out such sinful work in their houses'. Not only admitted prostitutes, but any woman 'who serves a priest or layman and lives with him publicly without marriage' was to wear the short coat and yellow band identifying her as dishonourable. No excuses that she was simply a housekeeper or practised another craft were to be tolerated, as long as it was 'widely known and recognized' that she was really 'that sort of woman'.[31] There was to be no grey area between women who were honourable and those who were not.

Despite, or perhaps because of, their marginal status, throughout the fifteenth century prostitutes appeared often in public. A chronicle from 1471 reports on the stay of Emperor Friedrich III in Nuremberg:

> [The Emperor] rode behind the grain houses and looked at the weapons and the grain, and while he was leaving the grain houses, two whores caught him with a silver chain and said 'Your Grace must be captured.' He said 'We haven't been captured yet and would rather be released,' and gave them one gulden. Then he rode to the *Frauenhaus* where another four were waiting and he gave them another gulden.[32]

Although chroniclers often exaggerate, this may not have been far from the truth. Prostitutes were allowed to come to dances at the city hall in Nuremberg whenever they wished for another twenty-five years.

In Frankfurt, prostitutes brought flowers to the city council at their yearly festive meal and were then allowed to eat with the councillors until 1529, though the council members' wives were not invited. After this, the prostitutes still received a free dinner from the council, brought to them in the brothel. The Würzburg fire ordinance required prostitutes to help put out the fires that broke out in the city until 1528; and in Frankfurt, they gave flowers

31. Ibid., Vol. 2, fol. 137 (1497).
32. *Die Chroniken der fränkischen Städte* (Leipzig, 1874), Vol. 4, p. 328.

and congratulations to newly married couples.[33] In Memmingen they, along with the city's midwives, were given a special New Year's gift every year.[34]

The ambivalence of official attitudes toward prostitution in the fifteenth century is reflected in city councils' attempts to draw women out of the brothel to more 'honourable' callings; at the same time they tolerated them at or even invited them to public events. In many cities, anyone who married a prostitute was given free citizenship, as long as the couple maintained an 'honourable way of life'. In Nuremberg an endowed fund was set up by Conrad Khunhof to provide support each year for four women who wanted to leave the brothel and join the sisters at the nearby convent at Pillenreuth. After the Reformation, when the convent at Pillenreuth was forbidden to take in any new women, the city council decided to continue support for the women who were already there but in the future to look into other ways to use the money that would correspond with Khunhof's aims. Two years later, it finally decided to provide dowries of 20 gulden annually to each of four women from the brothel who had worked in the city's main hospital. The council also used some of Khunhof's money for a quite different purpose, setting up a stipend fund of 52 gulden a year for university students.[35]

The same kind of opportunities were offered in other cities by 'Magdalene houses', small houses specifically set up to provide homes for prostitutes who had decided to give up their former lives or were too old to work. Most of these were similar to Beguinages, the religious associations of women devoted to charitable works which had grown up in the Middle Ages, so that the women did not take actual vows, and many of them were endowed by women who felt this was a particularly appropriate form of charity for a woman.[36]

Many of the clauses in early brothel ordinances were included to prevent violence and bloodshed in the house. The innkeepers in the area around the houses in Nuremberg were limited to the amount of wine they could sell, either to the women or their customers.[37]

33. Anton Kriegk, *Deutsches Bürgerthum im Mittelalter* (Frankfurt, 1871), Vol. 2, p. 322; Helmut Wachendorf, *Die wirtschaftliche Stellung der Frau in den deutschen Städten des späteren Mittelalters* (Quackenbruck, 1934), p. 120.

34. Memmingen Stadtarchiv, Ratsprotokollbücher, 19 December 1526.

35. NB, Ratsbuch 19, fol. 252 (1539); Ratsbuch 20, fol. 255 (1541).

36. K.A. Weith-Knudsen, *Kulturgeschichte der europäischen Frauenwelt* (Stuttgart, 1927), p. 173.

37. NB, Ratsbuch 1b, fol. 324 (1455); Ratsbuch 7, fol. 59 (1499).

In 1478 the Frankfurt city council put two iron bands in the brothel for imprisoning men who had got out of hand and specifically allowed the manager to carry a knife in order to defend himself or the women. Men who had beaten up or injured prostitutes were supposed to be given longer jail sentences than those given for normal assault.[38] In Nuremberg, the council also forbade women to have favourite customers, for it felt this brought 'clamour, indigna- tion, discord, and displeasure' and could lead to fights, though the men often identified one of the women as 'theirs'.[39]

Customers were also to be protected from disease, so cities made some attempts to guard the cleanliness and health of the women in the brothel. They were to be allowed at least one bath a week and, in some cities, had a special separate bathing room at the public baths, another indication of their marginal status. In Ulm, a mid- wife regularly conducted examinations of all prostitutes, both to check if they were pregnant and to make sure they were 'fit, clean, and healthy women'.[40]

Though promulgated for the benefit of the brothel's customers, these ordinances regarding violence and disease also worked to the women's advantage. Most ordinances also included clauses designed specifically to protect the women from exploitation by their relat- ives or by the brothel manager. All ordinances forbade parents and other people to place women in a brothel as payment for a debt to a brothel manager; later editions repeat and strengthen these clauses, a clear indication that this was occurring despite the prohibition. The manager also freely traded women who had become endebted to him after coming into the house. A 1488 Munich ordinance forbade a manager to trade away a woman for more than the debt she owed him, and later ordinances from Strasbourg, Nuremberg, and Frankfurt forbade him to sell or trade away any woman no matter how much she owed him. They attempted to take away all temptation to do so by forbidding him to loan the women more than a small amount at any one time. The manager was forbidden to force women into the house as well, though the burden of proof in such cases was on the woman, not on the manager.[41]

38. Kriegk, *Deutsches Bürgerthum*, Vol. 2, p. 306; FF, Bürgermeisterbücher, 1510, fol. 19b.

39. Joseph Baader, 'Nürnberger Polizeiordnungen aus dem XIII. bis XV. Jahrhundert', *Bibliothek des Literarische Verein Stuttgart* 63 (1861): 119–20.

40. Kriegk, *Deutsches Bürgerthum*, Vol. 2, p. 308.

41. MU, Zimilien 41, Eidbuch 1488; AMS, Statuten, Vol. 3, fol. 4 (1500); FF, Bürgermeisterbücher, 1545, fol. 47; Baader, 'Polizeiordnungen', 119–20.

The women were to pay the manager a designated amount per customer, usually more if the man stayed all night; the amount the customers were to give the women is not mentioned in any of the regulations, though we can assume it was fairly low, as badly paid journeymen were the most frequent customers. The women were to receive two or three meals a day in the house and were not required to pay any rent when they did not have customers, though they still had to pay for their meals. If a woman owed money to the manager or he felt she was not giving him his fair share, he could seize her clothing and personal effects until the case was brought to trial but theoretically could not force her to stay in the house.

The women were to be allowed out of the house whenever they wanted to go to church and were not to be forced to work at any time. An ordinance from Nuremberg reads: 'The manager, his wife, or his servants shall not force, coerce, or compel in any way any woman who lives in his house to care for a man when she is pregnant or menstruating [*mit weiblichen Rechten beladen*] or in any other way unfit or want to hold back from bodily work.'[42] In Munich, menstruating women were to have their normal meals augmented by a couple of eggs, as this was felt to ease any pain that might accompany a menstrual period, a good example of what anthropologists term *sympathetic magic.*[43]

The city councils also set minimum age limits for women in the brothels. Usually the minimum age was fourteen, although the treatment of girls found to be too young was hardly gentle. A regulation from Strasbourg in 1500 notes: 'Whichever daughters are found whose bodies are not yet ready for such work, that is who have neither breasts nor the other things which are necessary for this, should be driven out of the city with blows and are to stay out under threat of bodily punishment until they reach the proper age.'[44] Apparently the city council saw no contradiction in its judgment that these girls were too young to be prostitutes but old enough to be banished out of the city on their own.

The city of Ulm went the furthest in protecting its prostitutes. All of the money that the women made went into a common box and was then distributed each week by a woman who was not herself a prostitute, according to the needs of each woman. This box had three separate locks, with one key held by the manager, one

42. Baader, 'Polizeiordnungen', 119–20. Similar clauses in AMS, Statuten, Vol. 3, fol. 4.
43. MU, Zimilien 41, Eidbuch 1488.
44. AMS, Statuten, Vol. 3, fol. 5.

by one of the prostitutes, and the third by this outside woman, so that no one could get money from it illegally. Ulm also had a second fund, into which all prostitutes and the manager paid a portion of their incomes, which was supposed to be used to support prostitutes who were too old or sick to work any longer.[45] In return for this old-age pension, the women were required to spin two spindles of yarn every day for the manager. They did spinning in other cities as well, but the amounts and purposes were never specified.

Toward the end of the fifteenth century, city councils became more uncomfortable with the idea of municipally sanctioned prostitution and attempted to hide prostitutes from public view. In 1472 and 1478, Frankfurt prostitutes were ordered not to sit at the door of their house and call out to prospective customers.[46] In Strasbourg the women were not to sit directly in front of the altar at church, for they often spent the time talking or turning around so that their faces were visible to those behind them. If they were found there, they were to be followed when leaving the cathedral, their coats or shawls taken from them, pawned, and the money given to the poor; the council recognized that they were probably too poor to pay a fine outright. They were also forbidden to come to dances where honourable women were present, with the additional proviso that there would be no punishment for anyone who attacked the prostitute or the person who brought her, unless the attack led to a serious wounding or death.[47]

In Nuremberg the first restrictions came in 1508, when the brothel manager was ordered to keep all women off the street in their 'whore's clothing'; if they went to church or elsewhere they were to wear a coat or veil. Later, the brothel was closed until noon every day and at sunset on Saturday night and the eves of holidays. In 1544, on a complaint of the neighbours, the council ordered a special door to be built on the brothel so that no one could see inside and held the manager responsible to make sure it was always shut. Two years later, prostitutes were no longer to be allowed at public dances or at the wine market; if a number were found out of the house, the manager was to be thrown in jail. The neighbours grumbled again that they had to walk by and 'bear their [the

45. Kriegk, *Bürgerthum*, Vol. 2, p. 316; Bauer, *Liebesleben*, p. 134.
46. Kriegk, *Bürgerthum*, p. 306; Bauer, *Liebesleben*, p. 133.
47. AMS, Statuten, Vol. 2, fols. 75, 78.

prostitutes'] annoying and unsightly presence', so the door was ordered locked shut during the day. It was to be opened only at night, so city officials could go in easily if there was a problem.[48]

Guilds were also growing more concerned about the conduct and morality of their members and increasingly forbade all contact with prostitutes. In 1521 in Frankfurt, all masters and journeymen were forbidden to dance with prostitutes or other 'dishonourable' women, or even stand next to them in a public place. Similar clauses were added to many guild and journeymen's ordinances through- out Germany beginning at about this time, a trend that resulted from guild attempts to limit memberships in a period of declining opportunities. Children born out of wedlock, children of parents with 'dishonourable' occupations, such as grave-diggers and execu- tioners, and those who had contact with prostitutes were all denied membership, as were those who married women 'tainted' by these factors. The guilds could thus keep their numbers down for eco- nomic reasons, while claiming to be upholding the honour and morality of the guild. The fustian weavers in Frankfurt went one step further, forbidding their members to dance with or give drinks to women who were simply suspected of being dishonourable. By 1546, under pressure from the guilds, the city council in Frankfurt had agreed to forbid the burial of prostitutes in hallowed ground; a special cemetery was opened for them near the city's gallows.[49] Even in death, honourable citizens were to be protected from con- tact with prostitutes.

By the middle of the sixteenth century, city councils determined that the public good demanded closing the brothels, not just trying to hide or ignore them. Augsburg led the way in 1532 – it had always had the most stringent limitations on the conduct of prostitutes – with Basel following in 1534, Nördlingen in 1536, Ulm in 1537, Regensburg in 1553, and Frankfurt in 1560.[50] No provision was made for the women or the manager; the Augsburg manager asked the city council where he should go now with the women but received no answer.

We can best trace the arguments for and against the closing of a city brothel in Nuremberg, which was always cautious about doing anything that might bring more harm than good. Not until 1562

48. NB, Ratsbuch 9, fol. 17 (1508); Ratsbuch 19, fol. 342 (1542); Ratsbuch 20, fol. 44, 87 (1544); Ratsbuch 23, fols. 202, 205 (1546).
49. Danckert, *Unehrliche Leute*, p. 150.
50. Kriegk, *Deutsches Bürgerthum*, Vol. 2, p. 340; Bauer, *Liebesleben*, p. 159.

did the city council begin to ask for opinions as to whether the house should be closed 'or if it were closed, if other dangers and still more evil would possibly be the result'.[51]

The discussion among the jurists and theologians is very interesting. Augsburg had reported an increase and spread in unchastity since it closed its brothel, so the jurists asserted that the closing could cause journeymen and foreign workers to turn to their masters' or landlords' wives and daughters. The theologians urged the council to think of Nuremberg's reputation as the leading free imperial city and not allow it to break 'the word of God' just because of the complaints against the closing of the house by foreigners who visited or lived in Nuremberg. One argued that the brothel caused young men to have impure thoughts about women; those who had no opportunity and were never introduced to sex wouldn't chase other women.[52] In this he agreed with Johannes Brenz, who wrote: 'Some say one must have public brothels to prevent greater evil – but what if these brothels are schools where one learns more wickedness than before?' Brenz, incidentally, goes on to say that if men were the more rational creatures and women the more sensual, as everyone believed in the sixteenth century, why shouldn't women also have brothels? 'If the authorities have the power to allow a brothel and do not sin in this, where not only single men but also married men may go, and say this does no harm. . . . Why do they not also permit a women's brothel where women who are old and weak and have no husbands may go?'[53] Brenz was not advocating this, of course, but using the turnabout to point out the absurdity of the arguments for the brothels.

The spread of syphilis was also given as a reason: 'If the house isn't closed in a short time, then it will be necessary to build three syphilis clinics instead of just one.'[54] The council recognized early that women in the brothel were more likely to get syphilis and pass it on to other people than the population as a whole. It usually attributed this to moral rather than medical reasons, however. When syphilis first swept through Nuremberg in 1496, a special clinic was set up for syphilitics, and prostitutes were readily taken in, though other non-citizens were not. Other cities were not so enlightened. In 1498 in Munich, journeymen stormed the brothel and tried to

---

51. NB, Ratsbuch 31, fol. 316 (1562).
52. NB, Ratschlagbuch 34, fol. 137–53.
53. Quoted in Roper, 'Discipline and respectability', 12–13.
54. Karl Sudhoff, *Die ersten Massnahmen der Stadt Nürnberg gegen die Syphilis* (Leipzig, 1912), p. 109.

kill the manager because they were angry about the introduction of syphilis. Thirty-five armed men had to watch the brothel day and night for a month and a half before things quietened down again.[55]

The Nuremberg council wanted an exact report from Augsburg of the number of illegitimate children conceived before and after the closing of the brothel, to see if the numbers had actually increased. It rejected the argument that closing the house would lessen the opportunities for men to perform meritorious services by marrying prostitutes; closing the house would also 'pull the women out of the devil's jaws'. Another jurist realistically noted that, since there were only ten to twelve women in the brothel, they couldn't possibly be taking care of the sexual needs of all the city's unmarried men, so the closing wouldn't make that much of a difference.[56]

Those arguing for the closing were more persuasive, and the council decided to follow the example of Augsburg and others:

> On the recommendation written and ready by the high honourable theologians and jurists, why the men of the council are authorized and obliged to close the common brothel, it has been decided by the whole council to follow the same recommendation and from this hour on forbid all activity in that house, to post a guard in the house and let no man enter it any more. Also to send for the manager and say to him that he is to send all women that he has out of the house and never take them in again. From this time on, he is to act so blamelessly and unsuspiciously that the council has no cause to punish him. When this has been completed, the preachers should be told to admonish the young people to guard themselves from such depravity and to keep their children and servants from it and to lead such an irreproachable life that the council has no cause to punish anyone for this vice.[57]

Unfortunately for the council, its final words were not heeded. The house was closed, but a short time later the council found that 'adultery, prostitution, fornication and rape have taken over forcibly here in the city and in the countryside', and wondered whether its move had been a wise one.[58]

The closing of the official brothels obviously did not end prostitution in early modern European cities, for many women continued to make their living this way, often combining prostitution

55. MU, Ratsgeschäft, 1498.
56. NB, Ratschlagbuch 34, fols. 137–53.
57. NB, Ratsbuch 31, fol. 350 (1562).
58. NB, Ratsbuch 36, fol. 15 (1577).

with piecework or laundering or with theft and other crimes. What it did end was the city council's ambivalent attitude toward prostitutes. For a short period of time, from the first laws protecting them from being sold or pawned to the closing of the brothels, the welfare of prostitutes was a concern of the city government, though they never totally lost their 'dishonourable' status. Once the brothels were closed, however, their well-being was no longer viewed as part of the general well-being of the city, and they could be treated like any other criminal. Indeed, they were perhaps worse than other criminals, for they seduced honourable citizens from a life of *Zucht*, the moral order that all city councils were trying to create in the sixteenth century. The public good now demanded that they be punished, not protected, for the paternalistic wing of the city government no longer sheltered them.

Conclusion

Throughout the Middle Ages, city governments addressed a wide variety of concerns when they considered the 'public good': health and hygiene, consumer protection, security from invasion, fair business practices, just wages and prices, fire protection, to name a few. Though moral considerations entered into their discussions and are often included in the introductions to ordinances or regulations, greater emphasis was placed on economic growth or stability and physical security. During the sixteenth century these emphases were reversed, and ordinances also were passed solely out of concern for decorum, order, and morality. Paternalistic concern for the good of the community now demanded a still wider range of legislation.

City councils recognized that they could not possibly enforce this moral legislation by themselves and enlisted the assistance not only of lesser officials but also of heads of households, whom they viewed essentially as the lowest-level officials in the city. Masters were to control their apprentices and journeymen, employers their servants, parents their children; the proper moral order was strictly hierarchical. Individuals who did not normally fit into a hierarchy, such as unmarried young adults, were to be forced into one and, more important, one that successfully controlled its subordinate members. Lax households were not functioning as agents of the moral order, and so were chastised and could even have their servants or children removed and placed elsewhere. Lenient heads of household or disobedient servants were still considered part of the community, however, and actions taken to control them viewed as contributing both to the public good, by promoting public decorum, and to their own private moral development, by convincing them to change.

Prostitution was initially handled in the same way. The opening of public brothels put prostitutes under the care of the brothel man-ager, who controlled their conduct and that of their patrons. Con-cerns for health and hygiene, security, and fair business practices extended to the residents of these somewhat unusual households. As city councils came to regard prostitution as morally unacceptable in and of itself, regulations or restrictions no longer sufficed in their considerations of the public good. A well-run, orderly brothel was still a brothel. Unruly domestic servants could be brought under con-trol and disturbed public order and decorum only by their actions. Prostitutes could not be fitted into any hierarchy that reflected an ideal moral order and disturbed the authorities' sense of propriety by their very existence. The only solution was banishment from the city, thus removing them physically from the community from which they had already been ideologically excluded.

CHAPTER SEVEN

War, work, and wealth: the bases of citizenship in early modern German cities

Most of the recent scholarship on the development of citizenship in early modern Europe has taken for granted that 'citizenship' means *state* citizenship and so focuses on the emergence of the centralized state. There is, of course, another type of citizenship, one which historians of the Holy Roman Empire have written a great deal about – urban citizenship. Beginning with Max Weber's massive *Wirtschaft und Gesellschaft*, published in the 1920s, theorists of urban development have argued that a new and distinctive type of city began in the medieval West.[1] Here is Weber's description: 'The city of the Medieval Occident was economically a seat of trade and commerce, politically and economically a fortress and garrison, administratively a court district and socially an oath-bound confederation.' As is often true with Weber, this was not simply a description, but a set of criteria which any 'true' city exhibited: in other words, an ideal type. Thus, in his words, 'An urban "community" [*Gemeinschaft*], in the full meaning of the word, appears as a general phenomenon only in the Occident.' Though German urban historians and sociologists since Weber – scholars such as Werner Schultheiss, Gerard Dilcher, Edith Ennen, Hans Planitz, and Otto Brunner – have modified their tone somewhat, many of them have agreed with Weber that the key factor distinguishing this city from those of other periods and places was the notion of citizenship

1. Max Weber, *Wirtschaft und Gesellschaft*, selectively edited and translated by Don Martindale and Gertrud Neuwirth and published as *The City* (New York: Free Press, 1958); Hans Planitz, *Die deutsche Stadt im Mittelalter* (Graz: Böhlau, 1965); Otto Brunner, 'Zum Begriff Bürgertums', in Thomas von Mayer, ed., *Untersuchungen zur gesellschaftlichen Struktur der mittelalterlichen Städte in Europa: Vorträge und Forschungen, 10* (Constance and Stuttgart: Jan Thorbecke, 1966), pp. 13–24; Edith Ennen, *Die europäische Stadt des Mittelalters* (Göttingen: Vandenhoeck und Ruprecht, 1972). The quotations in the following sentences are from Weber, *The City*, pp. 104, 80.

(*Bürgertum*). It was citizenship that created the urban 'community'.[2] Weber's stress on the distinctiveness and importance of this urban community has been highlighted in the English-language scholarship on his work, a tendency best seen in the fact that the best-known English translation of *Wirtschaft und Gesellschaft* is a selective edition entitled simply *The City*.

Urban citizenship has been studied more extensively in German scholarship than in that focusing on western Europe, where cities lost their independence to centralizing states earlier. (This may also be the reason that Weber's ideas about urban development are not as well known in English-language scholarship as the 'Weber thesis' or 'ideal types', both of which can be applied more easily to English and French developments.) In German scholarship, this interest has not been limited to the medieval period, for notions of urban community based on citizenship have also been a key part of research on the urban Reformation since Bernd Moeller's *Imperial Cities and the Reformation*; and a recent study of German towns between the Thirty Years War and Bismarck asserts: 'Any town's citizenship policy and citizenship grants are usually the best place to read its history.'[3]

This scholarship on the urban community has been joined over the last fifteen years by scholarship focusing on the rural community, particularly the Swiss and German village communes between 1400 and 1600.[4] Like cities, villages were also oath-bound confederations (*Gemeinde*), and by the sixteenth century these confederations had, in turn, formed themselves into larger federations of villages. Though their primary decisions were economic ones relating to

2. Brunner, 'Zum Begriff Bürgertums'; Werner Schultheiss, 'Das Bürgerrecht der Königs- und Reichstadt Nürnberg', in *Festschrift für Hermann Heimpel* Vol. 2 (Göttingen: Vandenhoeck und Ruprecht, 1972), pp. 159–94; Gerard Dilcher, 'Zum Bürgerbegriff im späteren Mittelalter: Versuch einer Typologie am Beispiel von Frankfurt am Main', in Joseph Fleckenstein and Karl Stackmann, eds, *Ueber Bürger, Stadt, und städtischen Literatur im Spätmittelalter* (Göttingen: Vandenhoeck und Ruprecht, 1980), pp. 59–105.

3. Bernd Moeller, *Imperial Cities and the Reformation* (Philadelphia: Fortress, 1972), first published as *Reichsstadt und Reformation* (Gutersloh, 1962). For a survey of studies of the urban Reformation since Moeller, see Kaspar von Greyerz, 'Stadt und Reformation: Stand und Aufgaben der Forschung', *Archiv für Reformationsgeschichte* (1985): 6–63. The quote in the second half of the sentence is from Mack Walker, *German Home Towns: Community, State and General Estate, 1648–1871* (Ithaca, NY: Cornell University Press, 1971), p. 139.

4. See the work of Peter Blickle, most recently *Communal Reformation: The Quest for Salvation in Sixteenth-Century Germany*, tr. Thomas A. Brady, Jr., and H.C. Erik Midelfort (Atlantic Highlands, NJ: Humanities Press, 1992), and Heide Wunder, *Die Bäuerliche Gemeinde in Deutschland* (Göttingen: Vandenhoeck und Ruprecht, 1986).

regulation of agricultural production, by the early sixteenth century they were also making religious demands, in particular demanding that 'we ought to have the authority and power for the whole community to elect and appoint its own pastor'.[5]

Who made up these urban and rural communities? In the cities – though there are some differences from town to town – citizenship was generally based on three factors: military obligations and an oath of allegiance formalizing these (a swearing of *Treue und Gehorsam*); property ownership (*Eigentum*); and an honourable means of support (*bürgerliche Nahrung*) – what we can in shorthand term war, work, and wealth. Existing studies of urban citizenship have concentrated on changes in these bases, tracing the substitution of pecuniary military obligations for personal ones, increases in the levels of wealth required for citizenship, and the exclusion of certain people on the grounds that their occupation was dishonourable.[6] These three bases also seem to be applicable to village communes, though in these the issue of property ownership was more complicated.[7]

At first glance, any of these three factors might have been used as a reason for limiting citizenship to men, which could explain why most studies of urban citizenship in the Empire or the development of the village commune have focused on the meaning of these for men. Women did not perform military duties in medieval cities or villages; they could lose their right to control property on marriage; the types of work available to them independently were as likely to be dishonourable as honourable or to provide less than an adequate means of support. The problem with this is that it didn't happen. Not only were women citizens, but the bases for accepting them as such – at least in cities where this is spelled out – were explicitly the same three as for men. I would like to provide some examples of this from several south German cities and villages, and then explore changes in female citizenship in the early modern period. I will argue that though women continued to be labelled 'citizen', the significance of their citizenship decreased as distinctions were increasingly drawn between male and female

5. Twelve Articles of the Peasants (1525), quoted in Blickle, *Communal Reformation*, p. 21.

6. Schultheiss, 'Bürgerrecht'; Dilcher, 'Bürgerbegriff'; Wilhelm Ebel, *Der Bürgereid als Geltungsgrund und Gestaltungsprinzip des deutschen mittelalterlichen Stadtrechts* (Weimar, 1958); Franz Gschwind, *Bevölkerungsentwicklung und Wirtschaftstruktur der Landschaft Basel im 18. Jahrhundert* (Liestal: Kantonale Druchsachen, 1970).

7. Robert H. Lutz, *Wer war der gemeine Mann? Der dritte Stand in der Krise des Spätmittelalters* (Munich: Beck, 1979).

citizens. Thus not only in state citizenship, but also in urban and village citizenship, gender became an increasingly important variable. First to look at the medieval period. When referring to citizens, many medieval sources are explicitly gender-inclusive – they use the phrase 'Bürger und Bürgerin' when referring to all the citizens of a town, or 'alle Bürgern, Mann und Frau' (all citizens, man and woman) or 'Bürgern, es sey mannisname oder wybisname'[8] (citizens, whether male or female). Legal records make clear distinctions between citizens and non-citizens when referring to women, and in no German town have I found the phrase, common in Danish sources, 'a citizen or a woman of this town'.[9] Women were listed on new citizens' rolls in Nuremberg, Frankfurt, Munich, Nördlingen, Memmingen, Strasbourg, Augsburg, and many other south German towns, and were obligated to swear an oath and provide soldiers and arms for the city's defence.[10] The number of men and the amount of equipment they were required to provide were assessed according to the value of the property they held, exactly as they were for male heads of household. After a male citizen died, his widow was obligated to take an oath and pay a separate citizenship fee, though this was often less than the amount normally required.[11] Just as they did with men, the new citizens' lists record the occupations of the women accepted – midwife, seamstress, weaver, candle-maker – and the amount they paid to be accepted.[12] Married women were occasionally listed separately from their husbands, and might even purchase citizenship rights for them, as for example in 1465 in Augsburg 'Grethe Sattlerin from Esslingen has bought citizenship rights for herself and her husband, Heinz Engel from Munich'.[13] Women as well as men were granted citizenship free of charge for special services to the city, or if they practised an occupation the city deemed desirable; midwives

8. See e.g. Frankfurt Stadtarchiv (hereafter FF) Verordnungen und Gerichtssachen; Nuremberg Staatsarchiv (hereafter NB) Ratsbücher, Rep. 60b; Memmingen Stadtarchiv (hereafter MM) Bürgerbücher; Munich Stadtarchiv (hereafter MU) Ratsitzungsprotokolle.

9. Grethe Jacobsen, 'Women's work and women's role: ideology and reality in Danish urban society', *Scandinavian Economic History Review* 31 (1983): 5.

10. NB, Amts- und Standbücher, Rep. 52b, nos. 299–300, 305–306 – Neubürgerlisten; MM, Bürgerbücher; Augsburg Stadtarchiv (hereafter AB) Nr. 269 – Bürgerbücher; FF, Bürgermeisterbücher, 1495, fol. 26a; 1505, fol. 15b; Beata Brodmeier, *Die Frau im Handwerk* (Münster: Handwerkswissenschaftliches Institut, 1963), pp. 14–20; Erika Uitz, *The Legacy of Good Women: Medieval Women in Towns and Cities*, tr. Sheila Marnie (Mont Kisko, NY: Mayer, Bell, Ltd, 1990), pp. 55–62.

11. MU, Ratsitzungsprotokolle, 1544; Dilcher, 'Bürgerbegriff', p. 74.

12. See NB, Neubürgerlisten; AB, Bürgerbücher.

13. AB, Bürgerbücher.

and their husbands, for example, were offered free citizenship in the same way that doctors and their wives were.[14]

When some cities began in the fifteenth century to devise special oaths for permanent residents who did not have enough money or property to become full citizens (these individuals were termed 'Beisassen' or 'Seldener'), women were again explicitly included.[15] Until the late sixteenth or early seventeenth centuries, women were able to pass citizenship rights on to non-citizen men whom they married, in the same way that foreign women who married male citizens also became citizens. (This ability to pass citizenship on to their husbands has often been the only aspect of female citizenship seen as significant in German studies, with women's citizenship thus termed 'passive'. Female citizens – paying taxes, buying property, and appearing in court – would no doubt have been surprised by this designation, just as they would by the fact that the benefits a woman gained by marrying a citizen are never mentioned.)

Thus in terms of the bases of urban citizenship, and to a large degree of the responsibilities and rights it entailed, there was less distinction based on gender in most south German cities before 1500 than one might have assumed. This rather off-hand acceptance of women as citizens began to change in the sixteenth century, however. In Nuremberg, for example, women made up 13 per cent of the new citizens in the 1460s, a share which declined to 4.6 per cent by the 1500s and to less than 1 per cent by the 1550s.[16] Beginning in the mid-sixteenth or early seventeenth centuries, women granted citizenship as a reward or the widows and daughters of male citizens were prohibited from marrying foreigners unless they got the approval of the city council.[17] In 1631 in Lutheran Strasbourg, a distinction was made between male and female citizens who married Calvinists; a woman was to lose her citizenship 'because she would let herself easily be led into error in religion by her husband and be led astray', while a man would not, 'because he can probably draw his spouse away from her false religion and bring her on to the correct path'.[18] Female citizens, even widows and unmarried women, were increasingly required to have male

---

14. FF, Bürgermeisterbücher, 1471, fol. 141; NB, Ratsbücher, 3, fol. 198 (1482); NB, Neubürgerlisten.

15. Dilcher, 'Bürgerbegriff', p. 79; Schultheiss, 'Bürgerrecht', p. 170.

16. NB, Neubürgerlisten.

17. Strasbourg, Archives Municipales (hereafter AMS), Statuten, Vol. 18, no. 3, fol. 74 (1557), and reissued in 1594, 1627, 1687. MM, Ratsprotokollbücher, 21 June 1602, 13 March 1616; AB, Bürgerbücher, 1580 and elsewhere.

18. AMS, Akten der XXI (XXI), 1631, fol. 40.

guardians represent them in legal matters, and prohibited from standing surety on loans for their husbands or third parties.[19]

What might account for these developments? I would first like to mention three factors that have been suggested previously, and then propose a series of possible additional reasons. First, many towns went through a period of economic decline in the sixteenth century, when they increased the standard fees for citizenship to bring in more money and prevent poor people from immigrating, and granted citizenship free of charge less often.[20] Because women were generally poorer than men, this meant that fewer of them were able to afford citizenship. In several instances, however, the concern about poverty led to a lessening, rather than heightening, of gender distinctions: in 1599, the entrance fees for citizenship in Basel were raised from 10 gulden to 30, and men who married a foreigner were to pay an additional 10 gulden just as had already been required of women who married foreigners; in 1623 the Frankfurt city council ruled that male as well as female citizens would be prohibited from marrying foreigners 'without first bringing us proof of her legitimate birth and her property and means of support'.[21]

Second, Martha Howell has concluded, based on studies of cities in north Germany and the Low Countries, that when citizenship brought political rights rather than simply economic ones, women were excluded. She notes: 'female registration fell off exactly when citizenship was redefined so as to make it directly or indirectly equivalent to access to rule'.[22] This has explanatory value in the cities she studies, and may also work in the south German cities where guilds gained access to government, but it doesn't explain the decline in Nuremberg, where citizenship *never* brought access to rule.

19. AMS, Der erneuerte grosse Rathsbuch, Vol. 1, no. 89: 'Wie es mit dem ungeerbten aussgohn hinfuhrter gehen soll'; AB, Schätze, Vol. 16, fols. 164–6 (1578) and reissued in 1615 and 1668; Karlheinz Rudolf Maier, *Die Bürgschaft in suddeutschen und schweizerischen Gesetzbüchern, 16.–18. Jahrhundert* (Tübingen: Mohr, 1980), pp. 207–24.

20. Schultheiss, 'Bürgerrecht'; Dilcher, 'Bürgerbegriff'; Gschwind, *Bevölkerungsentwicklung*; Hans R. Guggisberg, *Basel in the Sixteenth Century: Aspects of the City Republic before, during and after the Reformation* (St Louis: Center for Reformation Research, 1982), p. 39; Lyndal Roper, *The Holy Household: Women and Morals in Reformation Augsburg* (Oxford, 1989), p. 55.

21. Gschwind, *Bevölkerungsentwicklung*, p. 160; FF, Verordnungen, Vol. II, no. 57 (31 July 1623).

22. Martha C. Howell, 'Citizenship and gender: women's political status in northern medieval cities', in Mary Erler and Maryanne Kowaleski, eds, *Women and Power in the Middle Ages* (Athens: University of Georgia Press, 1988), p. 47.

Third, studies of state citizenship in western Europe and of Italian city republics have concluded that once the individual became more important politically than the kin or corporate group, women were excluded.[23] A number of factors have been suggested as to why the political individual was defined as male: humanism's respect for Athenian standards; Machiavelli's and others' stress on autonomy and action; Locke's emphasis on the centrality of property; bourgeois reactions against the power of noblewomen.[24] This does help to explain developments in England, France, and Florence, but it has less relevance for early modern south German cities and villages, where familial and corporate values remained strong or, as studies of ideas about the family and community during the century of the Reformation have argued, became even more important than they had been earlier.[25] In these cities, the central political unit remained the household in both theory and practice, a household of which women were part and which they very often headed.[26]

Not only does the shift to the individual not apply to early modern German towns, but emphasizing this as a source of new gender distinctions masks the fact that familial and corporatist values

23. The literature on this is vast. See especially: Joan Kelly-Gadol, 'Did women have a Renaissance?', in Renate Bridenthal, Claudia Koonz and Susan Stuard, *Becoming Visible: Women in European History*, 2nd edn (Boston: Houghton Mifflin, 1987), pp. 175–201; Mary Lyndon Shanley, 'Marriage contract and social contract in seventeenth-century English political thought', *Western Political Quarterly* 32 (1979): 74–96; Christine Fauré, *La democratie sans les femmes* (Paris, 1985); Margaret George, *Women in the First Capitalist Society: Experiences in Seventeenth Century England* (Urbana: University of Illinois Press, 1988), pp. 37–112; Joan Landes, *Women and the Public Sphere in the Age of the French Revolution* (Ithaca, NY: Cornell University Press, 1988); Sarah Hanley, 'Engendering the state: family formation and state building in early modern France', *French Historical Studies* 16 (1989): 4–27.

24. Ian Maclean, *The Renaissance Notion of Women* (Cambridge: Cambridge University Press, 1980), pp. 47–67; Shanley, 'Marriage'; Hanna Fenichel Pitkin, *Fortune is a Woman: Gender and Politics in the Thought of Niccolo Machiavelli* (Berkeley: University of California Press, 1985); Hilda Smith, *Reason's Disciples: Seventeenth Century English Feminists* (Urbana: University of Illinois Press, 1982), pp. 58–9; Diane Owen Hughes, 'Invisible Madonnas? The Italian historiographical tradition and the women of medieval Italy', in Susan Stuard, ed., *Women in Medieval History and Historiography* (Philadelphia: University of Pennsylvania Press, 1987), pp. 25–34.

25. Dilcher, 'Bürgerbegriff', p. 82; Heinrich Schmidt, *Die deutschen Städtechroniken als Spiegel des bürgerlichen Selbstverstandnisses im Spätmittelalter* (Göttingen: Vandenhoeck und Ruprecht, 1958); Steven Ozment, *When Fathers Ruled: Family Life in Reformation Europe* (Cambridge, MA: Harvard University Press, 1983).

26. Heide Wunder, '"L'espace privé" and the domestication of women in the sixteenth and seventeenth centuries', unpublished paper. For statistics on female heads of household see Merry E. Wiesner, *Working Women in Renaissance Germany* (New Brunswick, NJ: Rutgers University Press, 1986), pp. 4–5.

were also changing during this period to exclude women. I have elsewhere traced the change in craft and journeymen's guilds, for even those guilds which did not gain political power also became more emphatically male groups.[27] Notions of gender among German urban elites have not been analysed as they have for Italian ones, but the closing of the patriciate in cities like Nuremberg, which happened in 1521 and meant that a man could no longer gain a seat on the city council by marrying into a *ratsfähige* family, certainly made membership in the governing patriciate more male-defined.[28] Once women could not stand surety for their male relatives, kin business networks also became more exclusively male.[29]

To get a full explanation for the decline in the significance of female citizenship, then, we must explore why in the sixteenth century corporatist and family values in south Germany became more masculine, and then see what effects this had on female citizenship. Here I am going to be highly speculative, as this is an issue I have only begun to work on, and one which touches, as you will see, on a wide range of concerns and sources. I wish to mention in this regard five factors.

First, not only did humanism and the classical tradition view the political individual as necessarily male, but both Greek philosophy and Roman law put greater emphasis on the mental weakness of women, rather than their inability to bear arms, as the reason for their exclusion from politics and secondary legal status.[30] Thus city leaders educated as humanists and jurists trained in Roman law were able to justify making distinctions between male and female citizens by using a new standard rather than by reinterpreting war, work, and wealth in gender-specific ways.

Second, though urban values remained corporatist and family-centred, they were middle-class rather than noble, so that families in which women held independent power were regarded as disruptive and disorderly.[31] Adult women were to have authority over

27. See my essays, 'Guilds, male bonding and women's work in early modern Germany', and '*Wandervögel* and women: journeymen's concepts of masculinity in early modern Germany', elsewhere in this volume.

28. Schultheiss, 'Bürgerrecht', discusses some of the implications of closing the council, but does not consider gender distinctions.

29. Maier, *Bürgschaft*, pp. 211–24, who also notes that the prohibition of women standing surety for their husbands in Switzerland was not lifted until 1975.

30. Rudolph Heubner, *A History of Germanic Private Law*, tr. Francis S. Philbrick (Boston: Little, Brown, 1918), p. 67. For a longer discussion of this, see 'Frail, weak and helpless: women's legal position in theory and reality', elsewhere in this volume.

31. This has been argued most fully for Italy in Hughes, 'Invisible Madonnas?', and for France in Landes, *Women and the Public Sphere*.

dependent members of their households, but this authority was derivative, coming from their status as wife or widow of the male household head. The derivative nature of women's acceptable authority is made clear by referring to a woman as 'wife' rather than 'mother' even in legal documents describing her relations with her children.[32] The suspicion of women with independent power was not based solely on theories of sexual difference, but also on urban and village communities' actual experiences with noblewomen who held power. By the sixteenth century, this was generally during wartime, when the noblewomen led military forces acting against city or village interests, such as Bianca Maria Sforza and Elisabeth, the daughter of Duke George of Bavaria-Landshut and widow of Count Palatine Ruprecht, who both directed action against the Swabian League.[33]

Third, south German patricians modelled themselves on Italian ones, and may have picked up the increasingly patrilineal view of the family so common among the Italian urban elite as easily as they did business procedures and styles of domestic architecture. The family histories left by Germans have not been studied as systematically for concepts of gender as the *ricordanze* left by Italian patricians, but I would not be surprised if they revealed a similar, though perhaps not as pronounced, tendency toward patrilineality.[34]

Fourth (and again this is more a direction for further research than a summary of existing evidence), as the urban and village community was sacralized in the sixteenth century, a development traced in many studies of the communal Reformation, greater distinctions were made between male and female citizens because the

32. Roper, *Holy Household*, p. 59.

33. These incidents are described in Thomas Brady, *Turning Swiss: Cities and Empire, 1450–1550* (Cambridge: Cambridge University Press, 1985), pp. 63–4, 79. The fact that using arms to gain freedom from noble domination was seen as the 'Swiss way' has particular irony when those nobles are female, for even in the early modern period, Swiss cantons were more restrictive of women's legal and economic rights than their south German neighbours (Maier, *Bürgschaft*, pp. 211–24). Given the history of women's political rights in Switzerland since the early modern period, it is probably fortunate that the south German towns Brady investigates were foiled in their attempt to 'turn Swiss'.

34. Patrilineality in Italian elites has been traced by Christiane Klapisch-Zuber, 'The "cruel mother": maternity, widowhood and dowry in Florence in the fourteenth and fifteenth centuries', in her *Women, Family and Ritual in Renaissance Italy*, tr. Lydia Cochrane (Chicago: University of Chicago Press, 1985), pp. 117–31; Diane Owen Hughes, 'Representing the family: portraits and purposes in early modern Italy', *Journal of Interdisciplinary History* 17 (1986): 7–38; Sharon T. Strocchia, 'Remembering the family: women, kin, and commemorative masses in Renaissance Florence', *Renaissance Quarterly* 42 (1989): 635–54.

former regularly swore oaths to uphold the city's religion while the latter did not.[35] Thus not only did the difference between male and female citizens acquire religious connotations, but there was also a new distinction between male and female Christians: for the former, faith was also a ritualized civic matter, while for the latter it was not. This led to uncertainty about how to handle the citizenship status of certain women. In Protestant cities, one of the key political effects of the Reformation was the integration of the male clergy into the citizenry, ending the distinction between clerical and lay status. In most cases these priests also married, but this was not a requirement for obtaining citizenship. For nuns, however, it was. The only way they could become citizens was to marry, which meant, of course, they were no longer nuns. A priest could be both a citizen *and* a priest, but a nun could not be a citizen and a nun. In some cities there was debate about whether even this was enough to make a woman a citizen. In Nördlingen, for example, though priests were required to become citizens, there was great debate about whether the women who married them should be considered as such, for they were tainted with the 'dishonourable' status of priests' concubines.[36] Protestant nuns were another problem, now that convents were no longer islands of foreign sovereignty.[37]

Fifth, and somewhat in contradiction to the previous factors, urban and village corporatist values had always been somewhat male-defined, so that sixteenth-century developments were not a complete break with tradition. Though women swore oaths of loyalty on first becoming citizens and were otherwise obligated to perform most of the duties of citizenship, they did not participate in the annual oath-swearing affirming their loyalty which took place in most German towns and villages until well into the early modern period. That annual oath-swearing was not limited to male citizens, however, but was also expected of adolescent boys before they became citizens and male non-citizen permanent residents

35. See Moeller, *Imperial Cities*; Ebel, 'Bürgereid', p. 39; Richard Stauffer, 'Das Basler Bekenntnis von 1534', in Hans R. Guggisberg and Peter Rotach, eds, *Ecclesia semper reformanda: Vorträge zum Basler Reformationsjubilaum* (Basel: Friedrich Reinhardt Verlag, 1980), pp. 28–49.

36. Hans-Christoph Rublack, *Eine bürgerliche Reformation: Nördlingen* (Gütersloh: Gütersloher Verlagshaus Mohn, 1982), pp. 174–5.

37. The convents which survived the Reformation by becoming Protestant were generally located in rural areas, and the abbess was the political overlord, so citizenship was not an issue. See my essay 'Ideology meets the Empire: reformed convents and the Reformation' elsewhere in this volume for a fuller discussion of this. For the debate about what to do with the convents in Augsburg, see Roper, *Holy Household*, pp. 206–51.

(the *Beisassen*).[38] More clearly than citizenship, this oath-swearing (*Schwörtag*) determined membership in the political community.[39] This distinction was certainly understood by medieval urban and village residents, which is why they saw nothing incongruous about female citizenship. Modern historians, on the other hand, have generally equated citizenship and participation in the political community, which is why female citizenship has posed such a problem for them that they have ignored it, relegated it to a footnote, or tried to make it somehow distinctive from male citizenship with terms not found in early modern sources such as 'passive citizenship'.[40]

Lyndal Roper and Kristin Zapalac have already explored some of the implications of defining the urban community in male-specific terms, and I would like to add a few more.[41] Though women were never categorically excluded from citizenship in German towns and villages, notions of women's proper place within the family and community increasingly made the only type of female citizenship that was acceptable a derivative one. Fewer women were accepted for citizenship independently or allowed to pass it on to non-citizen husbands.

At first it was new intellectual and religious criteria which were used to make distinctions between female and male citizens, but gradually the traditional bases of urban citizenship – war, work, and wealth – also came to be interpreted in gender-specific ways. German Neo-Aristotelians in the seventeenth century added women's inability to bear arms and their economic dependence on their husbands to their mental and moral weakness as reasons for excluding them from all aspects of public life; in the eighteenth century, women in Prussia were ruled ineligible for one of the benefits of

38. Dilcher, 'Bürgerbegriff'; Schultheiss, 'Bürgerrecht' (though he reports that by the seventeenth century the oath-swearing was held only every seven years in Nuremberg); Lyndal Roper, ' "The common man", "the common good", "common women": gender and meaning in the German Reformation commune', *Social History* 12 (1987): 10–12. The participation of citizens' adolescent sons is similar to the custom in English towns of boys being sworn into a tithing.

39. Though they approach it from vastly different perspectives, this is the conclusion of both Ebel, 'Bürgereid', and Roper, 'Common man'.

40. Schmidt, *Städtechroniken*, and Schultheiss, 'Bürgerrecht', ignore female citizenship, Ebel, 'Bürgereid', relegates it to a footnote, and Christopher Friedrichs, *Urban Society in an Age of War: Nördlingen, 1580–1720* (Princeton: Princeton University Press, 1979), uses the term 'passive' (p. 39).

41. Roper, 'Common man'; Kristin Zapalac, *'In His Image and Likeness': Political Iconography and Religious Change in Regensburg, 1500–1600* (Ithaca, NY: Cornell University Press, 1990), pp. 135–66; idem, 'Engendering (republican) virtue' (unpublished paper).

citizenship, a pension, because their labour was not judged to be 'work', even though it was exactly the same as that of men; women who had, by virtue of property ownership, participated in citizen's assemblies in Glarus were excluded in the mid-seventeenth century (and would not be readmitted until 1972).[42] Thus by the time state citizenship became an issue in Germany, war, work, and wealth appeared to be natural and long-standing reasons for excluding women, as the writings of the nineteenth-century jurist Carl Welcker make clear.[43]

42. MacLean, *Renaissance Notion*, pp. 52–5; Jean Quataert, 'The shaping of women's work in manufacturing: guilds, households and the state in central Europe, 1648–1870', *American Historical Review* 90 (1985): 1124; Louis Carlen, *Die landsgemeinde in der Schweiz: Schule der Demokratie* (Sigmaringen: Jan Thorbecke, 1976).

43. Heide Wunder, 'Von der Frumkeit zur Frömmigkeit: Ein Beitrag zur Genese bürgerlicher Weiblichkeit (15.–17. Jahrhundert)', in Ursula A.J. Becher and Jorn Rusen, eds, *Weiblichkeit in geschichtlicher Perspektive* (Frankfurt: Suhrkamp, 1988), p. 175. By the late eighteenth century, women as well viewed bearing arms as essential to citizenship. Olwen Hufton points out that club women during the early stages of the French Revolution demanded the right to bear arms, and that debates about wearing the cockade revolved around whether only those citizens who bore arms (i.e. men) should be required to wear it, or whether women should as well (Olwen H. Hufton, *Women and the Limits of Citizenship in the French Revolution* (Toronto: University of Toronto Press, 1992), pp. 23–4, 36–7). This point is also made in Claudia Opitz, 'Der Bürger wird Soldat – Und die Bürgerin? Die Revolution, der Krieg und die Stellung der Frauen nach 1789', in Viktoria Schmidt-Linsenhoff, ed., *Sklavin oder Bürgerin: Französische Revolution und neue Weiblichkeit 1760–1830* (Frankfurt: Joan Verlag, 1989), pp. 38–54.

PART THREE

Work

Introductory essay

When I wrote my first book on women's work, *Working Women in Renaissance Germany*, the word I worried most about in the title was 'Renaissance', as it carried with it much cultural baggage and was not often used to talk about economic developments in Germany; I stuck with it because I wanted a shorthand for the period I was investigating, 1450–1650. In the last ten years, however, feminist and economic analysis (and in particular feminist economic analysis) has also led to a rethinking of two other words in my title, 'women' and 'work'. Historians began to analyse the social construction of gender, and to investigate the interplay between gender hierarchies and other social hierarchies, such as those of race and class. They emphasized that any use of the word 'women' really only meant *some* women in any society, so that generalizations or chronological comparisons were never completely accurate; some theorists even suggested dropping the word 'women' altogether, as it was either essentialist in its definition (i.e. based on 'biology', which was itself a cultural construct) or exclusionary.

Along with doubts about 'women', there are also doubts about 'work'. Feminist economic historians, both Marxist and non-Marxist, argue that work and other economic activities cannot be detached from the family and other political and social institutions. This revisionist scholarship reminds us that, to be accurate and inclusive, an analysis of economic life in any period must include reproductive as well as productive activities; reproduction is defined not simply as childbearing, but as the care and nurturing of all family members, which allowed them to take part in productive labour. This is especially true for late medieval and early modern societies in which production often went on in the household, for all family members took part in both productive and reproductive labour. More recent studies of this period have thus paid greater attention to the ways in which family life and economic activities were intertwined, viewing such things as childbearing and service at a royal court as work.

Though contemporary historians are thus more willing to view a wide range of activities as 'work', they are also attentive to changes in the meaning of work and to people's work identity. We may choose to see childbearing and childrearing as 'work', but did early modern women view these as work? (Given the concerns about differences among women noted above, our next question would have to be: Which women? Women who put their children out to wet-nurses *and* women whose husbands hired them out as wet-nurses?) Did this change over time, and why? The recent research on the meaning of work has pointed out tremendous differences in the way tasks were defined and valued depending on whether they were done by women or men. This has led some historians away from simply investigating the impact of economic change on the lives of women and men – the focus of most research, including my own, ten years ago – to exploring also how gender hierarchies (or sometimes more pointedly stated, how patriarchy) shaped the development of capitalism.

Much of this questioning of definitions sounds very arcane and academic (don't we all sort of understand what 'women' and 'work' mean, and can't we just proceed from there?), but it has led research on the topic, especially in Germany, away from a con- centration on women whose structures of work were as close to those of men as possible – women in independent guilds or who were members of largely male guilds – to those who were tradition- ally viewed as 'marginal' – prostitutes, domestic servants, wet-nurses. There are very few published sources about any of these women, which has meant hundreds of hours in city, church, and state archives, but has also resulted in a much broader understanding of both the ideological meaning and the actual circumstances of women's work lives. By now I would think – though I could always be wrong – that no archivist would answer a researcher looking for information on women's work, as one did me fifteen years ago, 'Oh, we have no material on that. Women didn't work in this city in the sixteenth century.'

CHAPTER EIGHT

Spinning out capital: women's work in the early modern economy[1]

All societies draw distinctions between men's work and women's work. Cultural norms and prevailing values, as well as popular beliefs, all play a part in drawing those distinctions. Anthropologists have long recognized this, but historians have only recently turned to the study of the way the boundaries between women's work and men's change over time. The definition of women's work, what women did or did not do at a particular time, was affected not only by economic trends and technological development, but by changes in values, ideologies and political structures. These economic and cultural factors have at times shifted or blurred the lines between men's and women's work; they have also determined what sorts of activities will be defined as 'work' and how that work will be valued. This essay explores women's work from about 1500 to 1700, a time when the European economy and prevailing ideologies were both changing rapidly.

Work in the Middle Ages

In the medieval economy, the household had been the basic unit of production. Peasant families in rural areas raised crops and animals for their own and their landlords' use, and traded their surpluses in a nearby village or city for the items they could not produce themselves. They also made simple items such as brooms and wooden implements and agricultural products like butter and

1. Many of the direct quotations in this article are from unprinted sources located in archives in Germany and France. Specific references to these may be found in my book *Working Women in Renaissance Germany*, on the pages given in the footnotes. I would like to thank the American Council of Learned Societies and the Deutsche Akademischeaustauschdienst for their support in the research for this article.

cheese for sale at local markets. Urban households often included several servants, journeymen, and apprentices who worked and lived with a husband and wife and their children. All stages of production, from the purchase of raw materials and tools to the sale of the finished product, were carried out by members of the household. The goods produced were traded within the household's particular city or region. Tasks were not sharply divided by gender or status among members of the household, and both domestic and manufacturing tasks contributed to the success of the family enterprise. Even members of the household who were not family members, the servants, apprentices, and journeymen, stood to benefit from successful production and sales, for this generally brought more and better food and clothing, which formed the major part (if not all) of their wages.

During the thirteenth and fourteenth centuries, craft guilds were established in many cities to organize and regulate production, setting quality levels, terms of apprenticeship, and prices for goods which required a high degree of skill and training to produce. The guilds set standards for the finished product and limited competition between household workshops, but did not regulate what went on within a household.

There were some individuals in both the countryside and cities who worked for wages in the medieval economy, but they were often hired by a household and so were still part of an essentially family-based economy. Employed as servants, agricultural labourers, and pieceworkers, they were generally the poorest people in any community, and if they maintained an independent household, all family members had to work to assure survival.

The growth of capitalism

During the later Middle Ages, a new form of economic organization appeared in western Europe – capitalism. There is great debate among economic historians as to exactly when, where, and why capitalism started, but there is general agreement that it began among merchants, who traded luxury goods like spices and silk in an international market and often made enormous profits. Their businesses often began as family firms, but the opportunity for profit attracted non-family investors, and the firms gradually grew larger and more complex. As they grew, more and more of the actual labour was carried out by individuals who were paid wages rather than being rewarded with a share of the profits. This division between capital and labour is a hallmark of capitalism, and this initial stage is generally termed 'mercantile capitalism' because it involved merchants and their enterprises in commerce, banking, and trade.

Prosperous merchants throughout Europe gradually sought to expand their investments beyond commerce, and began to purchase raw materials, tools, and machinery, hiring workers to produce goods. They then sold these manufactured goods along with their other articles of trade in an international market, using the trading networks, systems of agents, and offices they had already developed. Merchants invested in manufacturing in some parts of Europe as early as the thirteenth century, particularly in cloth production in Florence and Flanders. They hired entire households to carry out one stage of production, such as spinning or weaving, sending out raw materials and often lending out the necessary tools; this is called the putting-out system or domestic industry. This putting-out system often employed rural households, and directly challenged traditional urban methods of production. The household thus remained the production unit, but it was paid wages solely for the labour of its members and had no share in the profits from production.

Some investors began to concentrate their capital in production, moving out of commerce. This is often viewed as a second stage of capitalism. It is generally termed 'protoindustrialization' because workers remained in their own homes or in very small workshops; only much later, in the eighteenth and nineteenth centuries, would industrial capitalism bring workers together into large factories.

Along with the putting-out system, the growth of capitalism brought additional changes to the rural economy. As cities grew, people in the rural areas surrounding them often turned to market gardening, producing fruits, vegetables, and other crops for urban consumers. Because of this development, such a region no longer produced grain, relying instead on imported grain from eastern Europe, where the landed nobility were enserfing the peasants to secure a steady supply of labour for their vast estates. The growth of agricultural capitalism thus had the opposite effect in western and eastern Europe; it brought the decline of serfdom in the west and the simultaneous rise of serfdom in the east. Because of these differences in the rural economies, rural women's work varied throughout Europe, and included both agricultural and protoindustrial production.

The early modern period was thus transitional in economic terms, with traditional domestic production existing side by side with both mercantile and protoindustrial capitalism. The household was still the basic unit of production, but increasing numbers of households depended on wages to survive, wages which were determined by international market conditions along with local demand for a product. There were great regional differences in the level of economic development, however, and some isolated areas remained largely bound to traditional patterns of production and trade.

The rise of capitalism brought ideological as well as economic change. During the Middle Ages, work was defined as an activity performed to support and sustain oneself and one's family. Domestic and productive tasks were both considered work, and all women, except perhaps those from very wealthy noble families, could be called working women. With the development of capitalism, work was increasingly defined as an activity for which one was paid, which meant that domestic tasks and childrearing were not considered work unless they were done for wages. Women's unpaid domestic labour freed men for full-time wage labour but was no longer regarded as work. As a result, the proportion of women who considered themselves working women and were considered as such by authorities shrank during the period as the definition of work changed, though women's actual activities changed very little.

There were other major ideological and political changes during the sixteenth and seventeenth centuries as well. This was the period of the Protestant and Catholic Reformations, which brought with them not only new ideas about theology and religion, but also different attitudes toward marriage and the family, public and private morality, and the value of certain occupations. It was the time of the rise of the nation state, when the rulers of western Europe began to depend on a professional army and bureaucracy instead of on feudal and kin ties and allegiances. Governments at all levels expanded the scope of their activities. City, state, and national governments took over many of the institutions and services that the church or private charity had maintained and provided in the Middle Ages, such as orphanages, hospitals, infirmaries, and poor relief. As governments secularized these services, they often created a centralized system so that they could more easily control who was receiving care and charity. The administration of these services and other government functions became increasingly professionalized, as did certain private occupations such as physicians, apothecaries, lawyers, and appraisers.

Economic change affected the lives of women very differently than the lives of men of their same social and economic class. It did not affect all women equally, however. Women's experiences varied according to social class, economic status, and geographic region, factors which have traditionally been taken into account when examining men's history. They also varied according to age, marital status, family size, and life span, factors which have rarely been noticed until very recently in standard histories.

Economic change affected the kinds of work women performed, but there was also continuity. The majority of women and men in early modern Europe continued to work in agriculture; at least three-quarters of the population remained in the countryside. Even in the cities, most of the economy was still 'precapitalist' and continued to operate in the same way that it had for centuries. Some occupations, such as domestic service and selling at the public market, changed very little during the period.

It is especially important to emphasize continuity when looking at women's work, for even dramatic changes in the structure and organization of institutions and industries may not have been evident to the women working in them, who were often clustered in the lowest-skilled jobs. Whether an industry was organized capitalistically or by guilds, or whether a hospital was run by the church or the city, made little difference to the woman who spun wool or washed bedding. Women remained in these low-status positions because they often fitted their work around the life-cycle of their families, moving in and out of various jobs as children were born and grew up, or as their husbands died and they remarried.

To analyse both change and continuity, I have chosen in this study to focus on women in the cities, principally because urban sources are clearer and begin earlier than rural ones. In many parts of Europe city governments began to keep records centuries before villages or states did.[2] A focus on the urban economy takes in the activities of many rural women, who were often the ones to sell agricultural products in the cities. Though urban residents travelled out into the countryside for the harvest, in general the cities offered a wider variety of occupations for both men and women.

2. This is not true in England, and recent studies of English peasants have used rural sources to explore women's labour in the countryside as early as the medieval period. See Barbara Hanawalt, *The Ties that Bound: Peasant Families in Medieval England* (New York: Oxford University Press, 1986), pp. 141–55; Judith Bennett, 'The village ale wife: women and brewing in fourteenth century England', in *Women and Work in Preindustrial Europe*, ed. Barbara Hanawalt (Bloomington: Indiana University Press, 1986), pp. 20–36.

Demographic patterns and the legal status of women

Another reason for a focus on cities in terms of women's history is that it appears women outnumbered men in the cities. This has been noted for late medieval and early modern cities by a number of authors, who have discovered that there were between 110 and 120 women for every 100 men in many cities.[3] Various explanations have been offered for this – men dying in the frequent wars and skirmishes, the large number of men in monasteries (who would not show up on city records), women living longer in cities as they did not have to perform physically taxing agricultural work, women moving into cities in search of opportunities for both employment and charity. These last two factors suggest that men would outnumber women in the rural areas, but this is difficult to document as there are almost no rural population counts which might indicate a preponderance of males in the countryside. Whatever the reasons, this skewed population balance continued into the early modern period, so there were a large number of urban women who could not make marriage their 'career', even if they had wished to.

Because of this preponderance of women in the cities, there were a large number of women who lived alone or in households headed by women. Many of these were widows, but a significant share were young women who had not yet married. On average, both men and women in western Europe during this period married in their mid-twenties – at least in the urban areas for which we have records.[4] In many cultures men wait until this age to marry, and then generally marry women who are much younger, often in their early teens. Late marriage for women is quite unusual, and there are several possible reasons for this peculiar marriage pattern. Married couples generally set up their own households, rather than moving in with the parents of one spouse, which meant that the husband had to be financially secure and the wife able to run

3. Friedrich Bothe, *Beiträge zur Wirtschafts- und Sozialgeschichte in der Reichsstadt Frankfurt* (Leipzig: Duncker and Humbolt, 1906); Karl Bücher, *Die Frauenfrage im Mittelalter* (Tübingen: H. Laupp, 1910); Gerd Wunder, *Die Stuttgarter Steuerliste von 1545* (Stuttgart: Klett, 1974).

4. Peter Laslett, *The World We Have Lost* (New York: Scribners, 1965), pp. 81–91; J. Hajnal, 'European marriage patterns in perspective', in D. Glass and D.E.C. Eversley, eds, *Population in History* (London: Edward Arnold, 1965); E.A. Wrigley and R.S. Schofield, *The Population History of England, 1541–1871* (Cambridge, MA: Harvard University Press, 1981).

a household, rather than relying on her mother or mother-in-law. Many guilds forbade apprentices and journeymen to marry, because they were supposed to live with the master-craftsman; on the other hand, the guilds required masters to be married, because two people were necessary to run a shop properly. Because the master's wife fed and clothed this large household, craftsmen often preferred to marry an adult woman rather than an inexperienced teenager. The preponderance of women in the cities meant that middle- and upper-class women were expected to provide dowries to their husbands, and delaying marriage gave a family and the woman herself an opportunity to save that dowry. Even a poor woman was expected to bring something as dower to her marriage – linens, dishes, and bedding, for example – which she could afford to purchase only after many years as a maid or pieceworker. In an era before effective contraception, delaying the marriage of women was one way to keep family size smaller. For poorer families, fewer children meant fewer mouths to feed, and for wealthier families, fewer dowries for daughters or training and education for sons.

Whatever the reasons for this unusual western European marriage pattern, it resulted in a large number of unmarried women living in cities. Households comprised of widows and unmarried women often made up between one-quarter and one-third of all households in many cities; such were generally the poorest households, often too poor to pay any taxes.[5] Their 'household' was not an entire house, but rather a rented room, cellar, or attic that no one else wanted.

During the medieval period, city and religious authorities had seen the large number of poor women living independently as an economic problem, because they recognized that these women would have to support themselves or would require assistance. Grudgingly, authorities allowed such women to make or sell various simple items, and left some low-skilled occupations such as laundering open to

5. Erich Maschke, *Gesellschaftliche Unterschichten in den südwestdeutschen Städten* (Stuttgart: Kohlhammer, 1967), p. 27; Christiane Klapisch, 'Household and family in Tuscany, 1427', in Peter Laslett, ed., *Household and Family in Past Time* (Cambridge: Cambridge University Press, 1972), p. 273; Barbara Diefendorf, 'Widowhood and remarriage in sixteenth-century Paris', *Journal of Family History* 9.2 (Winter 1982): 380; Grethe Jacobsen, 'Women's work and women's role: ideology and reality in Danish urban society, 1300–1550', *Scandinavian Economic History Review* 31, no. 1 (1983): 15; Diane Willen, 'Guildswomen in the City of York, 1560–1700', *The Historian* 46.2 (February 1984): 206; Mary Prior, 'Women and the urban economy: Oxford 1500–1800', in her *Women in English Society* (London and New York: Methuen, 1985), p. 105.

them. As tax records indicate, women living independently rarely earned more than enough to survive. Widows were generally better off than non-widows, because inheritance laws allowed a widow to keep at least her dowry and any property she had brought into the marriage, as well as a proportion of the property or assets acquired since the marriage. Despite this, the household income of a widow was generally much less than it had been when her husband was alive.

In the sixteenth century, civic and religious authorities began to regard women living independently in terms of morality as well as economics. Both Protestant and Catholic authorities became increasingly concerned with public order, propriety, decorum, and morality. In what is termed 'The Triumph of Lent', the authorities of cities throughout Europe expanded sumptuary laws, which attempted to regulate morality by limiting expenditure on dress, restricting public dances and carnivals, and prohibiting gambling and prostitution. In this new mood, governments toughened laws against vagrants, because of what was perceived as an increase in 'masterless' persons – wandering journeymen, servants between positions, mercenary soldiers and their campfollowers, 'sturdy beggars', itinerant actors and musicians. Whether economic changes were actually causing an increase in people moving from town to town or from household to household is difficult to say, but the perception of an increase on the part of civic and church authorities was very strong.

Migrants were suspect not only because they might engage in criminal activity or become a drain on community charitable endowments, but also simply because they were not part of a household. In a world that appeared to them to be becoming increasingly disorderly, authorities viewed the household as an institution of social control. Moreover, they felt that men as the heads of households were more effective than women at exerting that control. As these attitudes developed, authorities began to consider women who lived alone as 'masterless', lumping them in with other suspect groups. In Germany and France, laws were passed that forbade unmarried women to move into cities, required widows to move in with one of their male children, and obliged unmarried women to move in with a male relative or employer.[6] In Protestant areas, as convents were closed the nuns were encouraged to marry or move back to their families, and in Catholic areas, unmarried women not living under strict cloister were increasingly suspect.

6. Merry E. Wiesner, *Working Women in Renaissance Germany* (New Brunswick, NJ: Rutgers University Press, 1986), p. 6.

This hostility to unmarried women was further exacerbated by the Protestant emphasis on marriage as a woman's only 'natural' vocation, the Catholic church's increased concern (in response to Luther and other critics) with immorality among clergy and laity, and the increased currency of certain popular and scholarly notions about women's nature and proper role. The 'debate about women' that had begun in the late Middle Ages among churchmen and scholars, in which women's nature and character, virtues and vices were discussed and debated, had begun to make educated men increasingly view women as a distinct group.[7] Sweeping generalities about women's nature were made not only by moralists and preachers, but also by humanists and writers of popular satire. Many of these expressed or reinforced the notion that women suffered from uncontrollable sexuality and lacked the ability to reason. Women's sexual drive was thought to increase with age, so that older unmarried women were viewed as potential seductresses, willing to do anything to satisfy their sexual urges. This explained, in the eyes of authorities, their readiness to become witches, for the devil promised sexual satisfaction. It was also one of the reasons all unmarried women were viewed with such suspicion and hostility.

Despite all their attempts, the authorities never reduced the number of female-headed households; but the idea that women should be married or somehow under the control of a man had a profound and negative effect on women's work. Although it was recognized that some women would have to work for wages, authorities always viewed that work as a stopgap or temporary measure, until the women could attain, or return to, their 'natural', married, state. Thus the authorities were reluctant to establish policies that allowed women to practise any highly skilled occupation, and were suspicious when a woman made more than subsistence wages. A woman could work if she needed to support herself and her family, but she had no absolute right to work.

Although widows and unmarried women suffered from widespread suspicion, they did have distinct legal advantages over their married sisters. Women differed from men in their legal capacity to be witnesses, make wills, act as guardians for their own children, make contracts, and own, buy, and sell property. In addition, the legal status of an adult woman depended on whether she was

7. Joan Kelly, 'Early feminist theory and the Querelle des Femmes 1400–1789', *Signs* 8, no. 1 (1982): 4–28.

unmarried, married, or widowed, whereas adult males were generally treated as a single legal category. The kind of work each woman could do was thus determined to some degree by her marital status, although this varied from area to area depending on which city, state, or national law code applied.

Generally, in the early sixteenth century, an unmarried woman or widow had the right to dispose of her own property as she saw fit, using the assistance of a legal guardian only if she chose. When a woman married, she theoretically lost the right to make any contract without the agreement of her husband; she became, in French and English legal parlance, a *femme couverte*. However, married women who wanted to conduct business on a regular basis could appeal to the appropriate governing body for a lifting of this restriction. This was granted fairly easily, and the woman was allowed to act independently of her husband; such a woman was termed a *femme sole* in England and France, and a *Marktfrau* in Germany. City and state laws did not note that a husband's approval was necessary for a woman to become a *femme sole*, and often spelled out in great detail just which occupations were appropriate for women; a Nuremberg ordinance mentions 'female tailors, shop-keepers, money-changers, inn-keepers, wine-handlers, and market women'.[8] In addition to those women who received formal legal approval, urban records indicate that many other married women were carrying out business independently, although the law still allowed anyone to deny a loan or refuse to make a contract with a married woman.

Throughout the sixteenth and seventeenth centuries, because of the increasing emphasis on the household as an instrument of social control, and the rise in the belief that the proper household was headed by a man, the power of (male) guardians over widows and unmarried women in many areas increased. City councils often appointed these guardians, who then appeared in court on the woman's behalf, although, previously, women had often represented themselves in inheritance disputes and other cases. In a number of cities, the guardians decided whether a woman should retain control of her children if she remarried. Adult women were not yet the legal minors they would become by the Victorian period, but the laws grew decidedly more restrictive. Women's actual legal and

8. Joseph Baader, ed., *Nürnberger Polizeiordnungen aus dem 13. bis 15. Jahrhundert.* Bibliothek des Literarische Verein Stuttgart, Vol. 63 (Stuttgart: Literarische Verein, 1861), pp. 29–30.

economic activities, however, did not decrease proportionately – another example of the discrepancy between law codes and reality.

With this demographic and legal backdrop in mind, we can now examine women's work itself. In order to analyse the change or lack of change in various occupations, it will be useful to organize them by their function in the economy. Economists generally divide occupations into three basic types – production, sales, and service. This division derives from the organization of male labour in the modern economy, and is somewhat misleading for the early modern period, when, for example, individuals engaged in production often sold their own products. It is also somewhat artificial as a way of looking at women's work in any period, because women often participated in more than one type of occupation simultaneously and combined their productive and reproductive work. As long as we keep these limitations in mind, however, these occupational categories can still be useful, for the pattern of women's work in each of them differed significantly. In addition, the cultural values and economic reality that determined women's work operated somewhat differently in these three sectors.

Production

In the early sixteenth century, craft guilds controlled most production in many parts of Europe. In some cities, each craft had a separate guild, and as many as 150 or 200 different guilds might exist in a single city; in others, many crafts joined together in a few large guilds. In some cities, craft guilds had won representation on the city council by revolution or peaceful negotiation; in others, the city councils, made up of wealthy merchants and bankers, had blocked all such attempts. Whatever the guild structure or level of political participation, however, all guilds treated women in a remarkably similar fashion.

Craft guilds were, with the exception of a few female guilds in Cologne, Paris, and Basel, male organizations, organized according to the male life cycle. A boy studied for a set number of years as an apprentice, became a journeyman and usually worked under a number of different masters to perfect his skills, then finally made a 'masterpiece'. If it was judged acceptable by the current masters (and if they felt there was enough business to allow another shop to open) the young man settled down and opened a shop. Because guild members recognized that a master could not run a shop on his own – there were journeymen and apprentices to feed and clothe, raw materials and tools to buy, and merchandise to sell in the shop or at the public market – many guilds required that masters be married. Enterprising journeymen also recognized that the easiest way to acquire a shop complete with tools and customers was to marry a master's widow.

Though men dominated the guild structure, a large number of women could be found working in most guild shops. Besides the master's wife, his daughters and maids often worked alongside his journeymen and apprentices. Most workshops were small and attached to the master craftsman's house, so that women could easily divide their time between domestic duties and work in the shop. Early modern households were not self-sufficient; it was often more economical to purchase bread or finished clothing so that the women of the household could spend their time in production. The clothing and furnishings in all but the wealthiest houses in this period were few, simple, and rarely cleaned, so that there was relatively little of what we consider housework. This changed during the early modern period, as the sheer amount of consumer goods increased and the use of table linens, bed linens, and more elaborate clothing spread to the households of master craftsmen. By the late seventeenth century, a master's wife spent more of her time at domestic tasks because there were more things to take care of, and community social standards required fancier dress and more elaborate meals and table settings.

A woman's work in the craft guilds depended not on her own skill or level of training, but on her relation to a guild master and her marital status. A guild master was free to employ his daughter however he wished in the workshop, and she could learn the trade alongside his apprentices. She did not receive any formal apprenticeship certificate, but her skills could make her a more attractive marriage partner. Some women even continued working in their fathers' shops after they married, if the other masters did not object. If the master did not have enough daughters, he might hire additional women as maids or pieceworkers, particularly for the preparation of raw material or for simple tasks such as polishing or wrapping.

The most important woman in any workshop was the master's wife. Wives were often responsible for selling the merchandise their husbands made, collecting debts, and keeping the books. Wives, as well as husbands, were held responsible for the payment of fees and taxes and for the quality of the product. The wife also distributed salaries and food to the journeymen, which occasionally brought her into conflict with them, for they complained of being short-changed and underfed. Wives continued to operate the shop in the absence of their husbands when they were away, whether at war, purchasing raw materials, or selling finished products.

After the master craftsman died, his widow confronted restrictions on what she could do which increased over time. The earliest guild ordinances (thirteenth-century) made no mention of widows at all, who seem to have had unrestricted rights to carry on the shop, at least as long as they remained unmarried. Even in the heaviest industries, like iron-making and roofing, masters' widows ran the shop for as much as fifteen or twenty years after the deaths of their husbands. Although the widows could not take part in the guild's political functions or represent the guild in negotiations, they paid all guild fees, took part in festivities, and provided soldiers for the city's defence. Workshops run by widows often made up as much as 10 to 15 per cent of those in a particular craft.[9]

Beginning in the mid-fifteenth century, however, the length of time during which a widow could continue operating the shop was limited. In some cases widows could only finish work which they had already begun; often they could take charge of the business only if there was a son who could inherit the shop. By the mid-sixteenth century, widows in most crafts could hire no new apprentices, journeymen, or pieceworkers, and in some cases could not keep the ones they had. This often meant that a widow's workshop became so small that she could not produce enough to live on. Tax records from many cities indicate that over two-thirds of widows were in the poorest income category.[10]

One can easily understand why widows were allowed to carry on a business – the tools, equipment, and organization were already there, contracts had been made, the household still needed to be supported, and the widow was usually skilled enough to carry on the work. Why, then, would widows' work be restricted? Generally the guilds and city councils gave no explicit reasons, but occasionally records do give us a glimpse of both the official, publicly stated, justifications and the underlying reasons.

For example, in Frankfurt in 1624 a stonemason's widow asked to be allowed to continue working, as she had a large amount of

9. Rainer Stahlschmidt, *Die Geschichte des eisenverarbeitende Gewerbes in Nurnberg von den ersten Nachrichten im 12.–13. Jahrhunderts bis 1630.* Schriftenreihe des Stadtarchivs Nurnberg, 4 (Nuremberg: Stadtarchiv, 1971), pp. 186–7.

10. Same references as note 5 above.

stone left which her husband had purchased just before his death. The stonemasons refused her request, giving a number of justifications. First, other widows would want the same rights. Second, her husband had been the most successful stonemason in town, and the others felt bitter that he had taken business away from them. If his widow continued the shop, there would be many disputes between her and the other masters. Third, her husband had vigorously opposed allowing widows to work, so why should they go against his wishes in the case of his own wife? Fourth, she could not oversee the shop well enough and work might not be done properly, 'which would bring shame to her and to the whole guild'. Fifth, she could not control the journeymen, who might marry and have children, and later abandon their families with no means of support, making them a drain on the public treasury. Sixth, because she could not control the journeymen, they would want to work in her shop and not for other masters.[11]

In the stonemasons' answer, we can perceive a number of factors emerging: petty jealousy toward the most successful mason, suspicion between masters and journeymen, feigned or real concern about the guild's quality standards, and flagrant attempts to win over the city council with the spectre of more public welfare charges. Some of the reasons are economic, motivated by the desire to limit the number of stonemasons competing for customers. Some of the reasons are moral or ideological, motivated by the feeling that a woman could not or should not have authority over men or final responsibility for production processes. These kinds of considerations undoubtedly figured in other decisions to limit widows' rights in many crafts.

Widows often objected to these limitations, and city records are full of requests that they be allowed to continue working. They rarely argued that they, as widows, had an absolute right to work, but stressed factors they felt would be effective with the authorities: their poverty, old age, infirmity, and number of dependents; the authorities' Christian charity; the limited scope of their business. The widows who were successful were usually those who could make the most pitiful case. Although this accomplished what they wanted in the short run, in the long run it was harmful, because it reinforced the idea that woman's work was temporary, small-scale, no threat to the larger producers, and essentially something to keep one from needing public charity. By the seventeenth century,

11. Wiesner, *Working Women*, pp. 160–1.

fewer and fewer requests were being granted, and widows tended to sell the shop immediately after the death of their husbands.

This restriction of widows' rights was tied in with several larger trends in production. In many cities, the craft guilds themselves were declining in power and wealth – in central Europe with the general economic decline of the sixteenth century and in western Europe with the rise of capitalist production. Investors hired rural households to establish a putting-out system, thus avoiding the controls established by urban guilds and producing cheaper products. Guild masters often felt threatened, and sharply limited the number of workshops by restricting widows or allowing a journeyman to become a master only if he could inherit an existing shop.

As the opportunities for journeymen to become masters decreased, most became permanent wage workers rather than masters-in-training and formed separate journeymen's guilds. These journeymen's guilds demanded the right to determine who would work in a shop and refused to work alongside those who did not have their approval. At first, this meant men who were born out of wedlock, but it gradually came to include women. Journeymen demanded that the master's maids be excluded from all production-related tasks, and then that his wife and daughters be excluded as well. They thus assured themselves of more workplaces, and preserved a shred of their former dignity by sharply differentiating their work from 'women's work'. They also achieved a symbolic victory over the master. The master may have determined their hours and wages, but the journeymen kept his female dependents out of the shop. In addition, the journeymen made sure they would never have to take orders or receive their wages from a woman.

As journeymen fought against female labour in the shops, they also demanded the right to marry, for they often no longer lived in the master's household. Their disapproval of women working in a craft shop extended even to their own wives and daughters, and they never requested that their wives be allowed to join them in their trade. Because a journeyman's low wages could not support a family, his wife and daughters also had to work but were relegated to lower-paying domestic service, sales, or unskilled labour. Thus the journeymen's sentiment that working next to any woman was somehow dishonourable worked against their own economic interests, but was still fervently proclaimed.

As the guilds restricted opportunities for female employment, women turned to crafts that the guilds had never regulated or to employment in the new capitalist industries. They produced cheap and simple items such as soap, candles, thimbles, brooms, brushes, needles and pins, combs, and wooden bowls and spoons. They often made them as a secondary occupation, after working in the fields near the city or as laundresses or porters, or during winter when there was less agricultural or domestic work available. Because such products required little training, produced a meagre income, and could be made by one woman acting alone, guilds and city authorities rarely objected. In fact, city officials often viewed such labour as a preferable alternative to poor relief, and encouraged women to work rather than relying on public or private charity. This is evident in the official attitude toward seamstressing, for city councils often set up small endowments to provide poor girls with training in seamstressing. City orphanages had seamstresses as part of the staff, responsible for teaching as well as sewing.

Domestic industry, particularly cloth production, provided a more significant source of employment for both rural and urban women. In some cities, craft guilds controlled cloth production and gradually excluded women from most weavers', drapers', tailors', and cloth-cutters' guilds. The guilds generally allowed women to continue producing cheaper cloth made specifically for women's clothing, such as veils. Guilds in a few cities allowed only married women or widows to weave veils as they attempted to prevent unmarried women from living independently. In cities such as Florence, where weavers were not an independent guild but were hired by capitalist investors, women as well as men wove, because weaving did not bring high status or financial prosperity.[12] In the cloth industry, organizational rather than technological factors determined the sexual division of labour. Women carried out the stages of production that could be carried out in the home, required little or no assistance, and did not have a public or political function attached to them. In some cities, this included weaving; in those, such as Hamburg, that had a strong weavers' guild, it did not. The weaving industry presents another instance in which the political power of a guild affected women's labour.

The initial stages of cloth production, carding the wool (to produce straight fibres) and spinning, provided ever-increasing employment for women. Early modern techniques of production necessitated at least twenty carders and spinners per weaver, whether he or she was an independent guild master or hired by a merchant investor. Each weaver got his or her thread from a variety of spinners.

12. Judith Brown and Jordan Goodman, 'Women and industry in Florence', *Journal of Economic History* 40 (1980): 73–80.

Some of it was spun by female servants who lived in the employer's household; some of it by pieceworkers who worked but did not live in the weaver's house; some of it by pieceworkers spinning in their own homes, using wool provided by the weaver or investor; and some was purchased at the public market from urban or rural spinners who bought their own wool.

Authorities regarded spinning as the perfect female occupation because it required little capital investment or training and could be easily worked around family responsibilities – taken up and put down frequently with no harm done to the work. City councils expected women to keep spinning when in jail for various crimes, after the rest of their household had been sold to pay off debts, or, if they were prostitutes, between customers. Even wealthy or highly educated women were expected to spin; when a young woman who could speak and write Latin, Greek, and Hebrew was presented to James I of England his first question was, 'But can she spin?'[13] In Norwich, an eighty-year-old widow, 'a lame woman of one hand', still spun with her good hand, while in Memmingen a suicidal woman was to be chained in her hospital bed 'in a way that she can still spin'.[14] The Strasbourg city council was offered the prospect of a young woman 'with no hands and only one foot, but who can still do all sorts of handwork, like spinning'; the man who found her wanted to show her to the public, and the council agreed, allowing him to charge a penny an onlooker.[15]

As more and more women turned to spinning, wages were held down because the field was overcrowded, a phenomenon economists have discovered in many female occupations in the twentieth century. Spinners could not support a family on their wages, or in some cases even support themselves; as a woman in Frankfurt said, 'What little I make at spinning will not provide enough even for my bread.'[16] The growth of the putting-out system offered urban and rural women more jobs, but jobs with low pay, little security, and low status.

In production, therefore, the period saw a gradual proletarianization of women's work. In the early sixteenth century, though men

13. Quoted in Patricia Crawford, 'Women's published writings, 1600–1700', in Prior, ed., *Women in English Society*, p. 215.
14. Unpublished article by Diane Willen, 'Women and poor relief in pre-industrial Norwich and York'; Wiesner, *Working Women*, p. 182.
15. Wiesner, *Working Women*, p. 182.
16. Ibid., p. 184; Alice Clark, *Working Life of Women in the Seventeenth Century* (London: Routledge and Kegan Paul, 1919), p. 9; Donald Woodward, 'Wage rates and living standards in pre-industrial England', *Past and Present* 91 (May 1981): 39.

had hegemony over the public activities of the guilds, many women fulfilled essential functions in household workshops. The status of such women was recognized by the community, as was their authority over journeymen and apprentices as well as maids and children. Because this authority was not politically institutionalized, however, economic changes, combined with the rise of the sentiment that it was inappropriate for women to give orders to men, eroded women's position. By the late seventeenth century, many masters' wives and widows no longer took an active role in production, but concentrated their energies on domestic tasks. The wives of merchant capitalists rarely assisted their husbands in business, spending their time instead directing larger household staffs. The women who worked did so as wage labourers with much lower wages than men, and no supervisory authority. Of course, this proletarianization was also happening to most male workers, as we have seen in the case of the journeymen, but at least a few men had opportunities to increase their wealth, power, and prestige through business and investments, opportunities not available to any woman.

Sales

The market-place stood at the centre of economic life within any early modern city. Whether goods came from far away or close to home, they were usually bought, sold, or traded at the market, often a large open square in front of the cathedral or major church. Women conducted most of the business that went on at this market; they handled almost all retail distribution of food, used clothing, household articles, and liquor – things which made up the major share of most family budgets. In addition, the market-place served as a gathering place for women, who were the majority of customers as well as vendors; men exchanged news, information, and opinions in taverns, while women did this at the market place, at church, and at neighbourhood wells.

The sales sector of the early modern economy ranged across a wide spectrum in terms of wealth and prestige, from itinerant vendors and hawkers at the low end to major merchants with international trading networks at the top. Few women could amass the capital necessary for long-distance trade, or be absent from household and family for the time required, so women predominated on the lower end of the spectrum and men on the upper. Cities began to use merchants as ambassadors, envoys, and representatives, roles considered inappropriate for women.[17] As business procedures became more complex, major merchants relied more on formally trained accountants and bookkeepers with experience in double-entry bookkeeping, preparing contracts, and drawing up insurance agreements. Because women were excluded from such training, the wives and daughters of major traders retreated from an active role in the business.

In many ways, this was no different from the situation in the Middle Ages, however; although there were a few women who travelled and traded all over Europe, the important merchants' guilds and trading companies had always been male organizations. Most women in sales, whether in 1300, 1500, or 1700, were retail distributors who sold from a basket they carried, a small stand at the market-place, or a small shop bordering the market. City officials paid a great deal of attention to these women and what they sold, as they recognized the importance to their citizens of pure products, fair weights and measures, just prices and business practices, and legitimately obtained goods.

The poorest women were those who sold small items they had made or gathered, such as pretzels, nuts, wooden implements, cookies, candles, herbs, lace, and firewood. City councils often gave poor widows or other needy women special permission to sell such things so they would not need public charity; officials clearly saw this as an alternative to poor relief.

Women who had permanent stands might be slightly better off. Many of them sold fruits and vegetables, occasionally the products of their own gardens, but more often purchased from local farmers. Female peasants often brought their own produce into the city, and sold it along with eggs, cheese, and butter. City governments regulated prices, hours, and the variety of produce each woman could offer. They allowed each woman only one stand, because they wanted to prevent monopolies and keep a large number of women off

17. Martha C. Howell, 'Women, the family economy and the structures of market production in the cities of northern Europe during the late Middle Ages', in Hanawalt, ed., *Women and Work*, pp. 198–222. Jewish women may have been somewhat of an exception to this. As the memoirs of Glückel of Hameln indicate, she continued to assist her husband and sons in all aspects of their trade in luxury goods into the eighteenth century, occasionally even travelling to fairs or distant cities to buy and sell gold, pearls, and precious stones. This may in part be due to the fact that male Jewish merchants were never used by Christian political authorities as ambassadors and envoys, so women would not automatically be excluded because they could not perform a political role. (*The Memoirs of Glückel of Hameln*, tr. Marvin Loewenthal (New York: Schocken, 1977).)

charity. In the late sixteenth century, some cities also tried to limit stands to widows, to prevent 'young female persons who could easily do some other kind of work, like being a maid' from selling.[18] This is yet another example of the authorities' dislike of young women working – and thus perhaps living – independent of the household.

Female vendors continually broke restrictions and ignored regulations. They raised prices, withheld produce from the market in order to force up the price, and forced customers to buy less desirable merchandise before they could buy what they wanted. They sold house to house rather than at the market, a practice authorities disliked because it was hard to control and provided a good opportunity for selling stolen merchandise.

One such vendor, a woman named Anna Weyland, appeared before the Strasbourg city council many times over a thirty-year period. She was first charged in 1573 with illegally selling herring, but used an ongoing dispute between the city council and the fishers' guild to obtain the council's permission to continue selling. A short time later the fishers' guild complained that she refused to sell herring to people unless they also bought dried cod from her; they also complained that she bought her herring outside the city instead of at the public fish market, then sold it below the established price. She got into the candle business the same year, and was immediately charged with selling candles for less than the official price and with a number of other infractions of the candle ordinance. She answered she 'would not obey any ordinance, no matter what in God's name the council made for an ordinance'. At that the council ordered her to follow the ordinance and especially not to use children to sell candles illegally. If she spoke like that again the council threatened that she would be 'pinched with glowing tongs and if she works [illegally] she will be thrown in the water'.

Those threats apparently worked for a while, for she did not come before the council again for six years. At that point, she was charged with having candles that were underweight, but when the city inspectors checked them they were found to be all right. The council did not trust her, however, and decided 'that the inspectors should watch her and send unknown people to her to buy candles, to see if we can catch her hand in the sack (so to speak)'. This was done, and the candles were found to be too light. Attempting to anticipate all possible excuses, the council next ordered all her

18. Wiesner, *Working Women*, p. 123.

scales and weights to be checked secretly, and candles bought again 'so that she can be caught in the act'. Her scales and weights were found to be accurate, and the candles too light again.

Both she and her husband were ordered to appear before the council, but she pleaded some kind of illness, and he appeared alone. Despite his pleading, the council ordered him to shut the shop, after selling the things he had on hand already. His wife was to do nothing, 'neither buying or selling, changing money or anything else that has to do with the business' and was not even to let herself be found in the shop. He promised 'by the grace of God' never to do anything wrong again.

This time the promise lasted two years. In 1582 Anna Weyland was selling Dutch cheese illegally (she simply switched products whenever she was forbidden to sell something). This time the council sent out a representative to order her to stop or she would be banished – she had never yet come before the council to answer any of the charges against her. This was effective, for she never sold anything again, although she did ask for permission to do so in 1605, twenty-three years later. Still she was forbidden 'to sell anything at the public market'. Nearly a quarter century of good behaviour was not enough to make the council forget all the trouble she had caused.[19]

Wives and husbands often shared in food sales. Butchers, bakers, fishmongers, game handlers, and poultry dealers generally had strong guilds, but, unlike the manufacturing guilds, they did not feel the competition of capitalist production or pressure by journeymen. Masters' wives therefore remained important in the distribution of products, particularly as their husbands needed to be out of the city fishing or hunting – or in the case of bakers, busy at their ovens – and so could not do any selling. Masters' wives, widows, and other women also made sausage, prepared tripe, pickled meat, smoked game, and salted fish – all domestic processes.

Women produced and distributed all types of alcoholic beverages. In both cities and villages, female brewers made beer and ran small taverns to distribute their beverage. Apparently, brewers were also in the money-lending business to a small degree, for they incurred debts not only for beer, but for loans of money. Female brewers in Munich also took care of women in childbed, nursing them during the delivery with plenty of beer (this was felt to increase a mother's milk supply and help her quickly regain her strength).

Women made and sold mead and hard cider, and when the process of distilling was discovered in the mid-sixteenth century, distilled and sold brandy. They received licences to operate taverns and inns and ran small sleeping houses to accommodate poor people and students who could not pay normal inn prices.

The wealthiest and most powerful saleswomen were those who sold used merchandise of all types along with other small items such as dishes and pots. They received their merchandise from citizens who needed money, thus serving as pawnbrokers. During the sixteenth century, such women also served as appraisers, and sold the merchandise they had appraised if there were no heirs or cash was needed to pay back creditors. City councils required them to put up a certain amount of money as security, and investigated an applicant's reputation before giving her a licence, because market women were often suspected of being receivers of stolen merchandise.

These market women appeared frequently in court in disputes with various craft guilds, who accused them of selling new merchandise or fixing prices. In these conflicts the women used a wide variety of arguments and tactics to win their cases. They exploited rivalries and jealousies between guilds, often selling a commodity or product that two different guilds felt they had the sole right to, then turning the two guilds against each other when the case came up. The market women used conflicts between the city council and the craft guilds, turning to the council for protection from overzealous guild masters. These saleswomen used geographical conflicts within the city, for instance, selling from a place where selling was not allowed while knowing that the residents in that area would not complain – or would even defend them – because the residents wanted a market in that part of the city. As a last resort, they pleaded helplessness and incompetence, arguing that they could do nothing else and that their business was so small they couldn't possibly be hurting anyone by it, which may have been accurate, but promoted negative ideas about the nature and value of women's work.

Their businesses may have been small, but these women were far from helpless or reticent. Not only did they quickly bring anyone to court whom they felt was intruding on their territory, but they were also very frequently involved in slander and defamation cases. They called other women and men names – asshole, whore, and thief were the most common – and then refused to apologize until the case had gone all the way to the city's highest court. Even then, the woman's husband often came in first, pleading that she was 'only an irrational woman, who lets talk flow so freely and unguardedly out of her mouth without thinking about it': not until a fine was set did the woman herself come in, and then simply to ask that the fine be reduced.[20] In one case in Strasbourg, only after three weeks in prison on bread and water did the woman apologize, and agree to mutter the formulaic 'I know nothing but good and honour about this person'.[21]

As did the midwives, these market women developed a strong work identity and described themselves first as 'market women' rather than wives or widows; they often played a significant role in urban disturbances, from the iconoclastic riots associated with the Protestant Reformation to the French Revolution.

Services

The broad range of occupations that may be termed 'services' provided the most employment for women in the early modern period, as they do today. Part of the explanation for women's relative ease in finding employment in this area, whether in the sixteenth century or the twentieth, is that many of these occupations are considered stereotypically female or 'natural' for women. They were and are often viewed as extensions of a woman's function and work in the home – cooking, cleaning, childcare, nursing the sick, and care for the elderly. Such occupations often required little or no specialized training, so women could start and stop frequently, work only when financially pressed, or work part-time if they had a family to care for. Because of this flexibility and fluidity, women working in the service sector were (and are) often underpaid and rarely organized or protested to get higher wages or salaries.

A large number of women worked in health care, both in institutions, such as hospitals, pest-houses, infirmaries, and orphanages, and as independent practitioners, such as midwives, wet-nurses, and healers. During the early modern period, the administrations of most cities, both Protestant and Catholic, took over the operation of hospitals, infirmaries, and orphanages from the church or established new institutions for care of the sick, elderly, and infirm. As the authorities secularized these institutions, they often centralized them, setting up one major hospital to replace a number of smaller

20. Ibid., p. 142.
21. Ibid.

care centres. The city councils or officials appointed by them hired the staff and set forth the responsibilities and duties of each person.

These new institutions employed women in a variety of occupations, from administrative and medical to cooking and janitorial. The hospital mistress, or keeper, as she was occasionally called, was responsible for the physical needs of the hospital and patients. She made all purchases, occasionally including land for the hospital's endowments, and kept records of all income and expenditures. She oversaw the kitchen, ordered special diets for those too ill to eat regular food, and distributed excess food to the poor. Along with administrative functions, the hospital mistress – or mistresses, as in large institutions this job was divided among several women – also fulfilled medical and religious functions. She examined incoming patients and then visited them on a weekly basis, making sure they were ill enough to warrant being in the hospital. She led the patients in prayer and prayed for those who were dying.

Like male employees, female hospital personnel, no matter what their position, had to swear an oath of loyalty and agree to follow all directives laid out for the day-to-day operation of the institution. The city councils envisioned the hospital as a family, led by the hospital mistress who was to treat the patients 'as a mother would her children' and do everything 'that is appropriate for women to do'. The women who assisted her, nurses, cooks, laundresses and children's maids, were to treat each other as 'true and loving sisters'.[22] This family imagery meant that such women, even though they had a wide range of responsibilities, were not considered professionals, and were therefore poorly paid, often receiving little more than board and room.

The hospitals were for the chronically ill, the elderly, expectant mothers, the handicapped, foundling children, and mentally retarded or psychologically disturbed children and adults. Those with contagious diseases, such as the plague, leprosy, or smallpox, were consigned to small pest-houses outside the city. The pest-houses and plague hospitals also employed women, usually on a short-term basis when an epidemic swept through an area. Very little could be done for such patients except to keep them fed and clean; we can get an idea of the low level of early modern medical knowledge from the instructions given to women to simply air out the sheets and clothing of patients who had died, so that they could be used as bandages for those coming in.

22. Ibid., pp. 40–1.

The city orphanages were modelled after the family as well, with a married couple in charge. The 'orphan mother' taught the girls to spin, cook, and care for laundry; purchased food and clothing; oversaw servants; and took care of illnesses. She was responsible for the children's spiritual, as well as material, well-being, and instructed them in prayer. The orphanage did not admit very young children, who were given to wet-nurses living in the city or in the surrounding villages. Wet-nursing provided employment for women whose own infants made other occupation difficult, and evoked no negative comments during the period, though it would come under increasing attack in the eighteenth century.

Midwifery was the most important occupation open to women. Until the eighteenth century, very few male doctors or accoucheurs worked in obstetrics and gynaecology; midwives handled all births, from those of the very poor to those of the nobility. City councils recognized the importance of midwives, and paid them an annual salary to take care of poor women, granted them allotments of grain or wood, and encouraged trained midwives to move into the city. Individuals who could afford it also paid the midwife for her services, her fees varying with the social class of the mother. In the fifteenth century, city councils established organized systems of midwives, appointing upper-class women to oversee the midwives and, in conjunction with city doctors, to examine and license prospective midwives. Midwifery is the one field in which there was an organized hierarchy of women similar to that of men in the craft guilds or the city government. This hierarchy was not called a guild, and was less independent of city authorities than the craft guilds, who wrote their own ordinances and set limits on their own membership; in many ways, however, the hierarchy operated as a guild, particularly in the training and disciplining of midwives.

Midwives learned their skill through apprenticeship. They accompanied experienced midwives to births for a period of years, then took an examination with questions ranging from how to handle a breech birth to proper diets for newborns. After passing the examination, the midwife took an oath and received a midwife's licence. These oaths illustrate a wide variety of functions. Besides delivering babies, the midwife was to instruct new mothers in child care, perform emergency baptisms if she felt the child might die, and report all illegitimate children and try to discover the identity of the father 'during the pains of birth'.[23] She swore not to perform

23. Ibid., p. 63.

abortions, use implements to speed the birth, or repeat superstitions. In the eighteenth century, male accoucheurs and 'man-midwives' slandered female midwives as bungling, slovenly, superstitious, and inept, but earlier, in the sixteenth and seventeenth centuries, authorities held them in high regard. City councils often called upon midwives to give opinions in legal cases of infanticide and abortion and examine women charged with fornication or female prisoners who claimed to be pregnant in the hope of delaying their corporal punishment or execution. The midwives participated in the municipal welfare system, handing out food and clothing to needy women and serving as medical assistants during epidemics. More than women in any other occupation, they defended their rights against outsiders. Their testimony in court shows a strong sense of work identity, for they always proudly note that they are midwives when appearing in court, making an appeal, or acting in any other legal or public capacity.

Women, then, faced no opposition when working in hospitals or similar 'domestic' institutions. No tracts declared them unfit or too delicate to care for even the most horribly afflicted patients. There was opposition to women in medicine during the period, but this centred around their treatment of people who were not in hospitals. Physicians, barber-surgeons, and apothecaries claimed this was their province alone.

Until the late fifteenth century, women as well as men had been listed as physicians on the citizens' lists of many communities. From that time on, however, that title was increasingly given only to men who had received theoretical medical training at a university, a path that was closed to women. As physicians became more clearly 'professional', barber-surgeons and apothecaries who had completed formal apprenticeship attempted to identify themselves as also somehow professional. They drew increasingly sharp lines between those who had received formal training and those who simply practised on their own. Gradually, as these men convinced city and state governments to forbid 'women and other untrained people' to practise medicine, female physicians and barber-surgeons disappeared from official records.[24] Some women received permission to handle minor external problems, like eye infections, skin diseases, and boils, if they promised to charge only small fees and not to advertise. Even this was too much for some barber-surgeons, who complained that the status of their profession was irreparably damaged if any women

24. Ibid., p. 50.

could perform the same operations as they did. Some men hinted that the women's skills must be diabolical in origin, for God would certainly never bestow medical talents on a woman.[25]

Professionalization also affected other occupations. Women had long served as appraisers, for many communities required an inventory when a spouse died or an estate was being divided. Appraisers listed the value of everything from fields and vineyards down to the last dishtowel, a procedure that required extensive knowledge of merchandise and prices. During the sixteenth century, however, cities began to require more formal legal language, which made it difficult for women with little formal education to write out an acceptable inventory. The testimony of a male appraiser was increasingly viewed as more credible because female appraisers were held to be more likely to take bribes. During the late sixteenth century, the appraisers were made elected city officials, which ended the chances for women in the field.

In most cities, women could be found in several other service occupations – running small primary schools, overseeing charities, inspecting milk, grain, or vegetables, serving as gatekeepers and toll-collectors. Such positions were poorly paid, and city governments often rewarded needy widows with them to keep the women from depending on charity, much as they allowed poor women to bake pretzels or sew. Women worked alongside men as day labourers in construction and other types of heavy labour, often travelling to rural areas during harvest time, where their wages for harvesting, picking grapes or gleaning were set at one-half those of adult males.[26]

In the early sixteenth century, all major cities had public baths, with women serving as bath attendants, washing the customers' hair and bodies, trimming nails, and beating them with branches to improve circulation. Such women were often specifically designated as 'rubbers', 'scratchers', or 'beaters'. During the sixteenth century, public baths went out of style, and respectable people no longer celebrated weddings, christenings, and business agreements with a group bath as they had in the Middle Ages. During the same period, much of Europe was deforested to provide wood for ships and military equipment, leading to a dramatic increase in the price of firewood and making baths too expensive for journeymen and wage labourers. The increasing concern with public morality and

25. Ibid., p. 52.
26. Ibid., pp. 92–3; Michael Roberts, 'Sickles and scythes: women's work and men's work at harvest time', *History Workshop* 7 (Spring 1979): 3–29.

decorum led city councils to prohibit mixed-sex bathing, which combined with higher prices to force most public baths to close.

This same concern for public morality also led to a closing of municipal brothels in the sixteenth century. During the Middle Ages, most large cities and many smaller ones had opened one or more municipal brothels, hiring a brothel manager and prostitutes, and passing regulations concerning the women and their customers. Municipal authorities protected the women from violence and over-exploitation, and regarded prostitution as simply a necessary service for journeymen and out-of-town visitors. Such attitudes changed in the sixteenth century, and officials increasingly required prostitutes to wear distinctive clothing and prohibited them from appearing in public.[27] Eventually the municipal brothels were closed. Concern for 'public decency' and the spread of syphilis were given as the reason for this action. Illicit prostitution continued, but the women involved were prosecuted rather than protected.

Domestic service was the longest single employer of women. About 15 to 20 per cent of the population of most cities was made up of domestic servants; the larger commercial and manufacturing centres had a higher percentage of servants than the smaller cities whose economies were more dependent upon agriculture.[28] During the Middle Ages, many servants had been employed in noble house-holds, and men as well as women cooked, served at the table and did other domestic tasks; these were simply part of their duties as household retainers, regardless of gender. Gradually, servants' duties were increasingly specialized and divided by gender, with men and boys becoming responsible for the stables and grounds and women and girls for the kitchen and interior household. By the beginning of the early modern period, bourgeois urban house-holds employed the majority of servants in urban areas; since such employers rarely had extensive grounds or stables, they hired more women than men for the indoor domestic tasks that had come to be seen as female. Both women and men continued to be hired

27. Lyndal Roper, 'Discipline and respectability: prostitution and the Reformation in Augsburg', *History Workshop* 19 (Spring 1985): 3–28.

28. Maschke, *Unterschichten*, p. 29; Rudolph Endres, 'Zur Einwohnerzahl und Bevölkerungsstatistik Nürnbergs im 15./16. Jahrhunderts', *Mitteilungen des Verein für Geschichte der Stadt Nürnberg* 57 (1970): 249; J. Jean Hecht, *The Domestic Servant Class in Eighteenth-century England* (London: Routledge and Kegan Paul, 1956), pp. 33, 34; Judith Brown, 'A woman's place was in the home: women's work in Renaissance Tuscany', in *Rewriting the Renaissance: The Discourses of Sexual Difference in Early Modern Europe*, ed. Margaret Ferguson, Maureen Quilligan, and Nancy Vickers (Chicago: University of Chicago Press, 1986).

as agricultural servants in rural areas, but their duties were also increasingly defined by gender, with women taking care of the household and animals, and men performing more, though not all, of the field work.[29]

Service offered young women a chance to earn small dowries that enabled them to marry. In fact, many maids were not paid at all until the end of a set period of service, with the understanding that their wages were specifically to provide a dowry. For other women, service became a career. These women might work their way up in large households from goose-girl to children's maid to serving maid to cook. More typically, they remained with a family as its single servant for twenty, thirty, or forty years. Their wages were low, and inventories taken at the deaths of maids indicate they usually owned no more than the clothes in which they were buried. For many women, however, service was the only type of employment possible until they were married, or after the death of a husband left them penniless.

Because of the large numbers of people involved, some cities, such as Nuremberg and Munich, organized the hiring of servants through a system of licensed employment agents who found jobs for a girl (or boy) from the countryside. The agents were paid by both the servant and the employer and followed certain rules: they could not take gifts or bribes, let servants change positions more than twice a year, house any servants themselves, or store any servants' trunks (which might contain stolen goods). Most of the employment agents were the wives or widows of craftsmen or minor officials, and operated from a small stand at the market-place or out of their own homes, with a sign hung out in front just like any other occupation.

City officials also tried to regulate the conduct, salaries, and social activities of servants once they were hired. This meant admonishing servants not to leave positions without just cause, stay in public inns or live independently between positions. Like unmarried women, both male and female servants were subjected to the hostility toward 'masterless' persons. Those who married and tried to set up their own households could be banished, as could those who tried to live on their own as day labourers. They were to remain dependents, under the control of a preferably male head of a household. Wages were strictly limited, because servants in some areas were charged

---

29. Ann Kussmaul, *Servants in Husbandry in Early Modern England* (Cambridge: Cambridge University Press, 1981).

with causing the general inflation; the authorities in Stuttgart were horrified that 'these servants now demand a salary along with room and board'.[30]

In the late sixteenth and seventeenth centuries, regulations became harsher and more hostile to servants, and reflect a growing distrust between employer and servant. Servants who spoke against their masters or pretended to be ill were to be strictly punished, as were those who exhibited general 'disobedience and pride'. Sumptuary laws established clear class distinctions, with servants prohibited from wearing fancy clothing or jewelry even if this was a gift from an employer.

These ordinances paint a rather grim picture, but private household journals and accounts give a more peaceful view of employer/ employee relations. Wet-nurses and maids were made special guardians for children, and sometimes received substantial sums at the death of a master or mistress. Wealthy people often set up funds to provide small dowries or hope chests for maids who left their service to get married. Former servants often married late, had more freedom in choosing their own spouses, and played a more active role in courtship and marriage.

As opportunities for women to work in other occupations decreased, those in domestic service remained the same or increased as domestic tasks became feminized, larger household staffs became more fashionable, and maids were used for industrial tasks such as spinning. Men were more free to move in search of employment and opportunities, including those to be found in Europe's new overseas empires, while women had to look closer to home. By the seventeenth century, a greater percentage of the women who worked outside their own homes worked as servants in someone else's.

Conclusion

In all three areas of the economy there was sharper differentiation in the early modern period between women's work and men's work. Occupations which required university education or formal training were closed to women, as they could not attend universities or humanist academies, or participate in most apprenticeship training programmes. Women rarely controlled enough financial resources to enter occupations which required large initial capital outlay, and

---

30. Wiesner, *Working Women*, p. 88.

social norms kept them from occupations with political functions. Family responsibilities prevented them from entering occupations which required extensive travelling. Unfortunately, it was exactly the occupations with formal education, political functions, capital investment, or international connections, such as physicians, merchants, bankers, lawyers, government officials, and overseas traders, that were gaining in wealth, power, and prestige.

This increasing separation of men's and women's work was one consequence of several major economic and political changes: from household production organized by guilds to capitalist domestic industry; from a definition of work based on use to one based on monetary exchange; from loose training requirements to rigid professionalization; from political power based on feudal family ties to centralized states. It was also a product of the increased concern for public order, propriety, and decorum and the emphasis on male-headed households as instruments of social control. City authorities kept women out of occupations in which they would supervise men, work extensively out in public, or live independently. For ideological reasons, domestic service became the perfect female employment, though the economy still required women's labour in production and sales.

Increasingly, women worked at jobs which required few tools, minimal formal training, and no supervisory responsibilities – in short, jobs which were poorly paid and could be done part-time. Women changed occupations much more frequently than men, and moved in and out of the labour force as their individual and family needs changed, fitting their work around the life-cycle of their families. As they were restricted to fewer occupations, competition among them for workplaces increased and wages were held down.

Many men also worked in similar low-skill, low-paid occupations, but they increasingly felt a need to differentiate their work from 'women's work'. They increased training or investment requirements, and in some cases prohibited women from performing certain tasks. Men excluded women entirely from a shop or drew an artificial line between men's work and women's work down the middle of a workshop, leaving to women the tasks that were more domestic and reserving the productive tasks to themselves. As a result domestic tasks were devalued not only because they were not rewarded financially, but also because they were associated with women.

Women themselves often devalued their own work when appealing to authorities for the right to produce or sell. Recognizing that such arguments would be successful, they stressed that their work was temporary, small-scale, a stopgap, no threat to anyone, and essentially a substitute for poor relief. Unfortunately, authorities began to regard these qualities as intrinsic to all women's work, making it inherently inferior to men's work.

The line between men's and women's work gradually grew into a gulf, and eventually affected the definition of work itself. According to the German industrial code of 1869, women who spun, washed, ironed, or knitted in their own homes were not considered workers (and thus not eligible for pensions), even though they worked for wages, while male shoemakers or tailors who worked in their own homes were.[31] The devaluation of women's work begun in the early modern period was complete; nothing a woman did, or at least nothing she did within her own home, was truly work.

---

31. Jean H. Quataert, 'The shaping of women's work in manufacturing: guilds, households, and the state in central Europe, 1648–1870', *American Historical Review* 90, no. 5 (December 1985): 1146.

CHAPTER NINE

Guilds, male bonding and women's work in early modern Germany

Though they are featured prominently in studies of medieval urban life, craft guilds have received less attention from early modern historians, who often view them as institutions in decline which were trying unsuccessfully to prevent economic change. This view of the guilds' decay has been successfully challenged in the case of Germany by Mack Walker, who demonstrates that in most medium-sized German cities the time after the Thirty Years War was 'the period probably of their greatest power to impress their values and goals upon the society of which they were components'.[1] These values and goals primarily involved maintaining the local economy and upholding the honour of the guilds. Walker and others have analysed the guild notion of honour quite extensively without noting what is, in my opinion, the most important component of it: this was an honour among *men*, an honour which linked men together with other men and excluded women. Craft guilds became an excellent example of what sociologists and psychologists term 'male bonding'.

Male bonding is a concept rarely used by historians, perhaps owing to the fact that the male group so predominates as a subject of historical study that male bonding appears trans-historical and almost self-evident. In this case, however, the notion of male bonding can prove enlightening and help to explain some of the actions

---

1. Mack Walker, *German Home Towns: Community, State, and General Estate 1648–1871* (Cornell University Press, Ithaca, NY, 1971), p. 76. Richard MacKenney finds that guilds in Venice also played a very prominent and positive role in the sixteenth and seventeenth centuries, adapting to economic change much more readily than previously assumed. He extends his conclusions tentatively to guilds in other cities, and calls for a reassessment of the relationship between guilds and mercantile capitalism. (*Tradesmen and Traders: The World of Guilds in Venice and Europe, c. 1250–c. 1650* (Barnes and Noble, Totowa, NJ, 1987), pp. 113–25.)

of craft guilds in early modern Germany which are difficult to explain in terms of more standard social, economic, and political factors. It is an even more powerful determinant of the actions of journeymen's guilds, which were a new force in the economy of early modern German cities. I thus use the concept of male bonding to analyse the aims and actions of craft guilds and journeymen's guilds in German cities from the fifteenth to the eighteenth centuries. Though this exploration could go off in many directions, I will focus my discussion on two questions: How did the concept of themselves as a group of men determine the way craft and journeymen's guilds defined skilled work and the gender boundaries of work? How did male bonding affect women's access to skilled work and to other forms of economic power?

First a few words on theories of male bonding. The concept was first extensively discussed by Lionel Tiger in his now classic *Men in Groups*. In his words: 'Males consciously create secret groups for the gregarious and efficacious control of political, religious, and/or economic worlds, and for the enjoyment of male company under emotionally satisfying conditions. Such grouping exhibits the culturally learned and socially mediated manifestations of a broad biological feature of the male life cycle.'[2] Tiger's most controversial point is revealed in his use of the word 'biological' to describe the underlying reason for male bonding. He views men's need to associate with other men as stemming from cooperative hunting during prehistoric times, and sees it as so ingrained in the male character as to be practically genetic. All men in all cultures feel the need to bond at certain points in their lives; the only difference is the form those bonds will take. Tiger would even go so far as to say that for certain men, the need to bond with other men is stronger than their sexual needs. (Tiger, I might add, sharply distinguishes between male bonding and male homosexuality, though notes that the former might have a somewhat hidden erotic component.)

Tiger's stress on the trans-cultural, trans-historical nature of male bonding is not accepted by other scholars, who view certain periods as favouring the formation of tighter male groups. To cite just one example that has applications for an analysis of early modern guilds, Ruth El Saffar asserts that males in the sixteenth century are being socialized for the first time in milieus almost entirely without women – milieus that impose discipline and foster male camaraderie at

---

2. Lionel Tiger, *Men in Groups* (Random House, New York, 1969), p. 140.

levels previously far less common.[3] She uses professional armies, the universities, and the expanded government bureaucracy as examples of these milieus. This male camaraderie both caused and resulted from men's attempts to disidentify with their mothers, which she and several contemporary psychoanalysts view as the core issue in the establishment of the modern masculine identity.[4] Her sources are primarily literary, and give evidence of a preoccupation with the disordering influence of women. Though one might argue that she overstresses the novelty of all-male milieus in the early modern period – the Athenian gymnasium provides one much earlier example, and the medieval university another – the notion that women are a source of disorder and dishonour is not simply a literary conceit during the period. As we shall see, that idea becomes the basis for craft guild regulations and actions, and is taken up in the late sixteenth century with even more vehemence by the journeymen's guilds.

The earliest guild ordinances in Germany, from the late thirteenth to the early fifteenth centuries, did not regard skilled guild labour as a male preserve. Some of them mention both male and female masters, although it is difficult to tell if these women had been trained independently in all cases or were actually masters' widows. In some guilds the women may have been trained on their own, as the ordinances regulating apprenticeship talk about both boys and girls. Many medieval guilds went to great lengths to make sure that all women who practised their craft were members, subject to the normal rules and paying the normal fees, just as municipal laws required female heads of household to pay taxes.[5] Although it is impossible to tell from prescriptive ordinances just how many

3. Ruth El Saffar, 'Literary reflections on the "new man": changes in consciousness in early modern Europe', unpublished paper, p. 14.

4. Ibid., p. 20; Ralph Greenson, 'Dis-identifying with the mother: its special importance for the boy', *International Journal of Psychoanalysis* 49 (1968): 370–4; Robert J. Stoller, 'Facts and fancies: an examination of Freud's concept of bisexuality', in *Women and Analysis*, ed. Jean Strouse (Grossman Publishers, New York, 1974), pp. 343–64.

5. Rudolf Wissell, *Des alten Handwerks Recht und Gewohnheit*, 2. Einzelveröffentlichungen der historischen Kommission zu Berlin, 7 (Colloquium, Berlin, 1974), p. 441; Helmut Wachendorf, *Die wirtschaftliche Stellung der Frau in den deutschen Städten des späteren Mittelalters* (C. Trute, Quackenbruck, 1934), pp. 30–2, 57; Benno Schmidt and Karl Bücher, *Frankfurter Amts und Zunfturkunden bis zum Jahre 1612*. Veröffentlichungen der historischen Kommission der Stadt Frankfurt a.M., Vol. 6 (Joseph Baer, Frankfurt, 1914), p. 513; Gustav Schmoller, *Die Strassburger Tucher und Weberzunft, Urkunden und Darstellung* (Karl J. Trübner, Strasbourg, 1879), pp. 40–1.

women were actually involved in craft work, one study using tax records finds 10–15 per cent of the iron-working shops in Nuremberg to be headed by widows or other women.[6] This, of course, does not count all the women who worked in a male-headed shop, nor is it a trade which was likely to attract high levels of female labour. Other studies indicate that women were even more likely to work in trades such as weaving, needle-making, yarn-spinning and hatmaking, which depended on dexterity rather than strength.[7]

Beginning in the mid-fifteenth century, many crafts expanded their ordinances and began to use more exclusively male language; the words 'female master' and 'girl apprentice' were often simply dropped with no explanation of why this was done. It is dangerous to draw conclusions from this change alone, but in some cases change was accompanied by specific ordinances prohibiting the work of women. Generally restrictions on masters' widows were the first to appear: a widow was allowed to continue operating a shop for only a short period of time, or only if she had a son who could take over; she was not allowed to take on or retain apprentices or journeymen; she could only finish work that had already been begun.[8] These restrictions were followed by limitations on the work

6. Rainer Stahlschmidt, *Die Geschichte des eisenverarbeitende Gewerbes in Nurnberg von der ersten Nachrichten im 12.–13. Jahrhundert bis 1630*, Schriftenreihe des Stadtarchivs Nürnberg, no. 4 (Stadtarchiv, Nuremberg, 1971), pp. 186–7. Lyndal Roper also finds 10% of the population of Augsburg in a 1539 muster list to be widows, though not all of these ran craft shops. ('Urban women and the household workshop form of production: Augsburg 1500–1550', unpublished paper, p. 6.)

7. Wissell, *Des alten Handwerks*, Vol. 2, p. 139; Merry Wiesner, *Working Women in Renaissance Germany* (Rutgers University Press, New Brunswick, NJ, 1986), pp. 151–85; E. William Monter, 'Women in Calvinist Geneva', *Signs* 6 (1980): 204; Karl Bücher, *Die Berufe der Stadt Frankfurt im Mittelalter* (Teubner, Leipzig, 1914); Annette Winter, 'Studien zur sozialen Situation der Frauen in der Stadt Trier nach der Steuerliste von 1364', *Kurtrierisches Jahrbuch* 15 (1975): 20–5. The only all-female guilds in Germany, those of gold-spinners in several cities and yarnmakers and silk-weavers in Cologne, also demonstrate this trend in women's work. (Margaret Wensky, *Die Stellung der Frau in der stadtkölnische Wirtschaft im Spätmittelalter*. Quellen und Darstellung zur hänsische Geschichte (Böhlau, Cologne, 1981). Natalie Davis finds women most prevalent in the textile and clothing trades in Lyon as well. ('Women in the crafts in sixteenth-century Lyon', in *Women and Work in Pre-Industrial Europe*, ed. Barbara Hanawalt (Indiana University Press, Bloomington, 1986), p. 181.)

8. Munich Stadtarchiv (hereafter MU), Ratsitzungsprotokolle, 1461, fols. 39, 42; 1526; Nuremberg Staatsarchiv (hereafter N), Ratsbücher: 2, fols. 31 (1475), 282 (1479), 318 (1479); 11, fol. 324 (1520); 22, fol. 236 (1544); Frankfurt Stadtarchiv (hereafter FF), Bürgermeisterbücher, 1515, fol. 112b; 1580, fol. 189b; FF, Zünfte, Ugb. D–3 (1527, 1588 and 1596); Nuremberg Stadtarchiv (hereafter NB), QNG, no. 68/11, 506; no. 68/1, 115 (1535); Strasbourg, Archives municipales (hereafter AMS), Akten der XV, 1613, fol. 201b; Memmingen Stadtarchiv (hereafter MM), Zünfte, 451(3), Hutmachem (1613).

female servants could do in a guild shop, which was generally limited to unskilled tasks such as preparing raw materials, cleaning and packing finished goods and cleaning the shop. Guilds which had previously seen high levels of female labour, such as those of weavers, dyers, and small hatmakers (*Baretmachern*), allowed women to produce only lower-priced and lower-quality goods.[9]

When I first examined this gradual exclusion of women from craft guilds, I attributed it to a number of factors – attempts to limit the number of workshops as the economies of various towns declined, conflicts between guilds and city councils over who had the power to control what went on in the shop, inter-guild rivalries, real or fabricated concerns over the quality of products.[10] To these economic and political factors I would now add an ideological one – guild honour. Women were to be kept out of guild shops not only because they had not been formally trained or would work more cheaply, but simply because they were women.

Several historians, most recently Mack Walker, have pointed out that social exclusiveness and a concern for maintaining honour and morality became the hallmarks of craft guilds after the Thirty Years War.[11] He lists a number of qualities that could make an individual 'dishonourable' and therefore not acceptable in a guild – illegitimacy, servile ancestry, parents who had worked as barbers, skinners, millers, shepherds, or linen-weavers.[12] To this list we must add having worked next to a woman or in a guild which still accepted women. To give just one example: in 1649 the Frankfurt hatmakers refused to take on journeymen who had been trained in Fulda, because the hatmakers in Fulda continued to use 'all sorts of female servants, maids, women and embroideresses'. The abbot of Fulda replied that it had long been the custom in Fulda to employ women as assistants, but now, 'since the hatmakers here have been insulted and despised because of this, their children, journeymen and apprentices hindered, and the quality of their

---

9. Restrictions on weavers: Wissell, *Des alten Handwerks*, Vol. 2, p. 441; F.G. Mone, 'Die Weberei und ihre Beigewerbe vom 14.–16. Jhd.', *Zeitschrift für Geschichte des Oberrheins* 9 (1858): 174. Restrictions on dyers: NB, QNG, no. 68/I, 311; MU, Ratsitzungsprotokolle, 1558, fol. 133; FF, Bürgermeisterbücher, 1590, fol. 201a; AMS, Akten der XV, 1655, fols. 33, 34. Restrictions on small hat makers: NB, QNG: no. 68/III, 1302 (1597); 1303 (1603); MU, Gewerbeamt, no. 1020, 1603 Krämerordnung; MM, Zünfte, 451(3) (1613); AMS, Akten der XV: 1639, fols. 120, 154, 164, 171, 182; 1665, fol. 94.

10. Wiesner, *Working Women*, pp. 161, 168.

11. Walker, *German Home Towns*, p. 89.

12. Ibid., pp. 104–5.

work denigrated', he agreed to forbid women to work any longer.[13] Cases involving linen-weavers in Saxony, stonemasons in Frankfurt, and brewers in Munich use similar language.[14]

Why guilds which still allowed female labour should have been judged prima facie dishonourable is an interesting question. Jean Quataert proposes one reason, noting that in their attempts to maintain a monopoly on market production, craft guilds devalued all occupations which maintained their connection with household production. She comments: 'By the end of the Thirty Years' War, household production had become inextricably linked with women's work in the eyes of the threatened craftsmen', who attempted to define both as not really work.[15] The male/female dichotomy eventually became more pronounced than the guild/domestic one, so that in the nineteenth century women who spun, washed, or ironed in their own homes were not considered workers (and thus eligible for pensions according to the German industrial code), while male shoemakers or tailors who worked in their own homes were.[16]

I agree with Quataert, but would add male bonding as another reason why guild work was increasingly seen as 'a learned art and given to men alone'.[17] Not only were women excluded, but connections were explicitly established between men, connections which can be traced in the language of early modern guild ordinances. Whereas medieval guild ordinances often spoke about the duty of masters to uphold decorum (*Zucht*), by the eighteenth century masters were instructed specifically to uphold male decorum (a rather inelegant translation of *Manns-Zucht*). For example, an ordinance for the saddlers in Linz in 1750 reads: 'All city and rural masters shall take great pains to maintain proper male decorum among

13. FF, Zünfte, Ugb. C–36, Cc (1649-Huter).

14. Wissell, *Des alten Handwerks*, Vol. 2, p. 444; FF, Ugb. C–38, Z (1624); MU, Ratsitzungsprotokolle, 1599, fol. 164.

15. Jean Quataert, 'The shaping of women's work in manufacturing: guilds, households, and the state in central Europe, 1648–1870', *American Historical Review* 90 (1985): 1124. Quataert's conclusions can also help explain why linen-weaving was considered dishonourable in many parts of Germany, and is included in Walker's list noted above, though in most places wool-weaving was a perfectly respectable or even high-status occupation. Walker comments that linen-weaving was dishonourable because it was 'primitive' and had 'suspect rural overtones and connections' (*German Home Towns*, p. 104) while Quataert is more specific: 'Those activities, like linen weaving, that remained closely associated with the household economy never achieved high social value' ('Shaping', p. 1147).

16. Quataert, 'Shaping', p. 1146. This is a good example of the way in which gender can come to take precedence over all other variables, subsuming even those with which it was originally linked.

17. MU, Ratsitzungsprotokolle, 1599, fol. 164.

themselves, and to instruct their apprentices and journeymen in such male decorum . . .'; and one from the same city in 1742 for the bakers: 'This ordinance is proclaimed for the preservation of unity and honourable male decorum [*Ehrbarer Manns-zucht*] among masters, journeymen and apprentices.'[18]

There were limits to the level of male bonding that could be achieved in any craft guild, however, because masters were almost always married and one of their main aims was the support of their families. This was not a constraint on journeymen, however, who were usually unmarried, and the journeymen's guilds which grew up in Germany and elsewhere in Europe in the seventeenth century provide an even better example than craft guilds of strong male groups.

In the expanding economies of medieval cities, journeymen were simply part of the craft guild; they had finished their apprenticeship, and travelled from town to town working for different masters as they improved their skills. They looked forward to the time when they, too, could become masters, marry, and establish their own shop and household. This began to change in the sixteenth century as craft guilds became more restrictive and limited membership to sons of masters or those who married a master's widow or daughter. Many journeymen continued to work for a master all their lives, becoming essentially wage labourers. As their work became proletarianized, they began to think of themselves as a group distinct from the masters rather than as masters-in-training (*Gesellen* rather than *Knechte*) and began to form separate journeymen's associations. Tiger comments that the need to form all-male groups and to prove oneself a 'man among men' is strongest among men feeling 'relatively deprived';[19] given their declining social and economic position, the journeymen certainly fit the pattern here.

Because authorities worried they might provoke social and political unrest, journeymen's associations were illegal in some parts of Europe, so their guilds were secret, and often operated out of alehouses, which automatically excluded respectable women.[20] Tiger notes that 'the male bonding process may constitute a strong inducement to

18. Gerhard Danninger, *Das Linzer Handwerk und Gewerbe vom Verfall der Zunfthoheit über die Gewerbefreiheit bis zum Innungszwang. Linzer Schriften zur Sozial- und Wirtschaftsgeschichte*, Vol. 4 (Rudolf Trauner, Linz, 1981), p. 75.

19. Tiger, *Men in Groups*, p. 198.

20. Rudolf M. Dekker, 'Women in revolt: popular protest and its social basis in Holland in the seventeenth and eighteenth centuries', *Theory and Society* 16 (1987): 347; C.R. Dobson, *Masters and Journeymen: A Prehistory of Industrial Relations 1717–1800* (Croom Helm, London, 1980), p. 38.

sever family-of-origin ties and circumscribe reproductive-family activity'.[21] Whether an inducement or a consequence, both of these
tendencies may be seen among journeymen. Their wanderings often
took them from their home towns, and they gained status among
themselves according to how many places they had been to and
how much of the world they had seen.[22] They also expected one
another not to marry, and fervently opposed allowing any married
journeyman the right to work.

Journeymen had originally been forbidden to marry in most craft
guilds because they were expected to live with a master's family
until they could become masters themselves. As their opportunities
to become masters diminished in the sixteenth century, one might
have expected journeymen's guilds to push for the right to marry.
They did in a few cities, but in most they did not.[23] Instead of setting up their own households, they lived in all-male journeymen's
hostels and in some cases pressured guilds which had originally
accepted married journeymen to forbid them.[24] State authorities
trying to promote the free movement of labour in the eighteenth
century ordered journeymen to accept their married colleagues
and provided stiff punishments for those who did not, but opposition remained strong well into the nineteenth century.[25]

This hostility to married journeymen can be partially explained
as an attempt by unmarried journeymen to secure more work places,
but the vehemence with which married journeymen and the masters
who hired them were attacked hints at something deeper. As their
opportunities to become masters or to amass actual capital declined,
journeymen became increasingly obsessed by what Andreas Grießinger
has nicely called 'the symbolic capital of honour'. Craft guilds had
always been concerned about honour, and often demanded higher
standards of honour for membership than that required for citizenship or an official position; for example, guilds refused to allow

21. Tiger, *Men in Groups*, p. 135.
22. Andreas Grießinger, *Das Symbolische Kapital der Ehre: Streikbewegungen und
kollektives Bewußtsein deutscher Handwerksgesellen im 18. Jahrhundert* (Ullstein Materialen,
Frankfurt, 1981), pp. 67–8.
23. For an example of a city where journeymen did demand the right to marry,
see AMS, Akten der XXI, 1620 on.
24. Walker, *German Home Towns*, p. 83; Wissell, *Des alten Handwerks*, Vol. 2, p. 448;
Klaus Schwarz, *Die Lage der Handwerksgesellen in Bremen während des 18. Jahrhunderts*,
Veröffentlichungen aus dem Staatsarchiv der Freien Hansestadt Bremen, Vol. 44
(Staatsarchiv, Bremen, 1975), p. 38.
25. See, for example, the Imperial Trades Edict of 1731, translated in Walker,
German Home Towns, p. 448, and a proclamation of Maria Theresa in 1770, reprinted
in Wissell, *Des alten Handwerks*, Vol. 2, p. 449.

those legitimized after they were born to become members, until they were forced to by imperial ordinances in the eighteenth and nineteenth centuries.[26] Journeymen became the most vigorous guardians of a shop's honour, because they needed to be accepted elsewhere and thus 'their careers were more threatened by the taint of dishonour than an established master's was'.[27]

Because losing his honour meant a journeyman also lost the right to a work place, honour was an economic commodity for him in the same way as his training. At times their concern for honour caused journeymen to do things which worked against their own economic interests, however. They developed elaborate initiation rituals, and achieved high prestige by learning and transmitting these rituals, or by serving as a guild officer, even if the time spent resulted in a loss of wages.[28] They refused to work in the shops of masters who were suspected of moral infractions, though this meant a decline in the total number of work places available.[29] In some cases they refused to work for any master of a guild deemed less than honourable, simply avoiding certain cities in their travels, despite laws which prohibited this and prison sentences enforcing those laws.[30]

Journeymen forced one another to comply with their code of honour by refusing to work next to any journeyman who had broken the code, and reinforced their bonds with each other when they travelled.[31] Journeymen's practice of going from town to town assured that the names of those reprimanded or banned would be known throughout a broad area even if a formal guild did not exist; such banning often lasted for decades.[32] Though their local influence was less than that of craft guild masters, their transient status gave journeymen a great deal of influence throughout the Empire, perhaps more than they had in the centralized states of western Europe.

Not working next to women became an important part of journeymen's notion of honour. Journeymen originally objected to women's work for economic reasons, viewing women as taking work

26. Wissell, *Des alten Handwerks*, Vol. 1 pp. 253–4.
27. Walker, *German Home Towns*, p. 94.
28. Grießinger, *Symbolische Kapital*, p. 451.
29. Wissell, *Des alten Handwerks*, Vol. 1, p. 271; Frank Göttman, *Handwerk und Bundnispolitik: Die Handwerkerbände am Mittelrhein vom 14. bis zum 17. Jahrhundert*. Frankfurter Historische Abhandlungen, no. 15 (Steiner, Wiesbaden, 1977), pp. 153, 280; AMS, Akten der XV, 1628, fols. 152, 164.
30. Wissell, *Des alten Handwerks*, Vol. 1, pp. 269, 272.
31. Ibid., Vol. 1, p. 257.
32. Ibid., Vol. 2, p. 232; Walker, *German Home Towns*, p. 83.

places they regarded as rightfully theirs. During the sixteenth century, women's work also became a political issue for journeymen; as their opportunities to become masters declined, forcing a master's female servants, wife, and daughters out of a shop became one way of demonstrating their power *vis-à-vis* the masters. In order to accomplish this, journeymen began to argue that any shop or guild which allowed female labour was tainted.

Journeymen's attempts to differentiate their work sharply from that of women came at exactly the same time that their actual work situation was becoming more like that of women. No longer was the position of journeyman necessarily simply a stage in the male life cycle; rather it was a permanent state, leaving one dependent on a master for wages. Because journeymen generally had little or no real property or goods, their honour was their most important economic asset, in the same way that it was for women; for women, a loss of honour might also bring economic devastation because of the resultant loss of marital opportunities. Joan Kelly-Gadol has noted that courtiers during the Renaissance became more like women in their dependent status, and so may have been increasingly motivated to limit the independence of their female relatives.[33] Could something similar have been operating here with journeymen, at least on a subconscious level?

Whatever the reasons for their hostility to women's work, journeymen carried this idea with them from town to town, and forced guilds in many towns to prohibit work by female servants for the first time in the seventeenth and eighteenth centuries.[34] As with other parts of their code of honour, they enforced this by refusing to work with any journeyman who had worked next to a woman, forcing guilds in every city to comply. The first attempts by state authorities to compel journeymen to relax their code of honour precipitated a wave of strikes and riots in the 1720s, and an imperial edict of 1772 permitting women to work in crafts had little practical effect.[35] A later Prussian edict again allowing women to work

33. Joan Kelly-Gadol, 'Did women have a Renaissance?' in *Becoming Visible: Women in European History*, 2nd edn, ed. Renate Bridenthal, Claudia Koonz and Susan Stuard (Houghton Mifflin, Boston, 1987), p. 196.

34. Wissell, *Des alten Handwerks*, Vol. 2, pp. 448–9; Karl Heinrich Kaufhold, *Das Handwerk der Stadt Hildesheim im 18. Jahrhundert*, Göttinger Beiträge zur Wirtschafts- und Sozialgeschichte (Otto Schwarz, Göttingen, 1980), p. 118; NB, Quellen zur Nürnbergische Geschichte, no. 68/III, 1108.

35. Walker, *German Home Towns*, p. 84; Grießinger, *Symbolische Kapital*, passim; Wissell, *Des alten Handwerks*, Vol. 2, p. 445; Beata Brodmeier, *Die Frau im Handwerk*, Forschungsberichte aus dem Handwerk, Vol. 9 (Handwerkswissenschaftlichen Institut, Münster, 1963), pp. 19, 36.

specifically ordered that journeymen were not to be punished or censured for working next to a woman, but this, too, probably had little effect.[36]

Once the notion that women made a *shop* dishonourable took hold among journeymen, it was not very far to the idea that all contact with women was dishonourable, which helps explain their hostility toward marriage and their married colleagues. This is also one reason why they banned any journeyman known to frequent prostitutes or engage in other forms of 'licentious behaviour'; not only was this dishonourable in the same way as any moral infraction, but it also meant that the individual had had contact with a woman. Though prohibitions of contact with prostitutes were certainly not effective everywhere, they did in some cases lead to a journeyman's being barred from work.[37] Combined with the hostility to marriage, this left journeymen with few sexual outlets, making journeymen's guilds a good example of a group in which the need for male bonding was 'functionally equivalent to, and probably more powerful than, the development of a sexual bond'.[38]

During the early modern period, then, skilled work in guild shops was increasingly defined as men's work, and the 'mystery' of any 'craft', the 'secrets of the trade' as something which should not be shared with women. (I put these words in quotes because they are often used interchangeably, though we usually forget the connotations of secrecy when using the word 'craft'.) The craft guilds themselves, and even more the journeymen's guilds which were both part of and in opposition to the craft guilds, became totally male groups.

Of course, the vast majority of those working in guild shops, and certainly the vast majority of masters, had always been male, so one might question whether this was really much of a change. Because so many female artisans were the wives, daughters, widows, and maids of masters, and because their participation in crafts was informal rather than regulated by the formal apprenticeship structure, it is difficult to quantify the effects of the exclusion of women. Nevertheless, one can find evidence that women's work in the crafts was actually declining, and that the goal of an all-male workshop was being achieved.

As crafts gradually imposed restrictions on the rights of widows during the fifteenth and sixteenth centuries, many widows appealed

36. Wissell, *Des alten Handwerks*, Vol. 2, p. 445.
37. Ibid., pp. 140, 271; Schmidt and Bücher, *Frankfurter Amts*, p. 280.
38. Tiger, *Men in Groups*, p. 172.

to city councils or other authorities for the right to keep working. In some cases they were allowed, and in others not, though nowhere in Germany did a city council categorically permit widows the right to continue their husbands' shops.[39] Continuing a shop was thus a special privilege based on a council's generosity and the merits of the case, not a widow's right, though, as noted above, 10–15 per cent of guild shops in some cities continued to be run by widows or other women during the sixteenth century. By the seventeenth century, however, some widows began to request the right to give up their shops, even though this ended their children's rights to remain in the guild.[40] As all guilds by this time had very high entrance fees, this also meant that the children would generally be reduced to doing piecework, working as servants or unskilled labourers, or working in an unregulated craft, with very little opportunity of entering the guild again. This affected sons directly, but also daughters, whose rights to pass on a guild membership to their husbands might have been worth more than any cash dowry.

Why would a widow give up her shop and impoverish her children? This was not her free choice, but the result of guild restrictions. Prohibited from utilizing journeymen or apprentices, she could not produce enough even to pay guild fees. A recent study of weavers in Augsburg around 1600 finds that 15 per cent of the master weavers were women, but they employed only 5 per cent of the journeymen and apprentices. As we would expect, tax records indicate that most of these women were very poor.[41] Widows were always vastly over-represented among the 'very poor' in every city.[42]

A more complicated question is why guilds would act against the interests of the widows and children of their own members. One of

39. FF, Zünfte, Ugb. D–2, F (1506); C–43, L (1600); C–59, Gg, no. 3 and Aa no. 4 (1672); AMS, Akten der XV: 1607, fol. 147; 1610, fols. 146, 156, 198, 225; 1618, fols. 8, 14, 20, 28, 119; 1617, fols. 84, 144, 247; 1633, fols. 88, 154, 173, 177, 178, 230, 232; MM, Ratsprotokollbücher: 15 September 1556; 8 November 1560. Inger Dübeck has discovered that in Denmark, as well, city governments did occasionally grant widows' privileges against the wishes of a guild. (*Københoner og Konkurrence* (Juristforbundets, Copenhagen, 1978), pp. 395–404.)

40. MU, Gewerbeamt, no. 2293; AMS, Akten der XV, 1608, fol. 22.

41. Claus-Peter Clasen, *Die Augsburger Weber: Leistungen und Krisen des Textilgewerbes um 1600.* Abhandlungen zur Geschichte der Stadt Augsburg, no. 27 (Muhlberger, Augsburg, 1981), pp. 23, 59.

42. Roper, 'Urban women', p. 6; MU, Steuerbücher (1410–1640). This was also true in English cities, as Diana Willen reports for Warwick, Salisbury, Ipswich and Norwich ('Women in the public sphere in early modern England: the case of the urban working poor', *Sixteenth Century Journal* 9 (Winter 1988): 562) and Mary Prior for Oxford ('Women and the urban economy: Oxford 1500–1800' in her *Women in English Society, 1500–1800* (Methuen, London, 1985), p. 106). Prior also notes that only a tiny share of masters' widows took on apprentices.

the main aims of the craft guilds had always been the maintenance of masters' families; numerous ordinances which favoured masters' sons and those who married masters' widows or daughters point out the importance of the familial and social aspects of a mastership in an era before pensions and social security. Preserving the male nature of the guild by restricting widows' rights worked at cross-purposes to this, but in this instance excluding women from skilled work seems to have been judged more important to many guilds. A statistical study of how businesses were passed down among the joiners and corset-makers in Vienna during the Thirty Years War indicates that roughly 10 per cent were handed down to sons, between 12 per cent and 18 per cent to journeymen who married a widow or daughter, and more than 70 per cent were simply purchased by strangers.[43] Christopher Friedrichs' sample of the occupations of brides and grooms in early modern Nördlingen also shows that only a small minority of men married within the same occupation or took the occupation of their bride's father or former husband.[44] Connecting through women was not a typical way of moving from one all-male group to another, nor did marriage 'serve as a mechanism to promote occupational solidarity'.[45]

Just as widows no longer had any real 'rights' to continue operating a shop, they also had no rights to support in the way male members did. Supporting one's guild brothers in times of need was a way of reinforcing trade solidarity, while supporting widows was a way to show the guild's devotional philanthropy, a distinction evidenced by the fact that guilds often supported needy women who were not widows of guild masters, while they never supported non-guild men.[46] Widows asking for support or for special consideration were most successful when they pleaded extreme poverty and need rather than craft ties: 'How heavy and hard the hand of God, himself burdened with the cross, has come down on me, and in what a pitiful situation I find myself after the all-too-sudden death of my late husband, with my young and helpless child still nursing at my breast.'[47]

43. Heinz Zatschek, 'Aus der Geschichte des Wiener Handwerks während des 30 jährigen Krieges: Eine soziologische Studie', *Jahrbuch des Verein für Geschichte der Stadt Wien*, 9 (1951), p. 33.
44. Christopher R. Friedrichs, *Urban Society in an Age of War: Nördlingen, 1580–1720* (Princeton University Press, Princeton, 1979), p. 86.
45. Ibid., p. 87.
46. Roper, 'Urban women', p. 9. MacKenney also found this to be true in Venice (*Tradesmen and Traders*, p. 70).
47. FF, Zünfte, Ugb. D–24, L4 (1698).

Journeymen's efforts to force masters' wives, daughters, and female servants out of guild shops also appear to have been quite successful, at least judging by the number of times such restrictions are upheld by city councils.[48] Though this often put the councils in opposition to guild masters, the councils justified their actions by commenting that other cities had already given in to the journeymen, so that they would have to follow suit or risk economic decline from journeymen boycotts. In fact, some cities were even more active in courting journeymen, offering them the right to decide who would be hired in a workshop (the *Schenkwesen*), to draw them away from cities where masters held this right.[49] Given the journeymen's attitude toward women's work, their holding the *Schenkwesen* was not beneficial to women's employment. In 1607, for example, journeymen cord-makers in Frankfurt forced the masters there to stop employing female servants in the shop, and only to use their daughters for finishing and cleaning; in 1701, journeymen bookbinders in Nuremberg were able to exclude all women.[50] As noted above, only with the growth of more centralized state power in Germany were laws passed against journeymen; no city had the economic power to do this alone. Women were thus relegated to work outside the craft guilds in the expanding domestic industries or in trades which were not organized as a guild, trades which did not demand a high level of skill.

One might argue that the changes discussed here were not all that significant for women. Weren't craft guilds themselves in decline during this period? Wouldn't journeymen's guilds lose their meaning and eventually disappear with industrialism? What did it matter that women were excluded from a vanishing part of the economy?

There are three ways to answer these objections. First, as Mack Walker has so ably demonstrated, craft guilds remained the most important part of the economy in many cities of Germany,

48. NB, QNG, no.˜68/II, 663, 674, 847, 853, 873; no. 68/III, 1093, 1107, 1189; Augsburg Handwercksordnungen, 1550, Nestler and Huter: Wachendorf, p. 63; Martha Howell, *Women, Production and Patriarchy in Late Medieval Cities* (University of Chicago Press, Chicago, 1986), p. 91.

49. Ernst Mummenhoff, 'Frauenarbeit und Arbeitsvermittlung: Eine Episode aus der Handwerksgeschichte des 16. Jahrhunderts', *Vierteljahrsschrift für Sozial- und Wirtschaftsgeschichte* 199 (1926): 157–65.

50. Schmidt and Bücher, *Frankfurter Amts*, pp. 417–20; Wissell, *Des alten Handwerks*, Vol. 2, p. 448. Alice Clark has discovered that journeymen's organizations and their ability to 'bargain advantageously with the masters' had similar effects on women's work in seventeenth-century England (*Working Life of Women in the Seventeenth Century* (Routledge and Kegan Paul, London, 1919), p. 298).

particularly those slow to industrialize, well into the nineteenth century. They determined the economic policies of many towns, and 'bore political and civic factors into economic practice'.[51]

Second, guilds left a tremendous legacy to industrialism. The craft tradition of reserving skilled work for men continued in the artisan shop, and then the factory, as jobs there which were better paid and required some training went to men, leaving the least skilled jobs for women. Gender divisions within the factory thus mirrored those among artisans outside it. Journeymen's guilds also made important contributions to the development of trade unions.[52] One of their less positive contributions was the hostility toward women's work which many trade unions exhibited, though this also had other roots in the industrial economy.

Third, the guild concept of the strongest bonds being those between men had implications far beyond the realm of economics, which has been my main concern here. The guild notion that the workshop was a male preserve gradually became a more generally accepted ideal, predating, as Jean Quataert notes, 'by at least a century the related Romantic notions of separate spheres for males and females'.[53] As R. Po-Chia Hsia has pointed out, 'patriarchal sacred kinship received its inspiration partly from the Old Testament and partly from the social practices of the guilds . . . the artisans of the guild community lived in a social world in which an extra familial male corporation, with its ideology of a fictive kinship, a fraternity, reinforced their own positions as heads of households, as fathers and husbands, within the nuclear family'.[54] Though Anthony Black strangely never mentions the masculine nature of guilds, his description of them as 'a seedbed of *fraternity* as a popular belief' is here particularly apt.[55] The male bonds created by craft and journeymen's guilds are in many ways still with us.

51. Walker, *German Home Towns*, p. 77.

52. The links between journeymen's guilds and trade unions have merited surprisingly little study by labour historians. One of the few works which does examine them is R.A. Leeson, *Travelling Brothers: The Six Centuries' Road from Craft Fellowship to Trade Unionism* (George Allen and Unwin, London, 1979), whose title unconsciously supports my point in this paragraph.

53. Quataert, 'Shaping', p. 1147.

54. R. Po-Chia Hsia, 'Münster and Anabaptists', in *The German People and the Reformation*, ed. R. Po-Chia Hsia (Cornell University Press, Ithaca, NY, 1988), p. 69.

55. Anthony Black, *Guilds and Civil Society in European Political Thought from the 12th Century to the Present* (Methuen, London, 1984), p. 31 (my emphasis). Black also notes (p. 55) the connection between guild moral values and city values stressed by both Walker and Hsia.

CHAPTER TEN

Wandervögel *and women:*
journeymen's concepts of masculinity
in early modern Germany[1]

The early modern period has recently been described as a time of the triumph of patriarchy, patrilineal identity and Protestant domestic ideology.[2] Both feminist and non- (or anti-) feminist scholars agree that there was a strengthening in the power of the male head of household through legal and institutional changes, though they often disagree on the merits of these changes and the resulting effects on women's roles and status.[3] The male head of household was not the only model of masculinity which developed in the early modern period, however. Journeymen created their own definition

1. I first began thinking about these issues for a session titled 'Aspetti economici della emarginazione e della discriminazione' for the XXI Settimana di Studi, 'La Donna nell'Economia secc. XIII–XVII', held at the Istituto Internazionale di Storia Economica 'F. Datini' in April of 1989. My remarks there have been translated into Italian and published in *Memoria: Revista di storia delle donne* 27 (1989): 44–67. I would like to thank the Datini Institute for its support in allowing me to attend this conference, and also the conference participants, especially Grethe Jacobsen, Christina Vanja, Hilde Sandvik, Liliane Mottu-Weber, and Brigitte Schnegg, whose comments have greatly influenced this article.

2. Michael Mitterauer and Reinherd Seider, *The European Family: Patriarchy to Partnership from the Middle Ages to the Present*, tr. K. Oosterveew and M. Horzinger (Oxford, 1983); R. Po-Chia Hsia, *Society and Religion in Münster, 1535–1618* (New Haven, CN, 1984); Christiane Klapisch-Zuber, *Women, Family and Ritual in Renaissance Italy*, tr. Lydia Cochrane (Chicago, 1985); David Underdown, 'The taming of the scold: the enforcement of patriarchal authority in early modern England', in Anthony Fletcher and John Stevenson, eds, *Order and Disorder in Early Modern England* (Cambridge, 1985); Margaret Ezell, *The Patriarch's Wife: Literary Evidence and the History of the Family* (London, 1987); Susan Cahn, *Industry of Devotion: The Transformation of Women's Work in England, 1500–1660* (New York, 1987).

3. Natalie Davis, 'Women on top', in her *Society and Culture in Early Modern France* (Stanford, CA, 1975); Lawrence Stone, *The Family, Sex, and Marriage in England 1500–1800* (London, 1977); Steven Ozment, *When Fathers Ruled: Family Life in Reformation Europe* (Cambridge, MA, 1983); Lyndal Roper, *The Holy Household: Women and Morals in Reformation Augsburg* (Oxford, 1989). See also my essay 'Frail, weak, and helpless: women's legal position in theory and practice' elsewhere in this volume.

of manhood, a definition achieved not only in opposition to notions of womanhood, but also to the ideal of manhood proposed by religious and political authorities. This definition, I hope to show in this article, was at the same time anti-patriarchal and anti-female, providing those of us who have also criticized early modern patriarchy with some rather embarrassing bedfellows.

I became interested in journeymen during my research on early modern working women in Germany, when I discovered that journeymen frequently strenuously opposed any women working in guild shops. Though often this can be explained fairly easily as resulting from a desire to secure more work places for themselves, at times journeymen's opposition to women worked to their own economic disadvantage. For example, their demands that widows who were running craft shops should not be able to hire any journeymen limited the number of work places available to them. As they demanded that all tasks in a shop, even the most unskilled such as preparing raw materials or packing finished products, be reserved for a journeyman or apprentice, their own wages suffered as such tasks were paid at a lower rate than the more highly skilled ones. Journeymen's opposition to female labour thus cannot be explained solely on economic grounds; the violence of their attacks makes it clear that there is something else at work here.

Some of journeymen's hostility to women working grew out of more general craft guild restrictions on women, which began in Germany during the mid-fifteenth century.[4] Though the timing of these restrictions and their specifics varied from craft to craft and from city to city, in general masters' widows were increasingly limited in the length of time they could keep operating a shop, female servants were prohibited from doing any production-related tasks, and all women were limited to producing lower-priced, lower-quality goods. This gradual exclusion of women from craft guilds was motivated in part by economic pressures, but also by an ideology of guild honour which held that the workshop was a male preserve, and that working next to a woman or in a guild which still accepted women made one just as dishonourable as being born out of wedlock or having servile ancestry.[5] Female labour made a guild

---

4. See my essay 'Guilds, male bonding and women's work in early modern Germany' elsewhere in this volume for a longer discussion of this, and also Martha Howell, *Women, Production and Patriarchy in Late Medieval Cities* (Chicago, 1986), for an analysis of women's declining role in the crafts in Leiden and Cologne.

5. Mack Walker, in *German Home Towns: Community, State, and General Estate 1648–1871* (Ithaca, NY, 1971), discusses the idea of guild honour extensively.

dishonourable in part because it was linked with household production in the eyes of craftsmen who were attempting to maintain
a monopoly on market production.[6] Craft guilds were also coming
to view themselves explicitly as a group of men, and whatever they
did as 'a learned art and given to men alone'.[7] No longer was a
good shop one in which there was simply decorum (*Zucht*), but
'honourable male decorum' (*ehrbarer Manns Zucht*).[8]

Though they increasingly viewed their shops as a male preserve
craft guilds, or more properly said, guild masters, could not go
too far in judging women as a group dishonourable. Most guilds
required that masters marry, as they recognized that a wife was
essential in allowing a shop to function. She not only fed and clothed
the journeymen and apprentices, but often sold the products of the
shop at the city market and purchased raw materials. In her husband's absence she ran the shop. Other women might taint the
shop, but not the master's wife; the restrictions on women's work
imposed by the guilds themselves pointedly did not include the
master's wife.

Ideology also set a limit on the guild masters' disparagement of
women, particularly after the Protestant Reformation. Martin Luther's
critique of celibacy and championing of marriage made the ideal
woman in much of Germany the wife and mother.[9] Protestant pamphleteers extolled the family as the foundation of society, and later in
the sixteenth century Catholic writers also somewhat begrudgingly
began to praise marriage as a perfectly honourable Christian way of
life. In fact, this positive evaluation of marriage had begun before
the Reformation with some of the Italian and English civic humanists, so that German Catholic authors had acceptable authorities
to quote and did not have to admit that they were responding to
Protestant views.[10] Books and pamphlets advising men on how to

6. Jean Quataert, 'The shaping of women's work in manufacturing: guilds, households, and the state in central Europe, 1648–1870', *American Historical Review* 90
(1985): 1122–48.

7. Munich Stadtarchiv, Ratsitzungsprotokolle, 1599, fol. 164.

8. 1742 baker's ordinance in Linz, quoted in Gerhard Danninger, *Das Linzer Handwerk und Gewerbe vom Verfall der Zunfthoheit über die Gewerbefreiheit bis zum Innungszwang.*
Linzer Schriften zur Sozial- und Wirtschaftsgeschichte, Vol. 4 (Linz, 1981), p. 75.

9. Merry E. Wiesner, 'Luther and women: the death of two Marys', in James
Obelkevich, Raphael Samuel, and Lyndal Roper, eds, *Disciplines of Faith: Religion,
Patriarchy, and Politics* (London, 1986).

10. John Yost, 'The value of married life for the social order in the early English
Renaissance', *Societas* 6 (1976): 25–39; Margo Todd, 'Humanists, puritans and the
spiritualized household', *Church History* 49 (1980): 18–34; Katherine Davies, 'Continuity and change in literary advice on marriage', in R.B. Outhwaite, ed., *Marriage
and Society: Studies in the Social History of Marriage* (New York, 1981).

be good husbands, fathers, and heads of household abounded (the *Hausväterbücher*), all of which recommended that husbands treat their wives with respect.[11] Women could not be part of the *Mannszucht* of a shop, but they had their own sources of honour in sexual fidelity, obedience, motherhood, and piety. Because so much of his self-identity was that of husband and head of household, a guild master could not criticize women too sharply without implicitly criticizing himself.

These economic and ideological limits to hostility to women's work and women in general did not apply to journeymen, who for most of the medieval and early modern period were unmarried and in most trades were explicitly prohibited from being heads of households. Journeymen began forming associations independent of masters in Germany in the early fourteenth century in weaving, and in the early fifteenth century in other trades. These associations were first studied in Germany over a century ago, as part of an interest in the roots of what were then contemporary industrial workers' organizations.[12] Despite some voices to the contrary, the general conclusion seems to have been that they, like craft guilds, did not really represent 'the working class', and thus, because they were not truly 'protoproletariat', they were largely ignored until very recently by historians of labour. This lack of attention has changed in the last decade, and a number of German and American scholars have made both regional and more broadly based studies of journeymen and their organizations.[13]

11. Cyriacus Spangenburg, *Ehespiegel* (Strasbourg, 1556); Andreas Musculus, *Wider den Eheteuffel* (Frankfurt, 1556).

12. G. Schanz, *Zur Geschichte der deutschen Gesellenverbände* (Leipzig, 1876; reprinted Glashütten in Taunus, 1974); B. Schoenlank, *Soziale Kämpfe vor dreihundert Jahren: Altnürnbergische Studium* (Leipzig, 1907).

13. Andreas Grießinger, *Das symbolische Kapital der Ehre: Streikbewegungen und kollektives Bewußtsein deutscher Handwerksgesellen im 18. Jahrhundert* (Frankfurt, 1981); Wilfried Reininghaus, *Die Entstehung der Gesellengilden im Spätmittelalter* (Wiesbaden, 1981); Karlheinz Bade, 'Altes Handwerk, Wanderzwang und Gute Policey: Gesellenwanderung zwichen Zünftökonomie und Gewerbereform', *Vierteljahrsschrift für Sozial- und Wirtschaftsgeschichte* 69 (1982): 1–37; Knut Schulz, *Handwerksgesellen und Lohnarbeiter: Untersuchungen zur oberrheinischen und oberdeutschen Stadtgeschichte des 14. bis 17. Jahrhunderts* (Sigmaringen, 1985); Michael Neufeld, 'German artisans and political repression: the fall of the journeymen's associations in Nuremberg, 1806–1868', *Journal of Social History* 19 (1985–86): 492–502. Journeymen's associations in France and England have also been the subject of recent scholarly and popular studies. See especially: Eric Hobsbawm, *Labouring Men: Studies in the History of Labour* (London, 1964); Cynthia Truant, 'Solidarity and symbolism among journeymen artisans', *Comparative Studies in Society and History* 21 (1979): 214–26; R.A. Leeson, *Travelling Brothers: The Six Centuries' Road from Craft Fellowship to Trade Unionism* (London, 1979); C.R. Dobson, *Masters and Journeymen: A Prehistory of Industrial Relations* (London,

Only rarely in this new research, however, do the authors note what is to my mind the most striking thing about journeymen's associations – that these were associations made up almost exclusively of men. Other than a few female members in some of the early associations that were primarily religious in orientation and purpose (more on that in a moment), they were totally male bodies, but no one has considered how their masculine nature might have influenced their aims and actions.

This neglect of the obvious may come from the fact that we as historians are so used to studying groups of men that we only feel it necessary to comment when our focus of study is *not* a man or group of men. (Who calls Michelangelo a male artist, or the scholastics male philosophers?) In this case, however, gender is particularly important, for the journeymen not only were men, but came to define themselves primarily by their masculinity and their membership of an all-male group. Their opposition to women may have had some of its roots in craft guild restrictions on women's work, but they were able to carry their opposition much further than guild masters could, who were required to live and work with at least one woman.

When they were first founded, journeymen's organizations had a variety of aims, none of which was the explicit restriction of women's work. They were to provide financial support for journeymen who had been injured or were not able to find a position, arrange for memorial masses and hold regular memorial services, bargain for better wages and working conditions, help journeymen who were new in town find positions, erect an altar in or establish a special relationship with a local church or chapel. In order to accomplish their aims, they began to collect small fees from journeymen, and to meet regularly to decide future actions and how to deal with those who did not meet their obligations.

1980); Daniel Roche, 'Work, fellowship and some economic realities of 18th-century France', in Laurence Kaplan and Cynthia J. Koepp, eds, *Work in France: Representations, Meaning, Organization, Practice* (Ithaca, NY, 1986), pp. 54–73; Michael Sonenscher, 'Journeymen's migrations and workshop organization in 18th-century France', in Kaplan and Koepp, eds, *Work in France*, pp. 74–96, and 'Mythical work: workshop production and the *compagnonnages* of eighteenth-century France', in Patrick Joyce, ed., *The Historical Meanings of Work* (London, 1987); John Rule, 'The property of skill in the period of manufacture', in Joyce, ed., *Meanings*. There are also a number of older studies available for France: G. Martin, *Les Associations ouvrières au XVIII Siècle, 1700–1792* (Paris, 1900); E.M. Saint-Leon, *Le Compagnonnage, son Histoire, ses Coutumes, ses Règlements et ses Rites* (Paris, 1901); E. Coornaert, *Les Compagnonnages en France* (Paris, 1966).

The structure of these organizations and the balance between their religious/charitable aims and their economic aims varied widely throughout Germany. In some places two separate organizations were set up, a small one made up of only journeymen to handle strictly work-related issues, and a larger one, essentially a religious confraternity, which sometimes admitted individuals who were not journeymen. It was this larger group that before the Reformation occasionally admitted women, particularly during times when the number of current journeymen was not high enough to pay the costs of all religious services deemed necessary. The degree to which these two organizations were distinct from one another is hotly debated at this point, a debate which has become quite bitter and personal and which to a degree revolves around what a journeymen's organization chose to call itself.[14] This issue is part of a larger debate about what to call journeymen's organizations – associations, brotherhoods, guilds, societies – and whether contemporaries were making distinctions when they used different terms (e.g. *Genossenschaft, Gesellschaft, Verbände, Brüderschaft*). In some ways the whole debate is more about terminology than substance, and for our purposes quite pointless. The only groups which did admit even a few women were those which had simply religious functions; a woman might occasionally pay a group which had mixed religious and economic functions to light a few candles for her, but she was never considered a full member in terms of economic rights.

Both the craft guilds and the municipal authorities were often suspicious or openly hostile to these journeymen's organizations, but all attempts at suppressing them failed. If a city forbade the journeymen from organizing or attempted to restrict the actions of their organizations, the journeymen simply left that city and went elsewhere. This happened in 1551 and 1568 in Nuremberg and throughout the sixteenth century in other cities.[15] Even imperial edicts were not successful: the imperial diet (*Reichstag*) promulgated edicts against separate journeymen's associations in 1530, 1548, 1551, 1566, 1570, and 1577, with practically no effect.[16] The cities of the Empire were simply unable to develop a common policy toward the journeymen's demands, something which Swiss

---

14. Wilfred Reininghaus, 'Zur Methodik der Handwerksgeschichte des 14–17. Jhds', *Vierteljahrsschrift für Sozial- und Wirtschaftsgeschichte* 72 (1985): 369–78; Knut Schulz, 'Bemerkungen zur Diskussion um die Handwerksgesellen und über den Umgang mit Quellen', *VSW* 73 (1986): 355–61.

15. Schoenlank, *Soziale Kämpfe*, pp. 90–102.

16. Schulz, *Handwerksgesellen*, p. 149.

cities *were* able to do. In 1475 the Swiss cities stood up to a strike by journeymen, telling all those who were from the Empire that they would be forced to leave if they persisted in claiming the right to punish those who broke the rules of their organization. This was the last major action by journeymen in Switzerland, and many of their organizations there disappeared.[17]

The Swiss example points out what would become the key issue for both journeymen and those trying to suppress their organizations – the right to punish those who broke their rules, the right to have independent jurisdiction (*Gerichtsbarkeit*) over members. Without this right, journeymen's organizations would always remain more or less voluntary, a fact which was not lost on journeymen at the time. As they established separate organizations, they set up schedules of fines for those who broke group rules, and also demanded the right of placement. They, not the masters, would determine if a journeyman would be given a position in a workshop, and, more importantly, if journeymen would be sent to a workshop. Their right of placement gave them power thus not only over their own members, but also over the masters. The masters fought their claims to the right of placement bitterly, but were largely unsuccessful again because of the inability of German cities to unite on this.[18]

The journeymen's organizations built up group solidarity through a variety of means. New members went through an increasingly elaborate initiation ritual, modelled on Christian baptism, in which they were often given a new name and an older member who would be their 'godfather'.[19] There they learned a secret oath, secret originally because journeymen's guilds were ostensibly prohibited, but one which remained secret because this increased group cohesion. The organization met regularly, at least monthly and in some cases weekly, holding what was termed a 'Schenke' to welcome journeymen who were new in town, bid farewell to those leaving, and report any members who had violated rules. At first these meetings were held in public taverns, but many organizations arranged to

17. Anne-Marie Dubler, *Handwerk, Gewerbe und Zünft in Stadt und Landschaft Luzern*, Luzerner Historische Veröffentlichungen, Vol. 14 (Lucern, 1982), pp. 99–101.

18. Reininghaus, *Entstehung*, p. 156. Even areas which saw more political unity were generally forced to give in to the journeymen on this, however, for they won the right of placement in France and England as well, though somewhat later than they won it in the Empire. (Leeson, *Travelling Brothers*, p. 45; Cynthia Truant, 'Independent and insolent: journeymen and their "rites" in the Old Regime workplace', in Kaplan and Koepp, eds, *Work in France*, pp. 132, 139.)

19. Reininghaus, *Entstehung*, pp. 86, 214; Schulz, *Handwerksgesellen*, p. 137; Truant, 'Independent', p. 142.

have permanent private drinking rooms (*Trinkstube*) which they decorated and maintained. In addition to the regular *Schenke*, journeymen also held periodic memorial services where they remembered their dead colleagues as well as those who had simply moved away.[20] At this service, the names of both living and dead members were often read aloud, connecting the present with the past, and implying also a connection with the future because those listening knew that at some point they, too, would join the list of past members.

Nothing in the regulations and rituals described so far necessitated an all-masculine context, and, as mentioned, during the fifteenth century journeymen were not especially anti-female in their aims or actions. This changed in the sixteenth century when the economic situation of most journeymen worsened. In the late Middle Ages, journeymen had looked forward to the time when they, too, could become masters, marry, and establish their own shop and household. They formed or joined separate journeymen's organizations, but viewed their membership as temporary, ending when they opened their own shops. This began to change in the sixteenth century as craft guilds, feeling economically threatened, became more restrictive and limited membership to sons of masters or those who married a master's widow or daughter. Many journeymen continued to work for a master all their lives, becoming essentially wage labourers rather than masters-in-training. Their work became proletarianized and their affiliation with a journeymen's association became a life-long or at least very long-term one. They demanded the right to march as a separate group in municipal processions, clearly demarcating their distinction from the masters. Journeymen took two restrictions initially placed on them by the masters – the prohibition of marriage and the requirement of wandering – and made these the keys to their separate group identity. In doing so, they grew increasingly anti-family and anti-female, as I hope to show in the rest of this article.

Journeymen had originally been forbidden to marry in most craft guilds because they were expected to live with a master's family until they could become masters themselves. As their opportunities to become masters diminished in the sixteenth century, one might have expected journeymen's guilds to push for the right to marry, which they did in a few cities, but in most cases they did not. Instead they became the most vigorous enforcers of the laws against married journeymen, in some cases pressuring guilds which had

20. Reininghaus, *Entstehung*, p. 113.

originally accepted married journeymen to forbid them.[21] In 1578, for example, the journeymen potters received an imperial privilege for their association which forbade any married journeyman to make a masterpiece.[22] In 1597, the journeymen fustian weavers in Nuremberg forced the masters there to agree never to hire any married journeymen.[23] State authorities trying to promote the free movement of labour in the eighteenth century ordered journeymen to accept their married colleagues and provided stiff punishments for those who did not, but opposition remained strong well into the nineteenth century.[24] By marrying, journeymen automatically came to be considered *Bönhasen* (literally 'bin rabbits', a term used for all illegal workers who were regarded as stealing their food in a way rabbits or cats might from a storage bin) and were driven from jobs in the same way that men who had never been officially trained were.[25]

The hostility to married journeymen can be partially explained as an attempt by unmarried journeymen to secure more work places, but the vehemence with which married journeymen were attacked hints at something deeper. Part of this vehemence may be explained as a rather normal psychological reaction to the realization that they would never have the opportunity to have an independent shop, and, given the decreasing relative value of their wages in the sixteenth century, probably could never afford to have a family anyway. Downgrading what one can't attain seems to be basic human nature.

Another source of the hostility to marriage came from the living arrangements which journeymen developed once their economic situation worsened. Though before the sixteenth century most journeymen had lived in their masters' households, when their status grew more permanent they began to live in all-male journeymen's hostels (*Herberge*). A journeyman's move to such a hostel often occurred after a quarrel with his master or the master's wife,

21. Walker, *Home Towns*, p. 83; Rudolf Wissell, *Des alten Handwerks Recht und Gewohnheit*, Einzelveröffentlichung der historischen Kommission zu Berlin, 7 (Berlin, 1974), Vol. 2, p. 448; Klaus Schwarz, *Die Lage der Handwerksgesellen in Bremen während des 18. Jahrhunderts*, Veröffentlichungen aus dem Staatsarchiv der Freien Hansestadt Bremen, 44 (Bremen, 1975), p. 38.
22. Schulz, *Handwerksgesellen*, p. 158.
23. Schoenlank, *Soziale Kämpfe*, p. 137.
24. See, for example, the Imperial Trades Edict of 1731, translated in Walker, *Home Towns*, p. 448, and a proclamation of Maria Theresa in 1770, reprinted in Wissell, *Alten Handwerks*, Vol. 1, p. 449.
25. Wissell, *Alten Handwerks*, Vol. 2, pp. 446–50.

or when a master was being boycotted. It is important to remember that a strike or boycott by journeymen who lived with their employers meant more than just a work stoppage; it also meant having to find a new place of residence and severing ties with the master's family. Thus by living in a hostel, journeymen could keep strikes from becoming family quarrels. In many cities these hostels replaced the drinking room as the site of the *Schenke* and other ceremonies, and provided the journeymen with a substitute for family life. What began as a necessity was translated into a virtue as journeymen increasingly spent what little disposable income they had on ceremonies in their drinking room or hostel rather than saving it for a future family.[26] They attempted to limit their connection with the master's family by trying to get their meals sent to them in the hostel, a practice which most cities prohibited.[27] Apparently they were more comfortable eating with each other than with the master's family, where their demeanour and portions would be both observed and to some degree controlled not only by the master but also by his wife.

This increasing orientation toward their all-male residence fits in well with theories of male bonding developed by sociologists and psychologists. In the words of Lionel Tiger, 'Males consciously create secret groups for the gregarious and efficacious control of political, religious, and/or economic worlds, and for the enjoyment of male company under emotionally satisfying conditions.'[28] Tiger comments that the need to form all-male groups and to prove oneself a 'man among men' is strongest among men feeling 'relatively deprived'; given their declining social and economic position, the journeymen certainly fit the pattern here.

Several of Tiger's other findings about male bonding also appear to apply to journeymen. He notes: 'the male bonding process may constitute a strong inducement to sever family-of-origin ties and circumscribe reproductive-family activity'.[29] We know that journeymen had often broken ties with their birth families by travelling, and certainly opposed marriage in theory, but it is very difficult to document how totally they 'circumscribe[d] reproductive-family activity' in actuality. Most studies of marriage in early modern Germany focus, not surprisingly, on marital age and nuptial rates among women, because they are primarily interested in demographic

26. Grießinger, *Symbolische Kapital*, p. 451; Roche, 'Work', p. 65.
27. Schulz, *Handwerksgesellen*, p. 174.
28. Lionel Tiger, *Men in Groups* (New York, 1969), p. 9.
29. Ibid., p. 135.

questions.[30] A few local studies do look at differences in marital age for men, and age differences between spouses, but, though some of these are broken down by occupational group, they do not consider journeymen as a separate category.[31] Even highly detailed studies based on family reconstitution admit that the one weakness in their marital statistics is the inability to arrive at figures for the proportion of the population who never married.[32] Clearly, further study of marriage registers, where they exist for Germany, is needed to assess whether the hostility to marriage on the part of journeymen actually led to life-long celibacy; this is complicated, however, by the question of whether a journeyman who was marrying would label himself as such, or whether he would be hopeful about the impact of his marriage and call himself 'artisan', or realistic and call himself 'day labourer'. A focus on journeymen will also provide an important nuance in the current debate about the demographic impact of both proletarianization and migration.[33]

Though we can't know at this point how frequently journeymen continued to live in hostels all their lives, we do know that in the middle of the sixteenth century these journeymen's hostels became even more like families when the residents began to call the couple who ran them 'father' and 'mother', and included these individuals in their memorial services.[34] Journeymen might toast their 'mother' at their regular meetings, although I can find no report of these women attending ceremonies the way they apparently did in France.[35] Their apparent respect or fondness for their

30. For a study elsewhere in Europe which does focus on male rates of marriage and which finds a surprisingly high rate of permanent bachelorhood, see Stanley Chojnacki, 'Patriarchy denied? Patrician bachelors in Renaissance Venice' (unpublished paper). I would like to thank Professor Chojnacki for sharing this with me.

31. Arther Imhof, *Historische Demographie als Sozialgeschichte. Gießen und Umgebung vom 17. zum 19. Jhd.* (Darmstadt, 1975), pp. 304–12; John E. Knodel, *Demographic Behavior in the Past: A Study of Fourteen Germany Village Populations in the 18th and 19th Centuries* (Cambridge, 1988), pp. 130–5.

32. Knodel, *Demographic Behavior*, p. 129.

33. For a European-wide discussion, see Charles Tilly, 'Demographic origins of the European proletariat', in David Levine, ed., *Proletarianization and Family History* (New York, 1984), pp. 1–85. For Germany specifically, see Wilhelm Kaltenstadler, *Bevölkerung und Gesellschaft Ostbayerns in Zeitraum der frühen Industrialisierung (1780–1820)* (Kallmünz, 1977), esp. pp. 99–114, 157–89; W.R. Lee, *Population Growth, Economic Development and Social Change in Bavaria 1750–1850* (New York, 1977); Dieter Langenwiesche and Friedrich Lenger, 'Internal migration: persistence and mobility', in Klaus J. Bade, ed., *Population, Labour, and Migration in 19th and 20th Century Germany* (Leamington Spa, 1987), pp. 87–100.

34. Reininghaus, *Entstehung*, p. 160.

35. Truant, 'Independent', p. 143; Sonenscher, 'Mythical work', p. 34; Wendy Gibson, *Women in Seventeenth-century France* (London, 1989), p. 110.

'mother' might be seen as a relaxation of their anti-family stance, but in my opinion something else is at work here. The journeymen begin to use the terms 'father' and 'mother' only after the Reformation, at a time when, especially in the Protestant parts of Germany, the male-headed family was seen as the only acceptable living arrangement. Single-sex households were suspect, even all-male ones. Thus by stressing that they did have 'parents', the journeymen could somewhat mitigate the authorities' distrust of their hostels. With 'parents', they not only appeared more like a family, but also as more clearly under the control of an authority figure, something which both Protestant and Catholic authorities regarded as important in the late sixteenth century. The 'mother' had no voice in the actual running of the journeymen's organizations. She was a woman, yes, but one who provided the same sort of inspiration the Virgin Mary had before the Reformation to the many journeymen's confraternities specially dedicated to her honour.[36] (I would love to analyse the journeymen's relation with this mother in psychoanalytical terms, but think this is stretching the point a bit. I will note that many very male-orientated cultures, for example the highly developed *machismo* of contemporary Latin America, also have a strong veneration for actual mothers or mother figures.)

The anti-family sentiment built up in journeymen's hostels or drinking rooms led in some ways quite naturally to an anti-female stance, a stance that was further supported by economic change and the growing hostility to women on the part of the craft guilds noted above. Journeymen originally objected to women's work for economic reasons, viewing women as taking work places they regarded as rightfully theirs. During the sixteenth century, women's work also became a political issue for journeymen; as their opportunities to become masters declined, forcing a master's female servants, wife, and daughters out of a shop became one way of demonstrating their power *vis-à-vis* the masters. They argued that not only should female domestic servants be excluded from a shop, but that the master's female relatives and family members should as well. In their eyes, a shop or guild which continued to allow any female labour was tainted.

A good example of this attitude among journeymen can be seen in a mid-sixteenth century dispute among belt-makers. A Strasbourg

36. Reininghaus, *Entstehung*, p. 112. Her symbolic, rather than political, importance can be seen in reports from France that journeymen accompanied their 'mother' to church with great pomp on the day honouring their patron saint. (Sonenscher, 'Mythical work', p. 44.)

belt-maker, Hans Kranicher, employed his step-daughter until the journeymen protested, and the belt-makers' guild in Strasbourg ordered him to stop utilizing her. They agreed that he should be punished by being forced to work without journeymen for two years, a punishment which the journeymen did not regard as stringent enough. All five journeymen belt-makers left the city, worried that continuing to work there might make them dishonourable in the eyes of their colleagues elsewhere. The Strasbourg master belt-makers brought the issue to an inter-city meeting of belt-makers in Frankfurt, a meeting which included representatives chosen by journeymen. These representatives agreed that journeymen should return to Strasbourg, but they were not able to convince their rank-and-file of this, and ten years later the Strasbourg belt-makers were still working without journeymen, despite repeated attempts to end the boycott on the part of belt-makers in Frankfurt, Worms, Speyer, and Augsburg.[37] Similar cases, though usually not so drawn out, may be found in other German cities. In 1607 journeymen cordmakers in Frankfurt forced the masters there to stop employing female servants in the shop, and to use only their daughters for finishing and cleaning.[38] In 1701, journeymen bookbinders in Nuremberg were able to exclude all women, and in 1703 journeymen tailors successfully pressured the Nuremberg city council to allow them to refuse to work 'next to the masters' relatives or maids'.[39]

Occasionally a city attempted to stand up to the journeymen's hostility toward women. In 1530 the journeymen bagmakers in Nuremberg asked the city council to approve an ordinance regulating their association. (Nuremberg had no independent guilds; all craft guilds and journeymen's associations were under the control of the city council.) The council agreed to accept the ordinance word for word, except for two clauses which prohibited work by married journeymen or maids. Pressure by journeymen resulted in the exclusion of maids anyway, and by the seventeenth century the

---

37. Schoenlank, *Soziale Kämpfe*, pp. 58–66; Ernst Mummenhoff, 'Frauenarbeit und Arbeitsvermittlung: Eine Episode aus der Handwerksgeschichte des 16. Jahrhunderts', *Vierteljahrsschrift für Sozial-und Wirtschaftsgeschichte* 199 (1926): 157–65; Kurt Wesoly, 'Die weibliche Bevölkerungsanteil in spätmittelalterlichen und frühneuzeitlichen Städten und die Betätingung von Frauen im zünftigen Handwerk (ins besondere am Mittel- und Oberrhein)', *Zeitschrift für Geschichte des Oberrheins* 89 (1980), pp. 112–13.

38. Benno Schmidt and Karl Bücher, *Frankfurter Amts- und Zunfturkunden bis zum Jahre 1612*. Veröffentlichungen der historischen Kommission der Stadt Frankfurt a.M., Vol. 6 (Frankfurt, 1914), pp. 417–20.

39. Schoenlank, *Soziale Kämpfe*, p. 144; Wissell, *Alten Handwerks*, Vol. 2, p. 445.

council was approving journeymen's ordinances which specifically prohibited work by maids.[40]

The inability of even a strong city like Nuremberg, which had seen women assisting in craft shops throughout the Middle Ages, to allow work by female domestic servants to continue resulted from the same lack of concerted action that hampered most attempts to forbid journeymen's associations or limit their right of placement. Though craft guilds in Germany were independent in each city, they always paid great attention to what guilds in other cities were doing, and wanted to follow what appeared to be current trends and practices. This tended to militate against women's work in most crafts, as guilds hurried to prohibit or limit it once they realized their counterparts in other cities were doing likewise.[41]

Thus for economic and political reasons, not working next to women became an important part of journeymen's code of honour, at a time when, because their opportunities to become masters or amass actual capital were declining, they were becoming increasingly obsessed by what Andreas Grießinger has called 'the symbolic capital of honour'.[42] Because losing his honour meant a journeyman also lost the right to a work place, honour was an economic commodity for him in the same way that his training was; his career was 'more threatened by the taint of dishonour than an established master's was'.[43] The skills he had acquired were part of his honour – John Rule describes this as 'the property of skill' – but honour also involved knowing and following the very elaborate set of rules established by the journeymen's association.[44] At times their concern for honour caused journeymen to do things which worked against their own economic interests. They achieved high prestige by learning and transmitting the elaborate initiation rituals or by serving as a guild officer, even if the time spent resulted in a loss of wages.[45] They refused to work in the shops of masters who were suspected of moral infractions, though this meant a decline in the total number of work places available.[46] They left cities which tried

40. Schoenlank, *Soziale Kämpfe*, pp. 58–63.
41. See my *Working Women in Renaissance Germany* (New Brunswick, NJ, 1987), pp. 149–85, for a fuller discussion of this.
42. Grießinger, *Symbolische Kapital.*
43. Walker, *Home Towns*, p. 95.
44. Rule, 'Property'.
45. Reininghaus, *Entstehung*, p. 101; Grießinger, *Symbolische Kapital*, p. 451.
46. Strasbourg, Archives Municipales, Akten der XV, 1628, fols. 152, 164; Wissell, *Alten Handwerks*, Vol. 1, pp. 253–4; Frank Göttman, *Handwerk und Bundnispolitik: Die Handwerkerbände am Mittelrhein vom 14. bis zum 17. Jahrhundert.* Frankfurter Historische Abhandlungen, no. 15 (Wiesbaden, 1977), pp. 153, 280.

to restrict their actions or which tried to force them to do things judged less than honourable, despite laws which prohibited this and prison sentences enforcing those laws.[47] They fought other groups of journeymen who had somehow offended their honour, though this led to injury, inability to work, and occasionally even death.[48]

Journeymen carried their code of honour, including their hostility to women's work, with them when they travelled from town to town. Travelling had always been a tradition for journeymen, instituted originally to encourage the expansion of training and the transfer of skills. Most journeymen travelled at least some distance as early as the fourteenth century, and by the end of the sixteenth century journeymen were obligated to travel for a fixed period of years.[49] This obligatory period of travel was originally set by the masters in order to lessen competition for places – during their wanderings, some journeymen died, some turned to crime and others were drafted into one or another army, which made them ineligible for future guild membership.[50] Those who were assured of a place, generally masters' sons, were usually exempted from the requirement of wandering. Rather than opposing the requirement of wandering, however, the journeymen turned it into something positive. They gained status among themselves and thus increased their honour according to how many places they had been and how much of the world they had seen.[51] In their eyes, a *Wandervogel* (literally, wandering bird) was a hero and not the suspect creature he was to political authorities who favoured stability. Transforming what had been a tradition of moving from town to town into a requirement prevented their settling down, further decreasing their chance of a connection with any past, present, or future family.

Travelling was one of the reasons journeymen's guilds were created in the first place, and also assured that guild actions would be enforced even in areas where formal guilds did not exist. The names of individual masters or journeymen who had been reprimanded or punished were carried by journeymen on their travels, and such individuals were boycotted or excluded throughout a huge area.[52] Travelling also served to help journeymen reinforce their bonds

47. Wissell, *Alten Handwerks*, Vol. 1, p. 271.
48. Grießinger, *Symbolische Kapital*, p. 451; Sonenscher, 'Mythical work', p. 46.
49. Reininghaus, *Entstehung*, p. 49; Bade, 'Altes Handwerk', p. 10.
50. Bade, 'Altes Handwerk', p. 18.
51. Grießinger, *Symbolische Kapital*, p. 68.
52. Wissell, *Alten Handwerks*, Vol. 1, p. 257, Vol. 2, p. 232; Walker, *Home Towns*, p. 83.

with each other, as the most regular ceremonies were those in which an incoming member was welcomed or departing member sent on his way.

Though their local influence was less than that of craft guild masters, their transient status gave journeymen a great deal of influence throughout the Empire, perhaps more than they had in the centralized states of western Europe. They recognized this power, and were very unwilling to give it up. The first attempts by state authorities to compel journeymen to relax their code of honour precipitated a wave of strikes and riots in the 1720s, and an imperial edict of 1772 permitting women to work in crafts had little actual effect.[53] A later Prussian edict again allowing women to work specifically ordered that journeymen were not to be punished or censured for working next to a woman, but this, too, probably had little effect.[54] Recent studies of journeymen's associations in western Europe have not commented extensively on the effects of their hostility to women's labour, though years ago Alice Clark noted that journeymen's organizations and their ability to 'bargain advantageously with the masters' had similar deleterious effects on women's work in seventeenth-century England.[55] Their power may have been greater in Germany, but they certainly were not powerless elsewhere.

Once journeymen came to view women as making a *shop* dishonourable, associating with women in other contexts became similarly tainted. By the sixteenth century, journeymen known to frequent prostitutes were banned, whereas earlier mention of prostitutes in journeymen's ordinances had not totally forbidden contact, but had simply prohibited the women from being invited to ceremonies and dances, and limited the days journeymen might visit them in order to exclude holy days and Lent.[56] Though such prohibitions were not effective everywhere, they did occasionally lead to a journeyman's being barred from work.[57] Because they were also hostile to marriage, journeymen were left with no sexual outlet. Their guilds are thus a good example of the type of group Tiger analyses,

53. Walker, *Home Towns*, p. 84; Grießinger, passim; Wissell, *Alten Handwerks*, Vol. 2, p. 445; Beata Brodmeier, *Die Frau im Handwerk*, Forschungsberichte aus dem Handwerk, Vol. 9 (Münster, 1963), p. 19.

54. Wissell, *Alten Handwerks*, Vol. 2, p. 445.

55. Alice Clark, *Working Life of Women in the Seventeenth Century* (London, 1919), p. 298.

56. Reininghaus, *Entstehung*, p. 99.

57. Wissell, *Alten Handwerks*, Vol. 2, pp. 140, 271; Schmidt and Bücher, *Frankfurter Amts*, p. 280.

in which the need for male bonding is 'functionally equivalent to, and probably more powerful than, the development of a sexual bond'.[58]

Perhaps more than any other group of men in the early modern period, journeymen developed a self-identity which was tightly bound to an all-male group. Their notion of what it meant to be a man required that they limit contact with women both within and outside the shop, and that they cut off close family connections. Thus their sense of manliness and masculine honour was very different from that of the master craftsmen, for whom honour involved being the head of a household and family. Transience, prodigality, physical bravery, and comradeliness made one a true man among journeymen, in sharp contrast to the masters' virtues of thrift, reliability, and stability. The journeymen's masculine honour was very class-specific, setting them off not only from women, but also from their employers, whose own ideas of manhood had a religious as well as an economic base. By the end of the sixteenth century, both Protestant and Catholic moralists viewed the patriarchal household as the cornerstone of society, and the 'best man' as the head of that household. This view was echoed by political authorities, who increasingly questioned the wisdom of journeymen's wandering and debated closing the hostels.[59]

Though journeymen's notion of the 'best man' was increasingly at odds with that held by guild masters, religious leaders, and political authorities, it was one which lasted a long time. In assessing the importance of journeymen's identification of themselves as a group of men, we can first point to the survival of journeymen's associations well into the nineteenth century. Journeymen's associations carried out a series of strikes in many cities of Germany during the period 1790–1820, and were supporters, as a group, of many of the 1848 uprisings.[60] In Nuremberg they were still active

58. Tiger, *Men in Groups*, p. 172. Journeymen elsewhere in Europe also developed a growing hostility toward women. Prostitutes in London were the frequent targets of riots by apprentices and journeymen, who also attacked Quakers, a group also known for its 'deviant' women. (S.R. Smith, 'The London apprentices as seventeenth-century adolescents', *Past and Present* 61 (1973): 154–75; Barry Reay, 'Popular hostility towards Quakers in mid-seventeenth century England', *Social History* 5 (1980): 389.) I have not found evidence yet of journeymen in Germany being especially hostile to Anabaptist groups which allowed women to preach, though I would not be surprised if some surfaced. German Anabaptist groups were rarely as sexually egalitarian as the English Quakers, which may partially explain why they were not targets of hostility by journeymen or apprentices.

59. Bade, 'Altes Handwerk', p. 2; Neufeld, 'German artisans', p. 491.

60. Grießinger, *Symbolische Kapital*, passim; Reininghaus, *Entstehung*, pp. 235–43.

until the city repressed them in 1868.[61] Journeymen's opposition to female labour also survived; in the late eighteenth century journeymen silk-makers in Austria fought all attempts to bring women workers into shops, and in 1794 journeymen ribbon-makers in Berlin entered a new ribbon factory there, grabbed the young women who had been employed and beat them.[62]

This last incident points out what is, in my opinion, the greater significance of journeymen's conception of the honourable work place as a place for men only, and of workers as a group of men. This notion did not end when journeymen's associations finally died out, but was carried over into the trade unions that replaced them. The hostility of many trade unions to female labour is well documented and has some economic basis, for women (and children) were used by employers to drive down wages and were often brought in wherever an occupation was deskilled because of technological or organizational change.[63] As in the case of journeymen, however, trade unions also opposed female labour because it was seen as destroying the 'honour' of a shop. To have women working alongside one meant a reduction in one's 'property of skill', even if it brought no actual decrease in wages, for women's work was always judged less 'skilled' than men's, though the actual dexterity and facility required might be more than those in men's work. Jobs which normally went to women were termed 'unskilled' and thus lower paid, while 'skilled' jobs went to men. As in the division between guild work and domestic work noted above, gender became a more important determinant of the division between skilled and unskilled than the actual difficulty of the tasks concerned.[64]

Women could never be as fully excluded from factory work as they could from journeymen's associations, but trade unions often accomplished symbolically what they could not in actuality. In trade

61. Neufeld, 'German artisans', p. 498. In France the *compagnonnages* survived long after the guilds were officially abolished in 1791. Anthony Black, *Guilds and Civil Society in European Political Thought from the 12th Century to the Present* (London, 1984), p. 167.

62. Rita Bake, 'Zur Arbeits- und Lebensweise von Manufakturarbeiterinnen im 18. Jahrhundert', in Hans Pohl and Wilhelm Treue, eds, *Die Frau in der deutschen Wirtschaft*, Zeitschrift für Unternehmensgeschichte, Beiheft 35 (Wiesbaden, 1985), p. 58.

63. Alice Kessler-Harris, *Out to Work: A History of Wage-earning Women in the United States* (New York, 1982); Cynthia Cockburn, *Brothers: Male Dominance and Social Change* (London, 1983); Ava Baron, 'Questions of gender: deskilling and demasculinization in the U.S. printing industry, 1830–1915', *Gender and History* 1 (1989): 178–99.

64. Anne Phillips and Barbara Taylor, 'Sex and skill in the capitalist labour process', *Feminist Review* 6 (1980): 79–88; Paul Thompson, *The Nature of Work: An Introduction to Debates on the Labour Process* (London, 1983).

journals, union newspapers, posters, and illustrations, women were visually and verbally excluded, making 'worker' someone invariably male, and the 'working class' masculine.[65] Journeymen's associations are of course not the only root of the trade unions' hostility to women's work, but the fact that both groups thought of themselves, and represented themselves, as groups of men does point to some link.

Though ultimately craft guilds may have made more of an impact on German society as a whole and on European political philosophy, in terms of achieving a masculine sense of self which was also picked up by later groups, journeymen were more successful.[66] By turning restrictions imposed from the outside, such as the prohibitions of marriage and the requirement of wandering, into virtues, they defined themselves as a group and ultimately achieved power over those who had limited them in the first place. They created an ideal of masculinity separate from that of the masters and increasingly distinct from that proposed by religious and political authorities. The ideal was one not only cut off from women, but one in which women could not share in the least. Women could exhibit the qualities expected of an ideal head of household – permanence, honesty, thrift, control of children and servants – and were, of course, as widows quite regularly thrust into the position of household head. The qualities of the journeymen's ideal, the *Wandervogel* – transience, foolhardiness, bravery, spendthriftiness – were never seen as positive in any woman, and could in fact land her in jail or see her banished from a town. In the words of an anonymous sixteenth-century author, 'One thinks highly of journeymen who have wandered, but absolutely nothing of maids who have done so.'[67]

65. Eric Hobsbawm, 'Man and woman in socialist iconography', *History Workshop* 6 (1978): 121–38; William Sewell, 'Visions of labour: illustrations of the mechanical arts before, in and after Diderot's Encyclopedia', in Kaplan and Koepp, eds, *Work in France*, pp. 258–86; Joan Scott, *Gender and the Politics of History* (New York, 1988), p. 163; Elizabeth Faue, 'The dynamo of change: gender and solidarity in the American labour movement of the 1930s', *Gender and History* 1 (1989): 138–58.

66. For the impact of craft guilds, see Walker, *Home Towns*; Black, *Guilds*; R. Po-Chia Hsia, 'Münster and the Anabaptists', in his *The German People and the Reformation* (Ithaca, NY, 1988); Roper, *Holy Household*.

67. *Theatrum Diabolorum, Das ist: Warhaffte, eigentliche und kurtze Beschreibung allerley grewlicher, schrecklicher und abschewlicher Laster* . . . (Frankfurt, 1575), quoted in Wesoly, 'Weibliche', p. 77.

PART FOUR

In Conclusion

CHAPTER ELEVEN

Reassessing, transforming, complicating: two decades of early modern women's history[1]

When I wrote the essay that opens this collection, 'Women's defence of their public role', a bit over ten years ago, issues of the boundaries between public and private were a hot topic in women's history. There were a number of books with the phrase 'public and private' in the title, and the theme of the 1987 Berkshire Conference on the History of Women, the largest and best-established conference on women's history in the world, was 'Beyond the Public/ Private Dichotomy: Reassessing Women's Place in History'.[2] By ten years later this was no longer an issue, and the 1996 Berkshire programme included only one session with the phrase 'public and private' in the title.

Because the theme of the Berkshire Conference influences the way sessions are titled, it may not be totally fair to gauge trends in women's history from session titles, but the theme is also intentionally chosen to be as broad as possible and to capture key issues in women's history at that point.[3] The conference is held only every three years, a long span of time in a field that is developing as rapidly as women's history. For the first six Berkshire Conferences, held between 1973 and 1984, the field was so new that there was no theme; in 1987 it was, as noted, 'Beyond the Public/Private Dichotomy: Reassessing Women's Place in History', in 1990, 'Crossing

1. An earlier version of this paper was presented as the Erasmus Lecture at the Centre for Renaissance and Reformation Studies at Victoria University in the University of Toronto. I would like to thank Susan Karant-Nunn, Judith Bennett, and Heide Wunder for their comments on that version, and the Centre for its invitation.

2. See, for example, Eva Gamarnikow *et al.*, eds, *The Public and the Private* (New York: Heinemann, 1983).

3. I was one of the programme co-chairs for the 1996 Berkshire Conference, and can report that even though the theme that emerged appears very general and rather innocuous, it was the cause of several hours of debate.

Boundaries in Feminist History', in 1993, 'Transformations: Women, Gender, Power', and in 1996, 'Complicating Categories: Women, Gender, and Difference'. Like all descriptions and categorizations of knowledge, these titles both reflect and shape research.[4] The word 'difference', for example, so important to women's history in the mid-1990s, appeared in only a single session title in 1987, and that in a round-table discussion entitled 'The Politics of Women's History: Feminist Advocacy and the Meaning of Difference'. It appeared in no titles in 1984 or 1981.

Although the history of women in the United States has been the best-researched area of women's history over the last twenty years and has thus shaped the dominant questions and theoretical perspectives of the field to a great degree, studies of women in early modern Europe have also been very influential in establishing key topics and approaches. The themes of the last four Berkshire Conferences can therefore serve as a way to describe what has happened in the field over the last decade, and I would like to use them to explore three questions that have been central in explorations of early modern European women: Did women have a Reformation? What effects did the development of capitalism have on women? Do the concepts 'Renaissance' and 'early modern' apply to women's experience, and which is more fruitful? All of these questions hark back to the work of Joan Kelly, whose now twenty-year-old essay 'Did women have a Renaissance?' continues to be extremely fruitful as a springboard for discussion, both in her period of focus and in times and places far removed.[5]

The Reformation

Most considerations of women and the Reformation have tended to answer the question 'Did women have a Reformation?' with 'yes', and then go off in one of two directions. They either explore

4. Berkshire Conference titles even make their way onto doctoral dissertations. Lianne McTavish, who presented a paper at the 1996 conference, titled her 1996 dissertation from Syracuse University 'Complicating Categories: Women, Gender and Sexuality in Seventeenth-Century French Visual Culture'.

5. Joan Kelly, 'Did Women have a Renaissance?' in Renate Bridenthal and Claudia Koonz, eds, *Becoming Visible: Women in European History* (Boston: Houghton-Mifflin, 1997), pp. 137–164.

women's actions in support of or in opposition to the Reformation and women's spiritual practices during this period, or they explore the effects of religious change on women's lives. Those studies looking at women's actions have explicitly concentrated on what is rather unambiguously a public role, and found women active in the Peasants' War, preaching in the early years of the Reformation, defending convent life in word and deed, writing and translating religious literature. This scholarship has also explored the boundaries between public and private in the sixteenth century, noting that activities in which women engaged within the household – such as pastors' wives creating a new ideal for women or women converting their husbands or other household members – were not viewed as private, but as matters of public concern. Doing this kind of research tends to be very uplifting, confirming Mary Beard's assertion that women are a force in history, and seeing the Reformation as a female as well as a male creation.[6] It is carried out by scholars from many disciplines – religious historians such as Anne Conrad, Gerta Schaffenorth, Elsie McKee and Silke Halbach, literary scholars such as Barbara Becker-Cantarino, social historians such as Marian Kobelt-Groch and Siegried Westphal, intellectual historians such as Luise Schorn-Schütte and Peter Matheson.[7] Because English-language scholars were often the first to explore women's experiences, much of the theory has come from North America although in the last five years this has changed somewhat.

Research such as this – uncovering women's experiences – has in the last decade been supplemented by more complex gendered analysis, as some historians of the Reformation explore the issues of power and difference that were highlighted as Berkshire Conference (Berks) themes. This has been most noticeable, not in studies of women's actions, but in those of the effects of the Reformation on women. These studies began with explorations of the ideas of the reformers, and we now have both edited reprints, such as those of Joyce Irwin on the radical reformers and Erika Rummel on

6. Mary Beard, *Woman as Force in History: A Study in Traditions and Realities* (New York: Macmillan, 1946).

7. References to most of these authors may be found in the bibliography which follows this chapter; the two which are not listed separately there are Gerta Schaffenorth, ' "Im Geiste Freunde werden": Mann und Frau im Glauben Martin Luthers', in Heide Wunder and Christina Vanja, *Wandel der Geschlechterbeziehungen zu Beginn der Neuzeit* (Frankfurt: Suhrkamp, 1991), pp. 97–109; and Luise Schorn-Schütte, ' "Gefährtin" und "Mitregentin": Zur Sozialgeschichte der evangelischen Pfarrfrau in der Frühen Neuzeit', in Wunder and Vanja, *Wandel*, pp. 109–53.

Erasmus, and book-length analyses, such as the conflicting views of
Calvin's ideas on women presented by Jane Dempsey Douglass and
John Thompson.[8]

Discussions of the ideas of the reformers and those which explore
actual legal and social transformations (the theme of the 1993 Berks)
have provoked sharp disagreements. In covering these topics, one
is generally expected to have an opinion about whether the Reformation was a good thing or a bad thing for women. Those who think
that it was a good thing (and I am here stating this more baldly than
almost anyone would in their analyses) are generally either older
scholars focusing largely on marriage and the family, or younger
scholars who are intellectual or church historians trained in Germany. In this latter group I would put, most prominently, Luise
Schorn-Schütte, but also Gerta Schaffenorth, Christine Globig, G.
Maron, and Heidi Lauterer-Pirner.[9] Those who think that it was –
again speaking very generally – a bad thing, are generally social
historians or literary scholars trained outside Germany or with
extensive contacts with scholars outside Germany. In this group I
would put, most prominently, Lyndal Roper, and also Susan Karant-
Nunn, Sigrid Brauner, Dagmar Lorenz, and myself.[10]

What has not happened in Reformation scholarship, however, is
much integration of gender into more general analyses. The groups
that have been the focus of Reformation scholarship over the last
decade, such as peasants, city populations, and clergy, remain male
groups, though not explicitly so, for the only scholars of the Reformation interested in the very new research area of masculinity are

8. References to most of these works may be found in the bibliography; the one
which is not included there is Erika Rummel, ed., *Erasmus on Women* (Toronto:
University of Toronto Press, 1996). Though there are theses and articles, there is
still no book-length analysis – or even an edited collection – of Luther's writings
about women. This is certainly not due to any lack of material but, I would speculate, to trepidation, even outside Germany, about tackling so formidable a figure
and inviting what would no doubt be harsh attacks or at least a sharp discussion.

9. Christine Globig, *Frauenordination im Kontext lutherischer Ekklesiologie*, Kirche und
Konfession, Vol. 36 (Göttingen: Vandenhoeck und Ruprecht, 1994); G. Maron, 'Vom
Hindernis zur Hilfe: Die Frau in der Sicht Martin Luthers', *Theologische Zeitschrift* 39
(1983): 272–89; Heidi Lauterer-Pirner, 'Vom "Frauenspiegel" zu Luthers Schrift "Vom
ehelichen Leben": Das Bild der Ehefrau im Spiegel einiger Zeugnisse des 15. und
16. Jahrhunderts', in Annette Kuhn and Jorg Rüsen, eds, *Frauen in der Geschichte*,
Vol. 3 (Düsseldorf: 1983). For Schaffenorth and Schorn-Schütte see note 3.

10. References to most of these authors may be found in the bibliography; the
one which is not listed separately there is Dagmar Lorenz, 'Vom Kloster zur Küche:
Die Frau vor und nach der Reformation Dr. Martin Luthers', in Barbara Becker-
Cantarino, ed., *Die Frau von der Reformation zur Romantik* (Bonn: Bouvier, 1980),
pp. 7–35.

those who have already focused on women.[11] In the new *Oxford Encyclopedia of the Reformation*, Luther's ideas about women are included in the entry on women but not in the entry on Luther, in contrast to his ideas about Jews, which are in both 'Jews and Judaism' and 'Luther'.[12] Thus some categories have been complicated, but not others.

One of the most dramatic ways that categories *have* been complicated has been scholarship which answers the question 'Did women have a Reformation?' with a qualified 'no' rather than 'yes'. This has been done most effectively by Heide Wunder, who does not base her 'no' on the idea that women's lives did not change, but on a rejection of the Reformation as a major cause of that transformation. Wunder sees changes in family life and ideas about marriage, which are often viewed as the most important effects of the Reformation on women, as a result not of changes in religious ideology but of social and economic changes which allowed a wider spectrum of the population to marry and made the marital pair the basic production and consumption unit. Thus Reformation ideas about the family did not *create* the bourgeois family, but resulted from it.[13]

Capitalism

Wunder's turning on its head the standard explanation of new ideas about the family brings us to my second question: What effects did the development of capitalism have on women? In answering this, the first line of division is between those who see significant change and those who see more continuity – what we might in shorthand term the battle between capitalism and patriarchy.

Those who favour capitalism – who see, in other words, significant transformation in women's work and women's lives during this period because of the effects of 'capitalism' (however one may

11. For examples of the new scholarship on masculinity, see Stephens B. Boyd et al. (eds), *Redeenning Men: Religion and Masculinities* (Louisville, KY: Westminster John Knox, 1996). Clare Lees, ed., *Medieval Masculinities: Regarding Men in the Middle Ages* (Minneapolis: University of Minnesota Press, 1994); R.W. Connell, *Masculinities* (Berkeley: University of California Press, 1995); Mark Breitenberg, *Anxious Masculinity in Early Modern England* (Cambridge: Cambridge University Press, 1996).

12. Hans Hillerbrand, ed., *Oxford Encyclopedia of the Reformation* (New York: Oxford, 1995).

13. Heide Wunder, *'Er ist die Sonn', sie ist der Mond': Frauen in der frühen Neuzeit* (Munich: Beck, 1992), pp. 58–88.

choose to define or limit that word) – have tended to see these changes as negative. This, of course, is not a new idea, but was put forth by Alice Clark in *Working Life of Women in the Seventeenth Century* almost eighty years ago.[14] Though some of these studies see capitalism as an unremitting evil, pulling women down from a 'golden age' of pre-capitalist household production in which their labour and ideas were valued (here Caroline Barron and Susan Cahn are the clearest voices), most recent work has been more qualified.[15] Here 'difference' has emerged as a key issue, for newer scholarship has stressed that women's experience differed according to social class, economic status, and geographic region – factors that have traditionally been taken into account when examining men's experience of economic change – and also according to age, marital status, family size, and lifespan. These latter factors have only emerged as axes of difference in the last decade of research in women's history, and are rarely mentioned in works on men's work experiences. Thus in economic as well as religious history, women's categories are now more complicated than men's.

Those who argue that capitalism brought significant transformations also do not completely neglect continuity. The majority of women and men in Europe during these four centuries continued to work in agriculture, for at least three-quarters – and in some areas more like 95 per cent – of the population remained in the countryside. Historians such as Michael Roberts, Keith Snell, Ann Kussmaul, and Christina Vanja are investigating the rural scene more closely, where they trace both structures and techniques that were slow to change and innovations which directly affected women's lives, such as the introduction of the scythe, stall feeding, and silk production.[16] Historians who continue to concentrate on cities – where, of course, the sources are more prevalent and concentrated – stress that much of the economy was still pre-capitalist,

14. Alice Clark, *Working Life of Women in the Seventeenth Century* (London: Routledge, 1919, rpt. 1968, 1982, 1992).

15. Susan Cahn, *Industry of Devotion: The Transformation of Women's Work in England, 1500–1660* (New York: Columbia University Press, 1987); Caroline Barron, 'The "golden age" of women in medieval London', in *Medieval Women of Southern England* (Reading: Reading Medieval Studies, 1989), pp. 35–58.

16. Michael Roberts, 'Sickles and scythes: women's work and men's work at harvest time', *History Workshop Journal* 7 (1979): 3–29; Keith Snell, *Annals of the Labouring Poor* (Cambridge: Cambridge University Press, 1985); Ann Kussmaul, *Servants in Husbandry in Early Modern England* (Cambridge: Cambridge University Press, 1981); Christina Vanja, 'Frauen im Dorf: Ihre Stellung unter besonderer Berücksichtigung landgräflichhessischer Quellen im Mittelalter', *Zeitschrift für Agrargeschichte und Agrarsoziologie* 34 (1986): 147–59.

and many occupations, such as domestic service and selling at the public market, changed very little during the period.

For many historians, wide variety and strong continuities, however, do not negate the fact that this is an era of significant transformation in women's work. Some historians, such as Bridget Hill and Pamela Sharpe, have focused on the economic causes and effects of these changes, while others, such as Martha Howell, Michael Roberts, Jean Quataert, Maxine Berg, and myself, have been more interested in changes in meaning.[17] Ten years ago these changes in meaning were often conceptualized, as they are in my first essay in this book and in an essay by Martha Howell, 'Citizenship and gender: women's political status in northern medieval cities', as women's retreat from work that had public or political aspects, but now the issue is more complicated.[18] Recent research stresses that it is in the meaning of work as much as the actual tasks that women and men were doing that we can see the most change during this period. As Clark noted so long ago, women were excluded or stepped back from certain areas of production, but, more importantly, their productive tasks were increasingly defined as reproductive – as housekeeping – or as assisting – as helping out. Thus a woman who sewed clothes, took in boarders, did laundry, and gathered herbs – and who was paid for all of these activities – was increasingly thought of as a housewife, a title that became enshrined in statistical language in the nineteenth century, when her activities were also not regarded as contributing to the gross national product or other sorts of economic measurements.[19]

One of the clearest results of the last decade of scholarship on women's work is the discovery that transformations in meaning

17. For references to Howell and Quataert, see the bibliography. Bridget Hill, *Women, Work and Sexual Politics in Eighteenth-century England* (Oxford: Basil Blackwell, 1989); Pamela Sharpe, *Adapting to Capitalism: Working Women in the English Economy 1700–1850* (New York: St Martin's, 1996); Maxine Berg, 'Women's work, mechanization, and the early phases of industrialization', in R.E. Pahl, ed., *On Work: Historical and Theoretical Approaches* (Oxford: Basil Blackwell, 1988), pp. 61–94; Michael Roberts, ' "Words they are women, deeds they are men": images of work and gender in early modern England', in Lindsey Charles and Lorna Duffin, eds, *Women and Work in Pre-Industrial England* (London: Croom Helm, 1985), pp. 122–81. See also the essays in Patrick Joyce, ed., *The Historical Meanings of Work* (Cambridge: Cambridge University Press, 1987), and in the special issue, edited by Philippe Desan, on 'work in the Renaissance' of the *Journal of Medieval and Renaissance Studies* 25/1 (1995).

18. Martha Howell, 'Citizenship and gender: women's political status in northern medieval cities', in Mary Erler and Maryanne Kowaleski, eds, *Women and Power in the Middle Ages* (Athens: University of Georgia Press, 1988), pp. 37–60.

19. Marilyn Waring, *If Women Counted: A New Feminist Economics* (San Francisco: Harper and Row, 1988).

were not accompanied by a retreat from participation in the labour market, however. Peter Earle's recent study of the London labour market has found that 72 per cent of the women who served as witnesses in court in 1700 were doing paid work outside the home – most of it low status, but certainly not a withdrawal from economic activity.[20] A few voices, Heide Wunder's among them, note that the continuation or expansion of wage labour, despite its low-pay, low-status nature, may actually have benefited some women, as it allowed them to support themselves without marrying. She thus sees the great concern with 'masterless' women and the laws which attempted to force women into service or into male-headed households as a result of the expansion of wage labour (and again, *not* as the result of the Reformation, which is a common explanation); such laws had not been necessary earlier because the opportunities for women to live alone and support themselves by their labour were much fewer.[21]

Statistical data like Earle's, and also that which confirms women's lower wages for all types of tasks across centuries and countries, is often used by those who reject the notion that this is a period of dramatic change in women's work or who at least do not see capitalism as the most important agent of what change there was. Here Olwen Hufton, Katrina Honeyman and Jordan Goodman, Chris Middleton, and Judith Bennett have all been strong voices in favour of continuity, viewing gender ideology – what Honeyman and Goodman term 'gender conflict' and Bennett, more boldly, 'patriarchy' – as the most significant shaper of women's work experience.[22] They note that even dramatic transformations in the structure and organization of institutions and industries may not have been evident to the women working in them, who were often clustered in the lowest-skilled or poorest-paid jobs. Whether an industry was organized capitalistically or by guilds, or whether a hospital was run by the church or the city, made little difference to the women who spun wool

20. Peter Earle, 'The female labour market in London in the late 17th and early 18th centuries', *Economic History Review* 42 (1989): 338.

21. Wunder, '*Er ist die Sonn*'', pp. 187–90.

22. Olwen Hufton, 'Women, work, and family', in Natalie Zemon Davis and Arlette Farge, eds, *A History of Women in the West. Volume III: Renaissance and Enlightenment Paradoxes* (Cambridge, MA: Harvard University Press, 1993), pp. 15–45; Judith Bennett, 'History that stands still: women's work in the European past: review essay', *Feminist Studies* 14 (1988): 269–83; Chris Middleton, 'The familiar fate of the *famulae*: gender divisions in the history of wage labour', in R.E. Pahl, ed., *On Work* (Oxford: Basil Blackwell, 1988), pp. 21–46; Katrina Honeyman and Jordan Goodman, 'Women's work, gender conflict and labour markets in Europe, 1500–1900', *The Economic History Review* 44 (1991): 608–28.

or washed bedding. Women remained in these low-status positions because they often fitted their work around the life cycle of their families, moving in and out of various jobs as children were born and grew up, or as their husbands died and they remarried. Work for many women during this period was a matter of makeshifts and expedients, a pattern which some historians see continuing with only minor alterations until the twentieth century, or even until today, considering the role of ill-paid women and children in developing countries in today's global economy.

This position stems to some degree from the feminist critique of Marxism, and its exponents have been accused of being both depressing and ahistorical.[23] The first charge – being depressing – may be warranted, for it is one of the most common criticisms of *all* women's history, not simply of certain analyses of women's work. The second charge – being ahistorical – is not as warranted, however, for it is scholars who stress the importance of patriarchy (or the sex/gender system, or gender hierarchies, or gender structures, or whatever other term they choose to use), rather than those who deny its importance, who have over the last decades argued most forcefully for its changing nature and historical specificity. This has led Gerda Lerner and a host of feminist anthropologists, archaeologists, and political theorists such as Sylvia Walby, Peggy Sanday, Christine Gailey, Joan Gero, and Margaret Conkey to search for the origins of patriarchy, and – perhaps more prudently, and certainly with more sources – historians of more recent periods to explore its variety.[24] They have been joined by people who may not be quite as willing to accord patriarchy the prime place, but who have also gone beyond Joan Kelly's call for a 'doubled vision' (essentially gender plus class), and beyond the 'Holy Trinity' of race, class, and gender, to analyse axes of difference that were simply not part of historical scholarship twenty or even ten years ago, such as age, sexual orientation, place of residence, physical ability, or marital status.[25]

23. A recent example of this is the exchange between Bridget Hill and Judith Bennett, 'Women's history: a study in change, continuity or standing still?', in *Women's History Review* 2 (1993): 5–22 and 173–84.

24. Gerda Lerner, *The Creation of Patriarchy* (New York: Oxford University Press, 1986); Sylvia Walby, *Theorizing Patriarchy* (Oxford: Basil Blackwell, 1990); Irene Silverblatt, 'Women in states', *Annual Review of Anthropology* 17 (1988): 427–60; Christine Gailey, *Kinship to Kingship: Gender Hierarchy and State Formation in the Tongan Islands* (Austin: University of Texas Press, 1987); Joan Gero and Margaret Conkey, *Engendering Archaeology: Women and Prehistory* (Oxford: Basil Blackwell, 1991).

25. Joan Kelly, 'The doubled vision of feminist theory', in *Women, History and Theory: Essay by Joan Kelly* (Chicago: University of Chicago Press, 1984), pp. 51–64.

The Renaissance/early modern debate

Many of the axes of difference now standard for feminist historians are shared by our colleagues in other fields, as feminist sociology, economics, anthropology, psychology, and political science become increasingly more 'complicated' as well. As historians we have one more axis, of course, the one that we often accuse our colleagues in other fields of ignoring or neglecting – time. Ignoring time – being ahistorical – is perhaps the worst thing one can call a historian, which is why the charge emerges only in rather vigorous debates. I would thus like to turn directly to the issue of time in examining my third question: Do the concepts 'Renaissance' and 'early modern' apply to women's experience, and which is more fruitful? This, of course, takes us directly back to Kelly's original question and to its broader version: Was there a Renaissance at all?

Questions of periodization regarding this era, beginning with just what to call it, are a hot topic within both women's history and history at large at the moment – and also, judging by Leah Marcus's recent essay in *Redrawing the Boundaries: The Transformation of English and American Literary Studies*, in literary studies as well.[26] An entire session at the Berkshire Conference in June 1996 dealt with just this issue: 'Complicating Categories, Crossing Chronologies: Periodization in the History of Women from Medieval to Modern', as did a session at a conference on gender in the early modern period held in October 1996 in Frankfurt, 'Defining Moments: Feminist Stakes in the Late Medieval/Renaissance/Early Modern Conundrum'.[27]

This debate about the term 'Renaissance' is certainly not new. William Bouwsma surveyed earlier discomfort with it in his presidential address to the American Historical Association almost twenty years ago, when he felt historians' reservations about the term were part of a larger 'collapse of the traditional dramatic organization of Western history'.[28] Bouwsma was writing only a year after Kelly's essay appeared, and the critique of the term coming from women's history is not part of his considerations. His justification for resurrecting the Renaissance, however, nicely captures what has inspired

26. Leah Marcus, 'Renaissance/early modern studies', in Stephen Greenblatt and Giles Gunn, *Redrawing the Boundaries: The Transformation of English and American Literary Studies* (New York: Modern Language Association, 1992), pp. 41–63.

27. The Frankfurt Conference was held in October 1996 under the auspices of the Zentrum zur Erforschung der Frühen Neuzeit at the University of Frankfurt and titled 'Geschlechterperspektiven in der Frühen Neuzeit'.

28. William J. Bouwsma, 'The Renaisance and the drama of Western history', *American Historical Review* 84 (1979): 1–15.

feminist criticism of the label. Bouwsma advocates a return to the dramatic organization of history, with the Renaissance as a key pivotal event, important because it created an 'anthropological vision . . . that culture is a product of the creative adjustment of the human race to its varying historical circumstances rather than a function of universal and changeless nature, and the perception that culture accordingly differs from time to time and group to group'. So far this sounds simply as if the Renaissance created what we now call the 'new cultural history', but in a rewording of his idea later in the same article, Bouwsma notes: 'as the creator of language, *man* also shapes through language the only world *he* can know directly, including even *himself*. . . the notion of *man* as the creator of *himself* and the world was heady stuff' (my emphases). I am pointing this out not to criticize Bouwsma's gender-specific language, but to note that he was right. As countless discussions of 'self-fashioning' since have pointed out, it was *man* who was to be the creator of *himself*, *man* who was the measure of all things.[29]

The highly gendered nature of the Renaissance's 'anthropological vision' has been a steady theme in the work of Margaret King on women humanists, Constance Jordan on Renaissance feminism, and the huge number of studies of – mostly English – women writers.[30] Although it appeared originally that most of this feminist analysis of the Renaissance would be a further move away from the 'drama of history' (Bouwsma's words), dethroning the Renaissance yet again, in many ways it has not. The drama is still there, but the outcome is tragedy rather than triumph. The Renaissance is still the beginning of a trajectory, but that trajectory leads to Rousseau, the banning of women's clubs in the French Revolution, the restrictions of the Napoleonic Code, and separate spheres.[31]

29. Stephen J. Greenblatt, *Renaissance Self-Fashioning: From More to Shakespeare* (Chicago: University of Chicago Press, 1980).

30. Margaret King, *Women of the Renaissance* (Chicago: University of Chicago Press, 1993); Constance Jordan, *Renaissance Feminism: Literary Texts and Political Models* (Chicago: University of Chicago Press, 1990); Margaret Hannay, *Silent But for the Word: Tudor Women as Patrons, Translators, and Writers of Religious Works* (Kent, OH: Kent State University Press, 1985); Elaine Beilin, *Redeeming Eve: Women Writers of the Renaissance* (Princeton: Princeton University Press, 1987); Elaine Hobby, *Virtue of Necessity: English Women's Writing 1649–1688* (Ann Arbor: University of Michigan Press, 1988).

31. Though women's history of the nineteenth century rarely searches for roots in the Renaissance, that of the eighteenth century certainly does, with the eighteenth century painted in very gloomy terms. See Christine Fauré, *Democracy Without Women: Feminism and the Rise of Liberalism in France* (Indianapolis: Indiana University Press, 1991); Joan Landes, *Women and the Public Sphere in the Age of the French Revolution* (Ithaca, NY: Cornell University Press, 1988); Olwen Hufton, *Women and the Limits of Citizenship in the French Revolution* (Toronto: University of Toronto Press, 1992).

Perhaps using the term 'early modern' is the best way to escape these Renaissance trajectories, whether positive or negative? This is the route increasingly taken by historians; literary scholars are more loath to give up the Renaissance, partly, as Marcus and others have pointed out, because it allows them to preserve literature as a separate discipline in these days of ever-increasing interdisciplinarity.[32] But even the *Journal of Medieval and Renaissance Studies,* which publishes many articles on literature, has recently changed its name to *Journal of Medieval and Early Modern Studies,* and early modern is definitely the term of preference among scholars of women, myself included.[33]

Other analysts, including Bouwsma twenty years ago, have pointed to some general problems with the term 'early modern' – its assumption that there is something that can unambiguously be called 'modernity', its retaining of a notion of linear trajectory with a final act. As Judith Bennett has recently noted, many historians are questioning the 'master narrative of a great transformation' from pre-modern to modern. She uses examples from women's work experiences and other areas of life to challenge what she terms the 'assumption of a dramatic change in women's lives between 1300 and 1700' and asserts that 'women's history should ally itself with those who are questioning the master narrative' because 'the paradigm of a great divide in women's history is undermined by many factual anomalies'.[34] Thus pre-modern and modern could join public and private, nature and culture, work and family as one of the many dichotomies women's history should reject as it complicates categories.[35]

---

32. Marcus, 'Renaissance/Early Modern', p. 44, gives several examples of this.

33. The 'Statement of Purpose' which describes why the *Journal of Medieval and Early Modern Studies* changed its name provides evidence of Marcus's point that the term 'Renaissance' is increasingly used – perhaps defensively – to describe literature as a separate discipline. In a several paragraph explanation about why the journal 'is being retitled, reorganized, and redefined,' the editors use the words 'history' and 'theory' many times, but the words 'literature' or 'literary' never. (Though the word 'text' is used once.) Clearly 'Renaissance' would not fit with their new mission, and the change involves more than terminology. (*The Journal of Medieval and Early Modern Studies* 26/1 (1996), title page.)

34. Judith Bennett, 'Medieval women, modern women: across the great divide', in David Aers, ed., *Culture and History 1350–1600: Essays on English Communities, Identities and Writing* (London: Harvester Wheatsheaf, 1992), pp. 147–75. An abridged version of this appears in Ann-Louise Shapiro, *Feminists Revision History* (New Brunswick, NJ: Rutgers University Press, 1994), pp. 47–72.

35. For a discussion of the key dichotomies in women's history, see Gisela Bock, 'Challenging dichotomies: perspectives on women's history', in Karen Offen, Ruth Roach Pierson and Jane Rendall, eds, *Writing Women's History: International Perspectives* (Bloomington: Indiana University Press, 1990), pp. 1–24.

Perhaps women's history should reject periodization altogether? In this it could easily latch on to the Annales school historians, who have posited a *longue durée* stretching from the eleventh century to the nineteenth, a period Le Roy Ladurie termed 'motionless'.[36] In fact, as Susan Stuard has recently pointed out, women already appear in some Annales school works as the perfect example of motionless history, primarily part of a household, serving as a means of exchange between families.[37] This approach was adopted at least in part by Bonnie Anderson and Judith Zinsser in their survey of European women's history, for they discuss peasant women from the ninth century to the twentieth in a single section, going beyond the time-frame of even Le Roy Ladurie.[38] Motionless indeed.

Such wholesale rejection of periodization makes me and a number of other women's historians uneasy, however. In reviewing Zinsser and Anderson's textbook, Gianna Pomata comments: 'I perceive here the shade of essentialism, the idea of an unchanging female nature.'[39] In discussing women in Annales school works, Stuard notes: 'By such formulations gender for women, if not for men, was assumed to be a historical constant, not a dynamic category that changed in Europe's formative centuries and changed again with the transition into modern times.'[40] But here we are back to a medieval/modern transition again! We are thus not much further than we were with Kelly twenty years ago, critiquing periodization without finding a substitute with which everyone can agree.

Though you are probably now waiting for my answer to this conundrum – I have clearly indicated my stands on the first two questions in this essay, after all – I am going to end instead with what is the standard closing of every academic study, and call for more research. I opened this book by using the words 'explosion' and 'flood' to describe the amount of research in women's history over the last two decades, but this is only in comparison with women's history in the previous two millennia. In comparison with the amount of historical scholarship out of which the standard

36. Emmanuel Le Roy Ladurie, 'Motionless history', *Social Science History* 1 (1977): 115–36.

37. Susan Mosher Stuard, 'Fashion's captives: medieval women in French historiography', in Susan Mosher Stuard, ed., *Women in Medieval History and Historiography* (Philadelphia: University of Pennsylvania Press, 1987), pp. 59–80.

38. Judith Zinsser and Bonnie Anderson, *A History of Their Own*, 2 Vols (New York: Harper & Row, 1988).

39. Gianna Pomata, 'History, particular and universal: on reading some recent women's history textbooks', *Feminist Studies* 19 (1993): 7–50.

40. Stuard, 'Fashion's captives', p. 71.

schemes of periodization were developed, this is less than a trickle. We still know almost nothing about women's lives in this period – whatever we want to call it – in eastern Europe or Portugal, or about rural women in most parts of Europe. Even in areas in which it seems we must be buried in material by now – women's work in England, for example, which one would surely assume to be an over-researched field as everyone engages with Alice Clark – there has been only *one* book-length study of the period before 1500, *none* for the sixteenth or seventeenth centuries and only *two* for the eighteenth century.[41] No wonder Alice Clark has seen three modern reprints, and that her 1919 theories remain the chief master narrative for the field!

Though a call for more research on women might seem both depressing and unsophisticated, coming right at the time when gender has become more respectable than women as a field of research and when deconstructionist criticism has made many historians doubt their enterprise, I think that it is the only way we can develop a periodization, and a view of the past, that is drawn from the lives of women as well as men.[42] Only more studies will allow us to question all master narratives more effectively, including those we develop out of women's experience, such as the dichotomies of public/private or nature/culture which have been so forceful in women's history over the last two decades. Our categories are now much more complicated than they were twenty years ago, as we have crossed boundaries we did not then know existed. Women's history – and feminist scholarship more generally – has asked questions that now seem self-evident, but that until recent decades were rarely asked: Did women have a Renaissance, a Reformation, an Enlightenment? What effects did the development of capitalism, or industrialism, or democracy, have on women? That we can't yet answer all of these, or that we are less willing to answer them for all women than we were ten years ago, is a sign that we recognize how important these questions are.

41. P.J.P. Goldberg, *Women, Work and Life Cycle in a Medieval Economy: Women in York and Yorkshire c. 1300–1520* (Oxford: Clarendon, 1992); Hill, *Women, Work*; Sharpe, *Adapting to Capitalism.*

42. Amanda Vickery also recently advocated more research, noting that this would no doubt be interpreted as 'proof of my naive belief in a phantom of "real" history living in the Lancashire Record Office'. ('Golden age to separate spheres? A review of the categories and chronology of English women's history', *The Historical Journal* 36/2 (1993): 414.)

Bibliography

General

Those readers interested in further background on a range of issues in early modern Germany should consult Sheilagh Ogilvie and Robert Scribner, eds, *Germany: A New Social and Economic History*, 2 Vols (London: Edward Arnold, 1995). Those seeking to place the information on women and gender in a broader geographic context should see my *Women and Gender in Early Modern Europe* (Cambridge: Cambridge University Press, 1993), and Olwen Hufton, *The Prospect Before Her: A History of Women in Western Europe, 1500–1800* (London: HarperCollins, 1995). For an essay collection which covers a range of periods, see Lynn Abrams and Elizabeth Harvey, eds, *Gender Relations in German History: Power, Agency and Experience from the Sixteenth to the Twentieth Century* (London: University College London Press, 1996). For a slightly later period see Ruth Ellen B. Joeres and Mary Jo Maynes, eds, *German Women in the Eighteenth and Nineteenth Centuries* (Bloomington: Indiana University Press, 1986), and Ute Frevert, *Women in German History: From Bourgeois Emancipation to Sexual Liberation*, tr. Stuart McKinnon-Evans (Oxford: Berg, 1989).

The German Historical Institute has a good bibliography of works available in English: Helena Cole, ed., *The History of Women in Germany from Medieval Times to the Present: Bibliography of English-Language Publications* (Washington: German Historical Institute, 1990). References to both literary and historical studies can be found in Eda Sagarra, 'Recent feminist scholarship in the field of German studies: a review essay', *Internationales Archiv für Sozialgeschichte der deutschen Literatur* 3, Sonderheft 2 (1993): 113–58. The best discussion in English of recent historiographic trends in German-speaking countries is in Karen Offen, Ruth Roach Pierson and Jane Rendall, eds, *Writing Women's History: International Perspectives* (Bloomington: Indiana University Press, 1990), which includes chapters on the Federal Republic of Germany, the German Democratic Republic,

Switzerland, and Austria. For another view of trends in early modern German scholarship see Claudia Ulbrich, 'Aufbruch ins Ungewisse: Feministische Frühneuzeitsforschung', in Beate Fieseler and Birgit Schulze, eds, *Frauengeschichte: Gesucht–Gefunden? Auskünfte zum Stand der Historischen Frauenforschung* (Cologne: Böhlau, 1991), pp. 4–21.

The most important work for anyone interested in women and gender in early modern Germany is the recent magisterial study by the most prominent historian working in this area in Germany today: Heide Wunder, *'Er ist die Sonn', sie ist der Mond': Frauen in der frühen Neuzeit* (Munich: Beck, 1992). Wunder includes a 55-page bibliography which is a good starting point for any further research, and more than 60 illustrations, many of them engravings and woodcuts that have never been reprinted before, making this a book worth looking at even for those who don't read German; a translation is also forthcoming from Harvard University Press. Wunder, along with others, has also been the editor of several recent collections which include essays about women in early modern Germany: Heide Wunder and Christina Vanja, eds, *Wandel der Geschlechterbeziehung zu Beginn der Neuzeit* (Frankfurt: Suhrkamp, 1991); Karin Hausen and Heide Wunder, eds, *Frauengeschichte – Geschlechtergeschichte* (Frankfurt: Campus, 1992); Heide Wunder *et al.*, eds, *Eine Stadt der Frauen: Studien und Quellen zur Geschichte der Baslerinnen im späten Mittelalter und zu Beginn der Neuzeit (13.–17. Jhd.)* (Basel: Helbing und Lichtenhahn, 1995), which includes both sources and analysis for a range of topics; Heide Wunder and Christina Vanja, eds, *Weiber, Menscher, Frauenzimmer: Frauen in der ländlichen Gesellschaft 1500–1800* (Göttingen: Vandenhoeck und Ruprecht, 1996). Other useful collections include: Barbara Vogel and Ulrike Weckel, eds, *Frauen in der Ständegesellschaft: Leben und Arbeiten in der Stadt vom späten Mittelalter bis zur Neuzeit* (Hamburg: Kramer, 1991), which largely focuses on Hamburg and the other Hansa cities; Bea Lundt, ed., *Vergessenen Frauen an der Ruhr: Von Herrscherinnen und Hörigen, Hausfrauen und Hexen 800–1800* (Cologne: Bohlau, 1992); Gisela Bock, ed., *Lebenswege von Frauen im Ancien Regime* (Göttingen: Vandenhoeck und Ruprecht, 1992); *FrauenStadtGeschichte, Zum Beispiel: Frankfurt a.M.* (Königstein: Ulrike Helm, 1995). Lynne Tatlock and Christiane Bohnert, *The Graph of Sex and the German Text: Gendered Culture in Early Modern Germany*, Chloe: Beihefte zum Daphnis, Vol. 19 (Amsterdam and Atlanta: Rodolpi, 1994), includes a large number of essays on gender in early modern German literature and also several which consider historical topics.

Recent longer studies by a single author include: Silke Lesemann, *Arbeit, Ehre, Geschlechterbeziehungen: Zur sozialen und wirtschaftlichen*

Stellung von Frauen im frühneuzeitlichen Hildesheim (Hildesheim: Bernward, 1994); Peter Dinzelbacher, *Heilige oder Hexen? Schicksale auffälliger Frauen im Mittelalter und Frühneuzeit* (Munich: Artemis und Winkler, 1995); Barbara Becker-Cantarino, *Der Lange Weg zur Mündigkeit: Frau und Literatur (1500–1800)* (Stuttgart: J.B. Metlersche, 1987); Martha Schad, *Die Frauen des Hauses Fugger von der Lilie (15.–17. Jahrhundert), Augsburg–Ortenberg–Trient* (Tübingen: 1989); Margret Lemberg, *Landgräfin Juliane zu Hessen (1587–1643): Eine Kasseler und Rotenburger Fürstin aus dem Hause Nassau-Dillenburg in ihrer Zeit*, Quellen und Forschungen zur Hessichen Geschichte 40 (Marburg: Historische Kommission für Hessen, 1994); Sabine Alfing and Christine Schedensack, *Frauenalltag im frühneuzeitlichen Münster* (Bielefeld: Verlag für Regionalgeschichte, 1994).

New studies of men's ideas about women include Henricus Cornelius Agrippa, *Declamation on the Nobility and Preeminence of the Female Sex*, ed. and tr. Albert Rabil, Jr. (Chicago: University of Chicago Press, 1996), which is a new English translation of one of the strongest arguments for women written by a German writer, originally published in Latin in 1529. Sigrid Brauner, *Fearless Wives and Frightened Shrews: The Construction of the Witch in Early Modern Germany* (Amherst: University of Massachusetts Press, 1994), discusses the ideas of Luther and the playwrights Paul Rebhun and Hans Sachs. Maria Miller, ed., *Eheglück und Liebesjoch: Bilder von Liebe, Ehe, und Familie in der Literatur des 15. und 16. Jahrhunderts* (Weinheim: Beltz, 1988), covers a range of literature, and Joy Wiltenburg, *Disorderly Women and Female Power in the Street Literature of Early Modern England and Germany* (Charlottesville, London: University of Virginia Press, 1992), provides one of the very few comparative studies available. Gerhild Scholz Williams examines male opinion on one particular type of woman in *Defining Dominion: The Discourses of Magic and Witchcraft in Early Modern France and Germany* (Ann Arbor: University of Michigan Press, 1995).

Both women's and men's writings and ideas on a variety of topics regarding women have been collected and analysed in Elisabeth Gössman, ed., *Archiv für philosophie- und theologiegeschichtliche Frauenforschung*, Vols. 1–6 (Munich: Iudicium, 1984–94).

Religion

There are several extensive bibliographic essays that identify many resources about women in early modern religion, in both Germany and elsewhere: Kathryn Norberg, 'The Counter-Reformation and women, religious and lay', in John O'Malley, S.J., ed., *Catholicism in Early Modern History: A Guide to Research* (St Louis: Center for Reformation Research, 1988), pp. 133–46; Merry E. Wiesner, 'Studies of women, the family and gender', in William S. Maltby, ed., *Reformation Europe: A Guide to Research II* (St Louis: Center for Reformation Research, 1992), pp. 159–88. The best collection on the topic, with articles on many countries, is Sherrin Marshall, ed., *Women in Reformation and Counter-Reformation Europe: Public and Private Worlds* (Bloomington: University of Indiana Press, 1989).

The best book-length analysis in English about the changes in women's lives brought about by the Reformation is Lyndal Roper, *The Holy Household: Women and Morals in Reformation Augsburg* (Oxford: Oxford University Press, 1989). A briefer local study is Susan Karant-Nunn, 'Continuity and change: some effects of the Reformation on the women of Zwickau', *Sixteenth Century Journal* 13 (1982): 17–42. There are several local studies in German, most of which began as doctoral dissertations: Alice Zimmerli-Witschi, *Frauen in der Reformationszeit* (Zurich, 1981); Siegrid Westphal, *Frau und lutherische Konfessionalisierung: Eine Untersuchung zum Fürstentum Pfalz-Neuburg, 1542–1614* (Frankfurt: Peter Lang, 1994). For women's actions in the Peasants' War and among the Anabaptists more generally, see Marian Kobelt-Groch, *Aufsässige Töchter Gottes: Frauen im Bauernkrieg und in den Taüferbewegungen* (Frankfurt: Lang, 1993) and C. Arnold Snyder and Linda Huebert Hecht, eds, *Profiles of Anabaptist Women: Sixteenth-Century Reforming Pioneers*, Studies in Women and Religion 3 (Waterloo, Ont: Wilfred Lauries University Press, 1996). For changes in marriage, see Joel Harrington, *Reordering Marriage and Society in Reformation Germany* (Cambridge: Cambridge University Press, 1995); Thomas M. Safley, *Let No Man Put Asunder: The Control of Marriage in the German Southwest: A Comparative Study 1550–1600* (Kirksville, MO: Sixteenth Century Journal Publishers, 1984); and Uwe Sibeth, *Eherecht und Staatsbildung: Ehegesetzgebung und Eherechtssprechung in der Landgrafschaft kessen (-Kassel) in der frühen Neuzeit* (Darmstadt: Hessische Historische Kommission Darmstadt, 1994). The best example of an analysis of the interplay between Reformation ideas and notions of gender remains Lyndal Roper, ' "The common man", "the common good", "common women": reflections on gender and meaning in the Reformation German commune', *Social History* 12 (1987): 1–21. Those interested in psychoanalytical approaches to religious issues will want to see Roper's newest book, *Oedipus and the Devil: Witchcraft, Sexuality and Religion in Early Modern Europe* (London: Routledge, 1994), which also focuses largely on Germany, and for more general issues her 'Was there a crisis in gender relations in sixteenth-century Germany?', in Monika Hegmaier and Sabine Holt, eds, *Krisenbewusstsein und Krisenbewältigung in der Frühen Neuzeit/ Crisis in Early Modern Europe* (Frankfurt: Lang, 1992). For women's actions in religious groups in a slightly later period, see Barbara Hoffman, *Radikalpietismus um 1700. Die Streit um das Recht auf eine neue Gesellschaft* (Frankfurt: Campus, 1996).

Information about men's ideas about women in the context of the Reformation may be found in a number of studies. Susan Karant-Nunn, '*Kinder, Küche, Kirche*: social ideology in the wedding sermons of Johannes Mathesius', in Susan Karant-Nunn and Andrew Fix, eds, *Germania Illustrata: Essays Presented to Gerald Strauss* (Kirksville, MO: Sixteenth Century Journal Publishers, 1991), pp. 121–40, discusses the ideas of a typical early Lutheran pastor. Joyce Irwin, ed., *Womanhood in Radical Protestantism* (New York: E. Mellen, 1979), and Wes Harrison, 'The role of women in Anabaptist thought and practice: the Hutterite experience of the sixteenth and seventeenth centuries', *Sixteenth Century Journal* 23 (1992): 49–70, discuss ideas about women among Anabaptists and other radical reformers.

The ideas of John Calvin have been the focus of a number of good studies, including what is still the best example of how the traditional methods and sources of intellectual historians and theologians can be used to gain dramatically new insights: Jane Dempsey Douglass, *Women, Freedom and Calvin* (Philadelphia: Westminster, 1985). Douglass's conclusion about Calvin's being more open to women taking a greater religious role has been recently challenged by another insightful study, John Lee Thompson, *John Calvin and the Daughters of Sarah: Women in Regular and Exceptional Roles in the Exegesis of Calvin, His Predecessors and His Contemporaries* (Geneva: Droz, 1992). As yet there is no similar study of ideas about women and Luther in either English or German. The actual impact of Calvin's ideas on the lives of women has been investigated in Jeffrey R. Watt, 'Women and the consistory in Calvin's Geneva', *Sixteenth Century Journal* 24 (1993): 429–39, and Robert Kingdon, *Adultery and Divorce in Calvin's Geneva* (Cambridge, MA: Harvard University Press, 1995).

Studies of women's religious writings include Albrecht Classen, 'Frauen in der deutschen Reformation: Neufunde von Texten und Autorinnen sowie deren Neubewertung', in Paul Gerhard Schmidt, ed., *Die Frau in der Renaissance* (Wiesbaden: Harrasowitz, 1994), pp. 179–202. Merry Wiesner-Hanks and Joan Skocir, *Convents Confront the Reformation: Writings by Catholic and Protestant Nuns in Germany*

(Milwaukee: Marquette University Press, 1996), includes parallel English and German texts of four works by early modern religious women. Ute Braun, *Frauentestamente: Stiftsdamen, Fürstinnen-Äbtissen und ihre Schwestern in Selbstzeugnissen des 17. und 18. Jahrhunderts*, Beiträge zur Geschichte von Stadt und Stift Essen 104 (Essen: Historische Verein für Stadt und Stift Essen, 1991/92), uses abbesses' wills as evidence of their family relations and convent life. For writings by nuns from an earlier period, see Gertrud Jaron Lewis, *By Women, For Women, About Women: The Sister-Books of Fourteenth Century Germany* (Toronto: Pontifical Institute of Medieval Studies, 1996), which includes both analysis and texts.

Argula von Grumbach has been the focus of several recent studies, including several by Peter Matheson: 'Breaking the silence: women, censorship and the Reformation', *Sixteenth Century Journal* 27 (1996): 97–109, and 'A Reformation for women? Sin, grace and gender in Argula von Grumbach', *Scottish Journal of Theology* 49 (1996): 1–17. Matheson has also recently published a translation of many of her works: *Argula von Grumbach: A Woman's Voice in the Reformation* (Edinburgh: T. & T. Clark, 1995). Argula is also the subject of Silke Halbach, *Argula von Grumbach als Verfasserin reformatorischer Flugschriften*. Europäische Hochschulschriften, Reihe 23, Theologie; Bd. 468 (Frankfurt: Peter Lang, 1992).

Elsie Anne McKee is currently working on a biography of Katharina Zell and a critical edition of her writings, to be published by Wm. B. Eerdmans in 1997 or 1998. To date McKee has published: 'The defense of Zwingli, Schwenkfeld, and the Baptists, by Katharina Schütz Zell', in *Reformiertes Erbe: Festschrift für Gottfried W. Locher zu seinem 80. Geburtstag*, ed. Heiko A. Oberman *et al.* (Zürich: EVG, 1992), 1: 245–64; *Reforming Popular Piety in 16th Century Strasbourg: Katharine Schütz Zell and Her Hymnbook*, Studies in Reformed Theology and History, Princeton Theological Seminary 2/4 (Fall 1994); and 'Katharina Schütz Zell: Protestant Reformer', in Timothy J. Wengert and Charles W. Brockwell, eds, *Telling the Churches' Story: Ecumenical Perspectives on Writing Christian History* (Grand Rapids: Eerdmans, 1995), pp. 73–90. Zell is also discussed in Merry E. Wiesner, 'Katharine Zell's "Answer to Ludwig Rabus" as autobiography and theology', *Colloquia Germanica* 28 (1995): 245–54.

Studies of religious women include: Anne Conrad, *Zwischen Kloster und Welt: Ursulinen und Jesuitinnen in der Katholischen Reformbewegung des 16./17. Jahrhunderts* (Mainz: Philipp von Zabern, 1991); Lucia Koch, *Vom Kloster zum protestantischen Damenstift: Die Nassauischen Stifte Gnadenthal und Walsdorf in der 2. Hälfte des 16. Jahrhunderts* (MA thesis, Johannes Gutenberg-Universität Mainz, 1995); Ute Braun, *Frauentestamente: Stiftsdamen, Fürstinnen-Äbtissinnen und ihre Schwestern in Selbstzeugnissen des 17. und 18. Jahrhunderts*, Beiträge zur Geschichte von Stadt und Stift Essen (Essen: Historische Verein für Stadt und Stift Essen, 1991/92); Paula S. Datsko Barker, 'Charitas Pirckheimer: a female humanist confronts the Reformation', *Sixteenth Century Journal* 26 (1995): 259–72; D. Jonathan Grieser, 'A tale of two convents: nuns and Anabaptists in Münster, 1533–1535', *Sixteenth Century Journal* 26 (1995): 31–48; Ulinka Rublack, 'Female spirituality and the infant Jesus in late medieval Dominican convents', *Gender and History* 6 (1994): 37–57.

Cornelia Niekus Moore, *The Maiden's Mirror: Reading Materials for German Girls in the Sixteenth and Seventeenth Centuries* (Wiesbaden: Harrasowitz, 1987), includes extensive discussion of girls' religious training, and Elke Kleinau and Claudia Opitz, eds, *Geschichte der Mädchen und Frauenbildung, Bd. I: Vom Mittelalter bis zur Aufklärung* (Frankfurt: Campus, 1996), includes a number of essays on women's religious education.

There have been fewer studies of Jewish women during this period than of Christian, but this is a growing field of study. See Deborah Hertz, 'Women at the edge of Judaism: female converts in Germany, 1600–1750', in Menachem Mor, ed., *Jewish Assimilation, Acculturation and Accommodation: Past Traditions, Current Issues and Future Prospects* (Lanham, MD: University Press of America, 1992), pp. 87–109.

Law

The most thorough treatment of legal opinion about women in Germany is Elisabeth Koch, *Maior dignitas est in sexu virili: Das weibliche Geschlecht im Normensystem des 16. Jahrhunderts* (Frankfurt: Vittorio Klostermann, 1991), which summarizes the positions of hundreds of jurists during the period in which Roman law was being introduced in Germany. The regulation of sexuality and the growth of state power has been discussed for a slightly later period in Isabel V. Hull, *Sexuality, State, and Civil Society in Germany, 1700–1815* (Ithaca, NY: Cornell University Press, 1996).

The history of criminality is a flourishing field in Germany, and several recent studies use legal sources to discuss issues regarding gender and criminality: Ulrike Gleixner, *'Das Mensch' und 'der Kerl': Die Konstruktion von Geschlecht in Unzuchtverfahren der Frühen Neuzeit (1700–1760)* (Frankfurt: Campus, 1994); Otto Ulbricht, ed., *Von Huren und Rabenmütern: Weibliche Kriminalität in der Frühen Neuzeit* (Cologne: Böhlau, 1995); Richard von Dülmen, *Frauen vor Gericht: Kindsmord in der frühen Neuzeit* (Frankfurt: Campus, 1991); Gerd Schwerhoff, *Köln im Kreuzverhör: Kriminalität, Herrschaft und Gesellschaft in einer frühneuzeitlichen Stadt* (Bonn: Bouvier, 1991). Steven Ozment provides a biography of one woman's long legal case against her own father in *The Bürgermeister's Daughter: Scandal in a Sixteenth-Century German Town* (New York: St Martin's, 1996). Three specialized studies of prostitution are: Peter Schuster, *Das Frauenhaus: Städtische Bordelle in Deutschland 1350–1600* (Paderborn: Schöningh, 1992); Beata Schuster, *Die freie Frauen: Dirnen und Frauenhäuser in 15. und 16. Jahrhundert* (Frankfurt: Campus, 1995); and Lyndal Roper, 'Discipline and respectability: prostitution and the Reformation in Augsburg', *History Workshop Journal* 19(1985): 3–28.

Maria Boes includes considerations of gender in two recent articles, 'The treatment of juvenile delinquents in early modern Germany: a case study', *Continuity and Change* 11 (1996): 43–60, and 'Public appearance and criminal judicial practices in early modern Germany', *Social Science History* 20 (1996): 259–79. Legal cases have been used to study issues of honour in several articles, including Susanna Burghartz, 'Geschlecht – Körper – Ehre: Überlegungen zur weibliche Ehre in der frühen Neuzeit am Beispiel der Basler Ehegerichtsprotokolle', in Klaus Schreiner and Gerd Schwerhoff, eds, *Verletzte Ehre: Ehrkonflikte in Gesellschaften des Mittelalters und der Frühen Neuzeit* (Cologne: Böhlau, 1995), pp. 214–34, and Lyndal Roper, 'Will and honor: sex, words and power in Augsburg criminal trials', *Radical History Review* 43 (1989): 45–71. The recent literature on witchcraft in Germany is too extensive to begin listing here; the best bibliography for this may be found in Gerd Schwerhoff, 'Vom Alltagsverdacht zur Massenverfolgung: Neuere deutsche Forschung zum frühneuzeitlichen Hexenwesen', *Geschichte in Wissenschaft und Unterricht* 46 (1995): 47–71.

Work

There are two older studies in English which bring together materials from several cities: Merry E. Wiesner, *Working Women in Renaissance Germany* (New Brunswick, NJ: Rutgers University Press, 1986), and Martha Howell, *Women, Production, and Patriarchy in Late Medieval Cities* (Chicago: University of Chicago Press, 1986). To put developments in Germany in a wider European context, see the essays in Barbara Hanawalt, ed., *Women and Work in Preindustrial Europe*

(Bloomington: Indiana University Press, 1986), and Daryl Hafter, ed., *European Women and Preindustrial Craft* (Bloomington: Indiana University Press, 1995).

There are several studies of women in specific occupations: Eva Labouvie, in 'In weiblicher Hand: Frauen als Firmengründnerinnen und Unternehmerinnen (1600–1780)' in her *Frauenleben, Frauen-Leben: Zur Geschichte und Gegenwart weiblicher Lebenswelten im Saarland* (St Ingbert: Röhrig, 1993), presents material on women as entrepreneurs; Renate Dürr, *Mägde in der Stadt: Das Beispiel Schwäbisch Hall in der Frühen Neuzeit* (Frankfurt: Campus, 1995), on domestic servants; Susan Karant-Nunn, 'The women of the Saxon silver mines', in Sherrin Marshall, ed., *Women in Reformation and Counter-Reformation Europe: Public and Private Worlds* (Bloomington: University of Indiana Press, 1989), pp. 29–46, and Christina Vanja, 'Mining women in early modern European society', in Thomas Max Safley and Leonard N. Rosenband, eds, *The Workplace Before the Factory: Artisans and Proletarians, 1500–1800* (Ithaca, NY: Cornell University Press, 1993), both look at women in mining; Hilary Marland, ed., *The Art of Midwifery: Early Modern Midwives in Europe* (London: Routledge and Kegan Paul, 1993), includes several essays on midwives in German-speaking areas; and Waltraud Pulz, '*Nicht alles nach der Gelahrten Sinn geschrieben': Das Hebammenleitungsbuch von Justina Siegemund* (Munich: München Vereinigung für Volkskunde, 1994), discusses an instructional manual written by a German midwife.

Jean Quataert has investigated the way in which being associated with the household and women had a negative effect on many occupations in a very influential article, 'The shaping of women's work in manufacturing: guilds, households, and the state in central Europe', *American Historical Review* 90 (1985): 1122–48; she analyses a slightly later period in 'Survival strategies in a Saxon textile district during the early phases of industrialization', in Daryl Hafter, ed., *European Women and Preindustrial Craft* (Bloomington: Indiana University Press, 1995). Another view of women in early industrialization is Sheilagh C. Ogilvie, 'Women and proto-industrialisation in a corporate society: Württemberg woollen weaving, 1590–1760', in Pat Hudson and W.R. Lee, eds, *Women's Work and the Family Economy in Historical Perspective* (Manchester: Manchester University Press, 1990), pp. 76–103. Women's roles in early 'manufactories' have also been explored in Rita Bake, *Vorindustrielle Frauenerwerbsarbeit: Arbeits- und Lebensweise von Manufakturarbeiterinnen im Deutschland des 18. Jahrhunderts unter besonderer Berücksichtigung Hamburgs* (Cologne: Pahl-Rugenstein Verlag, 1984).

Several recent massive micro-histories of one particular village have included considerations of the division of labour and other aspects of gender relations in rural areas: David Sabean, *Property, Production and Family in Neckarhausen, 1700–1870* (Cambridge: Cambridge University Press, 1990); Albert Schnyder-Burghartz, *Alltag und Lebensformen auf der Basler Landschaft um 1700* (Liestal: Verlag des Kantons Basel Landschaft, 1992); Jürgen Schlumbohm, *Lebensläufe, Familen, Höfe: Die Bauern und Heuerleute des Osnabrückischen Kirchspiels Belm in proto-industrieller Zeit, 1650–1860* (Göttingen: Vandenhoeck und Ruprecht, 1994).

Index